D0254292

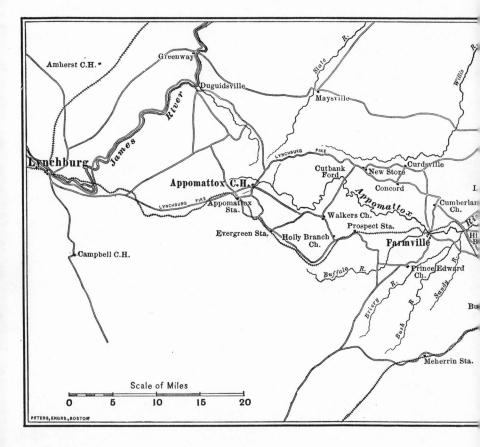

Amherst C.H.

Greenway

Duguidsville

Maysville

James River

State R.

Willis R.

Lynchburg

LYNCHBURG   PIKE

Cutbank
Ford

New Store

Curdsville

Concord

Appomattox C.H.

Appomattox

LYNCHBURG   PIKE

Appomattox
Sta.

Walkers Ch.

Prospect Sta.

Cumberland
Ch.

Evergreen Sta.

Holly Branch
Ch.

Farmville

Hi
B

Campbell C.H.

Buffalo   R.

Prince Edward
Ch.

Briery R.

Bush R.

Sandy R.

Meherrin Sta.

Bu

Scale of Miles

0   5   10   15   20

PETERS, ENGRS., BOSTON

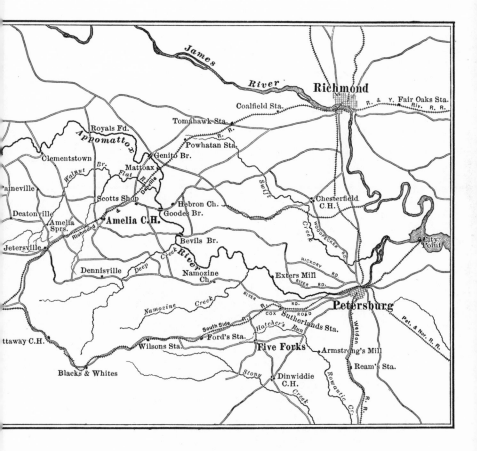

THE SUNSET OF THE CONFEDERACY

BY
CAPTAIN MORRIS SCHAFF

WITH MAPS

WITH A NEW INTRODUCTION BY
GARY W. GALLAGHER

Cooper Square Press

First Cooper Square Press edition 2002

This Cooper Square Press paperback edition of *The Sunset of the Confederacy* is an unabridged republication of the edition first published in Boston, Massachusetts, in 1912, with the addition of a new introduction.

New introduction copyright © 2002 by Gary W. Gallagher

All rights reserved.
No part of this book may be reproduced in any form or by any electronic or mechanical means, including information storage and retrieval systems, without written permission.

Published by Cooper Square Press
A Member of the Rowman & Littlefield Publishing Group
200 Park Avenue South, Suite 1109
New York, New York 10003-1503
www.coopersquarepress.com

Distributed by National Book Network

Library of Congress Cataloging-in-Publication Data Available.

ISBN 0-8154-1210-X (pbk. : alk. paper)

⊖™ The paper used in this publication meets the minimum requirements of American National Standard for Information Sciences—Permanence of Paper for Printed Library Materials, ANSI/NISO Z39.48–1992.
Manufactured in the United States of America.

This book is dedicated to my wife and children,
Harry, Rodman, Sally, *and*
long since departed blue-eyed
Charlotte
MORRIS SCHAFF

INTRODUCTION TO THE COOPER SQUARE PRESS EDITION

MORRIS SCHAFF'S name is not well known among modern students of the Civil War. Yet, during his lifetime he reached an appreciative audience with *The Sunset of the Confederacy* and other writings about the conflict that, through a combination of reminiscence and narrative history, sought to promote reconciliation between the North and South, forcibly united after years of war. His work stood alongside that of more famous reconciliationists such as Joshua Lawrence Chamberlain, the Union hero of Little Round Top, and John Brown Gordon, one of the ablest of Robert E. Lee's younger lieutenants. As a group, these men, and others who shared their point of view, created a literature that heavily influenced how generations of readers understood the Civil War.

Well before Schaff wrote *The Sunset of the Confederacy*, he had witnessed the disparate ways in which Americans reacted when four years of brutal slaughter ended. Many ex-Confederates—surveying the wreckage of their short-lived slaveholding republic and the disruption of their social and economic structures—nursed bitter feelings toward the North. They endorsed the sentiments expressed in the song "O, I'm a Good Old Rebel," which was composed shortly after Appomattox. "Three hundred thousand Yankees is stiff in Southern dust," proclaimed the song's lyrics: "We got three hundred thousand before they conquered us. They died of Southern fever and Southern steel and shot. I wish they was three million instead of what we got." For their part, many Union veterans agreed with a sergeant who bridled at evidence of continuing hatred toward the North among white Southerners. "There is not nine out of ten of these so called 'Whiped' traitors that I would trust until I saw the rope applied to their Necks," noted this man in the autumn of 1865, "then I would only have Faith in the quality of the rope."

Republican politicians sought to keep sectional antagonism alive for many years, as when one orator during the presidential election of 1876 reminded his audience that "Every man that endeavored to tear the old flag from the heaven that it enriches was a Democrat. Every man that tried to destroy this nation was a Democrat. . . . The man that assassinated Abraham Lincoln was a Democrat. . . . Soldiers, every scar you have on your heroic bodies was given you by a Democrat." Former Confederates similarly used the war, congressional actions during Reconstruction, and the presence of United States troops in the postwar South to gain advantage over Republican opponents.

While many veterans and civilians on both sides harbored long-term bitterness, others quite rapidly sought to promote reconciliation. Abraham Lincoln took a major step in this direction during the last week of March 1865. Meeting with Generals Ulysses S. Grant and William Tecumseh Sherman at City Point, Virginia, the president indicated that he hoped to close the war as gently as possible. He urged his generals to stop the killing and to offer generous terms of capitulation to the rebels. "Let them surrender and go home," Lincoln stated, "they will not take up arms again. Let them all go, officers and all, let them have their horses to plow with, and, if you like, their guns to shoot crows with. . . . We want these people to return to their allegiance and submit to the laws. Therefore, I say, give them the most liberal and honorable terms."

At Appomattox on April 9, 1865, Grant followed through on his commander-in-chief's wishes. He proposed to Robert E. Lee that soldiers in the Army of Northern Virginia lay down their arms, after which they would "be allowed to return to their homes not to be disturbed by United States Authority so long as they observe their parole and the laws in force where they may reside." These same terms were extended to the remainder of the Confederacy's forces as they surrendered over the next several weeks.

Sentiment in favor of reconciliation grew between the end of the war and the first decade of the twentieth century. Many white Americans, North and South, celebrated the bravery of soldiers on both sides as evidence of a superior national character. When the United States flexed its muscles as an emerging great power in the war against Spain in 1898, untold white Southerners—secure in the knowledge that influential Northern politicians and writers had acknowledged Lee's brilliance and the gallantry of Confederate soldiers—pronounced the Union victory in 1865 a good thing. Typically, reconciliationists played down the importance of slavery as a factor in the secession crisis and in the establishment of the Confederacy, and stressed restoration of the Union rather than emancipation as the principal accomplishment of the war.

Morris Schaff decided early in the twentieth century to add his voice to the chorus of reconciliation, approaching the task after a life of solid accomplishment. Born in Kirkersville, Ohio, on December 28, 1840, the son of John and Charlotte (Hartzell) Schaff, he entered the United States Military Academy in July 1858. He and his classmates labored over their studies against a backdrop of growing sectional tension. John Brown's raid on Harpers Ferry exploded into the national consciousness during the autumn of Schaff's second year at West Point, and the acrimonious election of 1860 followed thirteen months later. A Democrat, Schaff likely disapproved of the Republican platform in 1860 and regretted Abraham Lincoln's triumph. In 1861 he said goodbye to many Southern classmates, who left West Point to serve their states in what would become the Confederate army, and completed his final year of schoolwork while the war raged. His academic records show greatest proficiency in mineralogy, ordnance and gunnery, geology, chemistry, philosophy, English, and ethics. He ranked solidly in the middle of his class in artillery, cavalry, and infantry tactics and accumulated his share of demerits. He stood ninth among twenty-eight members of his graduating class in June 1862.

Commissioned a second lieutenant of ordnance in June 1862 and promoted to first lieutenant the following March, Schaff served in the Eastern Theater. A high point came in early May 1864 when U. S. Grant asked him to carry some dispatches during the Battle of the Wilderness. "It was not on account of any particularly great virtue of mine that I was made Gen. Grant's dispatch bearer," Schaff later recalled. With fighting reaching a ferocious pitch that spring day, the young lieutenant happened to pass by Grant's headquarters. "He was under a young pine tree whittling," noted Schaff, adding that the "battle was in a critical state. As I went by I heard him say: 'Where is the officer who was to carry these dispatches?' And then the dispatches were given to me." Schaff's "gallant and meritorious service in the Battle of the Wilderness" earned him promotion to brevet captain, to date from May 6, 1864 (formal promotion to captain, Schaff's highest rank in the United States Army, came in March 1867).

Schaff remained in the army only a few years past the end of the war before he resigned his commission in 1871. His postwar duty included a stint as commander of the arsenal at Mount Vernon, Alabama, from 1866 to 1867. In August 1868, he married Alice Page, with whom he had two sons and two daughters, and whose father was connected with the Berkshire Glass Company of Pittsfield, Massachusetts. Schaff accepted a position with that company after leaving the army and remained in Massachusetts for the rest of his life. Appointed inspector-general of the Massachusetts militia in 1882, he also served as a brigadier general on the staff of Governor John Davis Long until 1883. A decade later, Governor William E. Russell named Schaff to the state's gas and electric light commission, a post that he held until 1919. Schaff's strong sense of civic duty impressed fellow Democrats as well as members of the Republican Party (Long was a Republican; Russell a Democrat). Upon Schaff's retirement from the power commission, Governor Calvin Coolidge, a staunch Republican, lauded his "preeminent public service" and tendered the "thanks of the commonwealth."

Despite electing not to make his career in the regular army, Schaff treasured his connection with West Point. He was placed on the school's Board of Visitors in 1883 and in 1913 held the presidency of the Alumni Association and delivered the commencement address. In 1907, at the suggestion of *The Atlantic Monthly*'s editor, he wrote about his experiences as a cadet. First published serially in *The Atlantic Monthly* and later in book form as *The Spirit of Old West Point*, Schaff's memoir underscored his devotion to the institution and offered engaging vignettes of many young men who later earned fame in the Union and Confederate armies. One critic described the book, which avoided sectional bias, as "perhaps the most beautiful story ever inspired by cadet life at the academy."

Newspapers described Schaff as the second oldest living graduate of West Point when he died at the age of eighty-eight on October 19, 1929. Members of the West Point Alumni Association sent a wreath of chrysanthemums to honor their departed comrade.

An obituary observed that Schaff "came into public notice" in three ways: as a soldier with an excellent record during the Civil War; as an important public servant in Massachusetts; and as "a most interesting writer of Civil War history and military reminiscences." He achieved the widest attention in the last of these three roles. In addition to *The Spirit of Old West Point*, he published four other books. The first, *Etna and Kirkersville*, came out in 1905 and told the story of his home town. Like *The Spirit of Old West Point*, *The Battle of the Wilderness* ran in *The Atlantic Monthly* before appearing as a book in 1908. Part memoir and part tactical history, it remains a useful source on the first major battle in Grant's and Lee's Overland Campaign of 1864. *Jefferson Davis: His Life and Personality*, the last of Schaff's books chronologically, highlighted its author's devotion to the ideal of sectional healing. Published in 1922, it sought "to see justice done . . . to Jefferson Davis," a man who "has had unfair treatment by historians of the great war between the States . . . and against whose armies I fought on many fields, including the bloody ones of Chancellorsville, the Wilderness and Spotsylvania." Schaff wrote not out of sympathy for Davis's cause, he informed readers just five years removed from America's entry into World War I, but from a sense of magnanimity toward the leader of the Confederacy, the "sons and grandsons of whose gallant defenders helped so bravely to carry their united country's flag to victory on the fields of France."

In *The Sunset of the Confederacy*, published in 1912, Schaff explored the last phase of the war in Virginia. A long newspaper piece reviewing the author's life characterized this as "the favorite among all his books"—a description that left unclear whether it was Schaff's favorite or the title most appreciated by his audience. Whatever the answer to that question, it is beyond dispute that few topics held more potential for an author intent on promoting reconciliation. The meeting between Grant and Lee in Wilmer McLean's parlor at Appomattox Court House, which capped a campaign that began with the fall of Richmond and Petersburg a week earlier, had been described by countless authors who grasped its power as a symbol of sectional healing. Schaff follows a clear strategy in bringing readers of *The Sunset of the Confederacy* to that climactic scene. He avoids any harsh judgments about the Confederacy, pushes into the shadows ample evidence of deep-seated anger between the combatants, and anticipates a reunited country's journey toward national and international greatness. His is a story that many generations of Americans have taken to heart—a comforting celebration of how the North and South ended four years of enormous bloodshed with admirable grace.

Several themes emerge as Schaff weaves his narrative of the last days of the epic confrontation between Grant and Lee. In typical reconciliationist fashion, he pays little attention to slavery and emancipation. He blames those whom he deemed extremists—Northern abolitionists and Southern "fire-eaters"—for the coming of the war, alluding at one point to "a raving political delirium" in 1861. He points no finger at the mass of white Southerners for supporting a rebel government. Indeed, readers below the Mason-Dixon Line undoubtedly found comfort in Schaff's declaration that the descendants of the Army of Northern Virginia's veterans, as well as the people of the United States as a whole, would be proud of the Confederate soldiers' willingness to lay their "lives down for a political principle that is the very foundation on which our whole governmental system is based, namely, the Sovereignty of the States." *The Sunset of the Confederacy* goes further, offering "no veiled or surreptitious excuse for our armies in burning houses and barns of rich and poor, or pillaging and ruthlessly destroying the homes of those whose only offense was that their sons had dared to fight for honestly held principles." In these instances and elsewhere, Schaff's Democratic politics influenced his interpretation.

In this work Schaff expresses high regard for fellow reconciliationists Joshua Chamberlain and John Gordon, who had paid respect to each other during the famous surrender parade at Appomattox. As authors, Chamberlain and Gordon often employed colorful and emotional language, and Schaff matches them passage for passage in a sometimes effusive laudation of valorous soldiers in blue and gray. He urges his readers to "wave your laurel for Chamber-

lain," a gentle, knightly hero who saved Little Round
Top at Gettysburg and gallantly saluted the surrendering Confederates at Appomattox. In a similar
vein, Schaff detects a "natural eminence" and "indomitable courage" in Gordon, on whose hearth
"valor and honor" would feel at home. As for the soldiers commanded by Chamberlain, Gordon, and
other generals, Schaff repeatedly describes them as
gallant, valiant Americans who had served their respective causes nobly.

If anything, he bestows more praise on the Southern soldiers than on their Northern counterparts,
often echoing the Lost Cause writings of former Confederates who portrayed Lee's army as vastly outnumbered, poorly clad and fed, and exhausted. The
Confederates were "weak for want of food and sleep,
and low at heart," Schaff states in a representative
passage. "Toil on, veteran heroes; a few days more
and it will all be over," he continues, "and loving
hearts in days to come will testify their admiration
in monuments of bronze and marble."

But Grant's men also reached the edge of physical
endurance during the relentless pursuit from Petersburg and Richmond to Appomattox. Moreover,
the Federals did not enjoy so immense an advantage
in strength as Schaff suggested—"we had five men
to your one," he remarks in a parenthetical confes-
sion to Lee. The Army of Northern Virginia numbered about 60,000 when it began the trek

westward, and the principal components of Grant's trailing armies totaled about 80,000 (with another 30,000 or so within supporting distance).

Schaff admired both Grant and Lee, but presents a more flowery tribute to the rebel chieftain. "Never . . . was a great man less self-conscious than Grant . . ." he observed, ". . . under the depths of his quiet and artless reserve, lay a persistent and intense doggedness of purpose, as prompt and unconquerable as Lee's pride and burning enthusiasm." The roster of Lee's virtues, as laid out by Schaff, far surpassed that of the Union general-in-chief: "And now to those high moral standards, warmest family affections, imperial qualities—Lee had a bearing that would have made him at home among princes— add wealth, station, an imposing stature, a noble countenance, and abilities of the first order. . . ." Those attributes, together with a record of surpassing military accomplishment, concluded Schaff, combined to make Lee "the embodiment of one of the world's ideals, that of the soldier, the Christian, and the gentleman." Part of Schaff's idealization of Lee stemmed from an underlying uneasiness with what he perceived to be an overly materialistic, secular American society. The Virginian seemingly stood above what Schaff decried as a perverted American "commercial spirit" that, by the early twentieth century, had "grown into a sordid, money-gorged, godless, snoring monster."

Schaff exhibits a special warmth when writing of young West Pointers such as George A. Custer, Wesley Merritt, Ranald S. Mackenzie, James Dearing, and Frank Huger. *The Sunset of the Confederacy* includes an especially heartfelt tribute to Dearing, a Confederate brigadier who, after receiving a mortal wound near the end of the campaign, was comforted by his classmate Mackenzie. "Dearing asked after a number of his class," recorded Schaff, "and sent his love to all of us." After speculating that Custer and a pair of fellow West Pointers might have reflected on their days at the academy in the midst of the pursuit to Appomattox, Schaff noted that "no matter when or where we graduates meet, soon, very soon, we are back at that beautiful spot on the Hudson and living over the days of our youth."

A standard bibliography on the Civil War labeled *The Sunset of the Confederacy* a "somewhat sentimental treatment" of the Appomattox campaign, but found value in "its interpretation of the actions of Grant and Lee." True as far as it goes, this evaluation misses the book's primary importance as a classic example of the reconciliation genre. Schaff's handling of the causes of the war, his disinclination to ascribe superior virtue to either side, and his enthusiastic exaltation of the American fighting spirit illuminate one strain of public memory and interpretation of the conflict. Although Schaff largely ignored sectional anger that persisted in many hearts during the postwar decades, his book remains well worth the attention of anyone who would assess the ways in which Americans chose to remember the Civil War.

GARY W. GALLAGHER
University of Virginia
November 2001

GARY W. GALLAGHER is the John L. Nau III Professor of History at the University of Virginia. He has published widely in the field of Civil War history, most recently *The Confederate War*, *The Myth of the Lost Cause and Civil War History*, and *Lee and his Army in Confederate History*.

LIST OF MAPS

THE SUNSET OF THE CONFEDERACY

I

LONGER are the shadows, richer are the colors of the evening clouds, deeper is the feeling as the close of the day draws near and the sun goes down: so was it with the War of the Great Rebellion as its end drew near. That momentous struggle had gone on for four long years. Much gallant blood had been shed, thousands of graves had been filled; and now, Sunday, the second day of April, 1865,—a memorable month and a memorable year in the annals of our country, — had come, and the church bells of Richmond, the capital of the Confederacy, were ringing for the morning service.

Bright over the city was the sun in the bending sky, the jonquils were glowing in the gardens, the southern woods were sweet with the bloom of the jessamine, 'and the fields were gay with the voices of birds and brooks, — but the gloom of the people was deep indeed. For an army of the North, having fought its way from the bank of the Ohio to the bank of the Cape Fear River in North Carolina, a march of five or six hundred miles, had cut artery after artery of military supply, had brought the miseries and horrors of war to the door of many a home, and had left behind it, especially in Georgia and South Carolina, a track of vast and ruthless devastation.

The Confederate armies that had contested with it so valiantly the bloody fields of Shiloh, Perryville, Stone's River, Chickamauga, Missionary Ridge, Atlanta, Franklin, and Nashville, had been reduced by losses and repeated reverses to a disorganized and desponding fragment. And on that very day Sherman's army, every flag and bit of clothing scented with burning pine, crouched like a tiger for a final, savage leap. (A friend on duty in the Ordnance Office at Washington once told me that it was unnecessary for the officers of that army, coming to settle their accounts after the surrender, to tell him where they had served, for before they could speak, the odor of burning southern pine had told the story.)

So it may be said, and said truthfully, that on this fair Sunday morning all the territory of the Confederacy east of the Mississippi, with the exception of adjacent parts of Virginia and North Carolina, had been overrun and overpowered by the Federal forces; and although the people as individuals were unconquered, their hopes of success were fast turning to ashes. For the Confederacy — a martial embodiment of long and honestly held views of the Sovereignty of the States; a principle so sound and essential to the safety and dignity of our country, but

asserted, alas! so untimely and at the cost of so
much gallant blood and treasure by what we see
now was a raving political delirium — had met with
undreamed-of and untoward experiences. Her armies, to their surprise, had encountered forces equally
valiant; and, instead of going on from victory to
victory, had suffered repeated, almost mortal repulses. But keener, I am fain to believe, than the
defeat at the hands of underestimated and too
generally despised foes, was the disappointment and
humiliation the South had met with from the aris-
tocratic governments of the old world, which had
been counted on with absolute certainty to reach
out warm hands of welcome. But they, with satiric
politeness and despicable evasion, denied her recognition; and there was brought home the truth of
what had long ago been said: "Put not your trust
in princes."

Again, in the administration of civil affairs all had
not gone well. Finances which might have been
nursed into paramount strength had been terribly
bungled, practically thrown away; as a result,
hunger and want had become the tent-mates of
every Southern soldier in the field; and, as troubles
go in pairs, faction and cabal, the twin dusky-eyed
whelps of balked ambition, tore the Cabinet and Congress, day in and day out.

These surprises and adversities of four years were
not without profound and serious results. The

dearest and warmest lover of the Confederacy had
to confess, in the spring of 1865, that Fortune had
turned its face away from her, and that her strength
was almost gone. Having heard the cheers and beheld the joy with which she was hailed by the Southern friends of my youth at West Point, — and alas!
how many laid down their lives for her! — I am
free to say that I never think of her distressful last
days without a sense of pity. Eager and yearning
eyes of the Confederacy, are you looking for a friend
among the nations? Oh, you shall look in vain:
none, none will come; for the Spirit of the Ages has
written the hated word Slavery in big letters across
your breast; yet, in the memories of the sons and
daughters of the men who fell for you, you will
dwell transfigured as an image of sweet and radiant
splendor.

The South's only hope, her rock, shield, and horn
of salvation, now lay in the Army of Northern
Virginia, which, after four years of brilliant moves
and matchless courage, had been manœuvred and
forced back from the Rapidan by the lack of numbers, but not of spirit, to the defense of the lines
of Richmond. There, under severe fire, day and
night, hopeless of ever again flying their colors defiantly as of old on the banks of the Rapidan and
Rappahannock, the veterans of Gaines's Mill, Mal-
vern Hill, Manassas, Antietam, Fredericksburg,
Chancellorsville, Gettysburg, the Wilderness, Spott-

sylvania, and Cold Harbor — and every star that
shines and every wind that breathes over these
fields calls them fields of glory — had stood in rags
and hunger through the unusually cold winter days,
receiving pitiful letters daily, letters full of heart-
breaking home distresses, and often blurred and
dampened with the tears of loving eyes. But, notwithstanding their own sufferings and those keener
ones of hearth and cradle, they remained loyally,
illustriously steadfast to their colors, and for comfort and strength went to the source to which we all
go. Nightly they would gather, and on bended
knees, with palm to palm, tears channeling their
brave faces, ask God to guard and comfort their
homes and little ones and at last to own and bless
the Confederacy.

Since the Christian Era, what supreme hours
the believers in God have gone through! How the
beseeching, conflicting prayers have threaded suns
and moons and hosts of stars in their travels toward
Him! And He has heard them all, and wisely ruled
for the best; and to-day He blesses the Southland
with peace and plenty, and night and morning fills
her lap with the fruits of the field.

Such was the state of the army; and as the bells
were ringing that Sunday morning let the sweet
comforts of that other heavenly world gleam as they
may to the people of Richmond as in faith they
looked upward, yet sweep the Confederacy far and

wide, and their eyes would seek comfort in vain.
All the historic region of their beloved Virginia
east of the Blue Ridge, from the James to the Potomac, which had been one continuous battling ground,
was now so scourged and ravaged that it was a
pitiful scene. Moreover, in the previous autumn
the Shenandoah Valley, Virginia's granary and
gallery of beautiful views, which hitherto had been
spared, was despoiled; for, after practically obliter-
ating Early's army, — which, to weaken Grant's
hold on Petersburg, had threatened Washington
by way of the Shenandoah, — Sheridan laid waste
with the torch that mountain-cradled, wheat-bear-
ing, brook-singing valley.

But despite all these vicissitudes and the deepening
shadows of impending disaster, the people of Richmond, suffering for the necessaries of life and witnessing daily the wide-spread dying out of enthusiasm
for the Confederacy, as well as the rapid drying up
of the streams of its resources, had not given way entirely to despair; in fact, they were surprisingly
hopeful; their faith in the righteousness of their
cause, the genius of Lee, and the courage of his army,
was firm.

Sunday, — and the bells were calling the people
to worship. Old and noted Richmond families
uncovered at the door and reverently sought their
pews at St. Paul's, seven out of ten of the women
in mourning. In the solemn quiet sat the aged

fathers, their hair falling white, and many a mother with high-bred face, sorrowing for the boys who would never come home. There in the subdued light of the sanctuary they sat, while the bells, which had clanged so joyfully at the birth of the Confederacy, reluctantly and sadly boomed their final notes, as if they already knew, what the congregation little expected, that when they should ring again on the next Sunday, at that very hour, the Confederacy would be on its death-bed, breathing its last.

Jefferson Davis, President of the ill-fated cause, above middle height, lithe, distinguished, neatly arrayed in gray, came up the centre aisle with modest, dignified quietude of manner, entered his pew on the right and bowed his head in prayer. His spare austere face showed the effect of four years of care, as well it might, for who ever faced a longer and fiercer tempest? but he carried with him to St. Paul's, as everywhere, his habitual atmosphere of invincible courage and the never-failing bloom of urbanity.

From my point of view, and in this I may be very wrong, yet, notwithstanding all that may be said of his limitations, when I consider the bleak, inherent, and heart-breaking difficulties of his position, and how he met them, holding his turbulent forces intact and aggressive to the very end, far and away he soars above every public character, civil or military, of the Confederacy. Let this be as it may, the organ droned the last of the usual colorless *Venite*, and the service began.

Along the sunshiny side of the empty streets, here and there, convalescents from the hospitals sauntered, pale, some armless, and some on crutches. On its staff above the roof of the near-by capitol, the flag of the Confederacy drooped in the mild sunshine the stars of its blue saltier shining from its folds above steeple and chimney and over the spring-time gladness of the fields. Out in Holywood, where Stuart lay with so many of the best and the bravest, and where Mr. Davis's dust is now resting, the robins, sparrows, catbirds, redbirds, turtle-doves and mocking-birds were building their nests among the evergreens and native trees.

At the foot of the knolls of Holywood, the stately James flowed murmuring by, on by the shores of Belle Isle and the baleful walls of Libby Prison, from whose grated windows looked hollow-eyed, half-starved Northern prisoners of war, who, as they heard the bells of Richmond ringing, no doubt recalled the bells of home and longed for release and peace.

It was Communion Sunday, and the sacred ele-ments covered with a white cloth were on the table. Doctor Charles Minnegerode, the rector of St. Paul's, a diminutive, fervid, transplanted German, was de-livering his usual tense, extempore address, when the sexton, a portly aging man, with ruffles at his

wrists and bosom, and polished brass buttons on a
faded suit of blue, advanced up the aisle with soft
but stately tread, and after touching the President
on the shoulder with solemnity and his one-day-in-
the-week lofty importance, handed him a message.
Mr. Davis threw his blue-gray eyes rapidly over the
fatal dispatch, grasped his soft, creamy-white hat,
rose, and withdrew calmly.

Hardly had he left the door before the sexton again
marched up the aisle and, bending, spoke to General
Joseph Anderson, who at once took his leave. Then
followed two more grand entries — and I think the
Confederacy, though wan her cheek, smiled faintly;
for like everything born in America, she must have
had a sense of humor. Heaven be blessed for the
gift, and I hope they buried the dignified sexton in
his ruffled shirt and suit of blue with brass buttons
in due pomp; peace to his clay wherever it lies — .
At his fourth presageful march up the aisle, again
with a message to a prominent official, anxiety
seized the congregation, and like alarmed birds they
rose at once and left the church; and not until the
bewildered people cleared the door and mingled with
the throng that had already gathered in the modest
vestibule and on the pavement, was the purport of
the message to Mr. Davis revealed. There in consternation they saw government employees of a
department that occupied an opposite building
frantically carrying bundles of public documents out

into the middle of the street and setting them on fire.
Then the appalling significance of it all broke on
them, and they melted away to their homes in dread
and anguish. The smoke of the burning records soon
became the breath of panic, and by the time twilight
came on, the city was in tragic confusion.

When I was in Richmond at the unveiling of
Mr. Davis's monument, a few years ago, I went
into the historic church and sat awhile. The sun was
bright in the cloudless sky, the roses were fresh in
the gardens, for it was June, and sweet was the silence
in St. Paul's; and, thank God, sweet was the peace
of the land! As I sat there in the stillness, the solemn
past, as on a great and deeply shadowed river's
breast, went drifting by, and it seemed to me a
striking circumstance that the news of the breaking
of Lee's lines, foreshadowing as it did the immediate
collapse of the Confederacy, should reach its devout
President in a church on a Sunday, and, remarkably
enough, at the Communion service. Who knows
whether, since the earnest prayers of so many had to
be unanswered, it was not ordained in compensation,
that the sacred place and the sacred hour should
lend their serene and holy associations to this memory?

II

THE lines which Lee's army had held throughout the winter began on the north of Richmond, well out from its suburbs, and after circling them about to the east and south, led to Chaffin's Bluff on the James, some six or seven miles below the city. There they crossed to Drury's Bluff, uniting with a line of great strength that started on the bank of Swift Creek nearly opposite Petersburg, securing the railroad between it and Richmond, and barring all exit to our forces in the angle between the rivers. It was known as the Bermuda Hundred line. Those of Petersburg, the main or outer lines, began on the right bank of the Appomattox, ran eastward a mile or less on the crest of a ravine, then bore away southwestward to Hatcher's Run, and after crossing it turned westward till they came to what is known as the Claiborne Road, which they followed northward to the Run again. There they ended, seven or eight miles southwest of Petersburg, and at least thirty odd miles from where they started west of the Brooke Pike north of Richmond.

From Chaffin's Bluff, on the left bank of the James, back to Richmond, they were several deep, and consisted generally of strong, traversed breastworks, connecting what is known as detached earthworks with heavy parapets and deep ditches, all fronted with abatis and skirmish-line rifle-pits. They still can be traced; and had you, reader, seen our troops try to carry them, as I did, in front of Petersburg, on a hot July morning in the battle-summer of 1864, you would have discovered how truly formidable they were, and your heart would have beaten, I know, with mine, as the column, with flags flying, white and red bands rippling in the morning sun, moved to the assault and was mowed down by the enemy's guns. The gently upward-sloping ground over which the men advanced toward the Crater, for that was the action, was as blue with the bodies of the dead as a field of gentians. Yes, truly their line of works was strong and they had as brave men as ever lived to hold them.

Longstreet's two divisions, Field's and Kershaw's, were in the works north of the James; Mahone of Hill's corps, on the Bermuda Hundred front; while the rest of Hill's troops and a division of Ewell's old corps under Gordon, the one that struck us so hard in the Wilderness, occupied the long Petersburg lines; Lee's cavalry were veiling his right, but widely scattered, having to forage for themselves.

Richmond and its immediate defenses were under Ewell, a serious, long, lean-faced, doming-browed, pop-eyed man, and unconsciously amusing on ac-

count of his natural eccentricities, yet one of the
kindest, truest-hearted and most lovable that ever
lived. He had lost a leg during the War, and when
mounted, had to be strapped to his horse " Rifle,"
a flea-bitten gray, and was famous for his skill in
" deviling " turkey-legs. When well along in years
he married a Widow Brown, and always in introducing
any one to her, would say, " Mrs. Brown, allow me
to present my friend So-and-so." Ewell was the man,
too, who declared that he believed Stonewall Jackson was a lunatic for claiming that he could not use
red pepper on account of its giving him rheumatism
in his left leg!

What I am about to say in reference to Jackson
is of very little concern to my fellow men, for his
star is set high and will shine on long after this
narrative is forgotten and its writer turned to ob-
scure dust. But for some reason or other, brilliant
as were his military exploits, he never won my admiration as a man, like Ewell, Lee, Longstreet, Stuart,
and so many others; and had he died without uttering as sweet a sentiment as ever passed the lips of
a dying soldier, his career and personality would not
engage this pen for a single moment. But when that
cold ruminant nature, just on the point of exchanging
mortality for immortality, breathes softly between
his ashen lips, " Let us cross over the River and lie
down in the shade of the trees," and its spirit mounts
on its heavenly way, I am conscious of one of life's

mysteries, and feel another proof of God's abundance
in blessing the world with tender feeling. Without
this utterance, Stonewall Jackson would have been
nothing more to me than a belated, uninteresting
Roundhead, a dull, cast-iron military hero; but
with it he is transfigured; and may the last moments
of us all be attended with like visions of rest.

Besides a provisional force made up of employees,
clerks, convalescents, and the like, Ewell had a
small division of two brigades, chiefly heavy artillery,
commanded by Custis Lee, the great general's son,
to whom, while Custis was a cadet at West Point,
Lee wrote as good a letter as ever father wrote to son.

Such in general was the extent and character of
Lee's lines and the troops that occupied them just
before the final campaign began. Our lines, con-
forming to theirs in direction, were built like them,
and in many places were so very close that one could
almost tell the color of a man's eyes.

What was known as the Army of the James, consisting of the Twenty-fourth and Twenty-fifth corps
and a small division of cavalry under my classmate
Mackenzie, — peace to his ashes! — held the lines
north of the James and those of the Bermuda Hundred front. Facing Petersburg, with its right resting
on the Appomattox, was the Ninth corps, commanded by Parke; next came the Sixth, under
Wright; then Humphreys with the Second, joining
the Fifth, which had been led so long by the un-

fortunate Warren, and which now held the extreme left.

Sheridan, who had rejoined the Army of the Potomac with the First and Third divisions of his superb cavalry, having struck boldly across the country from the Shenandoah Valley, — and the ashes of its burned mills, barns, and stacks of harvested grain remember him yet, — had united them with their old comrade-division, which had remained with the army, and posted them all well to the front and left of Warren.

Besides these land forces, we had also a number of war-vessels, several of them heavy iron-clads, lying with steam up in the James, off City Point. That was our base of supplies; and at the edge of the bluff overlooking the James and Appomattox (for it is there they meet), was Grant's headquarters. I have no memory of the War more stirring than that which filled the eye from that bluff by day or by night. The broad rivers at our feet, dotted with craft of all kinds: noisy, stubborn tugs, barges, steamboats, steamships, and delicately-masted sailing ships, some coming, some going, threading their way slowly and carefully through the anchored vessels; the bank lined with wharves and storehouses; the narrow space between them and the sharply-pitching, clay bluff, a swarm of army wagons, ambulances, soldiers, laborers, black and white; the grave, steady rumble; the complaining

screech of lifting anchors; the whistles hoarse and
deep of the passing ships; and lo, plain coffins going
aboard the Washington boat on the way home; all
that and much more could be seen and heard from
sunrise to sunrise. It was pleasant, when all the
tumult was over and the hush of night had come,
to look down on the river and see the dim red, blue,
and yellow lights of the vessels, and all so still save
some busy, puffing tug. It was pleasant, but always
half-way sad, to hear the little bells on the men-of-
war striking the lonely hours.

Out in the river among all those lights, at the date
this narrative deals with, a trim steamboat called
the *Mary Martin* was lying; and aboard was Abraham Lincoln. Knowing from Grant that he was
about to move, the President's anxiety was so great
that he could not stay in Washington, so he came
down to be near his well-beloved army in its last trial.

Such then was the general character of our lines
and theirs, and the forces in them at the beginning
of the end.

Various figures have been given estimating the
strength of Lee's army. That it was nearer fifty
than forty thousand I am inclined to believe. But
however that may be, Grant had more than twice
as many; and, moreover, his army had had warm
clothing and food in abundance, while Lee's had
had neither sufficient food nor clothing, and the
winter had been one of rigorous, miserable cold.

The following letter from Lee to the Confederate Secretary of War lifts the curtain on his army's dismal state: " Yesterday, Feby. 7th, 1865 — the most inclement day of the winter — the troops had to be maintained in line of battle, having been in the same condition two previous days and nights. I regret to be compelled to state that under these circumstances, heightened by assaults and fire of the enemy, some of the men have been without meat for three days and all are suffering from reduced rations, scant clothing, exposed to battle, cold, hail, and sleet. Their physical strength, if their courage survives, must fail under this treatment."

Although they were true of heart and their faithfulness reached to the clouds, there was something more than the lack of food and clothing that wasted the spirits of his men. Defeat had drawn near and was staring at them, and the future was growing blacker and blacker.

" Eleven men of the 1st regiment," says the historian of McGowan's South Carolina brigade, " quitted camp in the early part of March, 1865, and started for home. Five were captured, four shot; one of these four had been an excellent soldier and bore that day the scars of three wounds received in battle."

On the other hand, for our men a sense of oncoming victory was kindling the sky of their hopes as the sun flushes the dawn.

III

GRANT, having resolved to bring the issue to its ultimate trial, on the night of March 27 brought Ord from north of the James with three divisions of infantry, two white and one colored, and Mackenzie's cavalry. When they reached Humphreys' and Warren's lines, Ord's troops slipped into them as these two veteran corps drew out preparatory to moving for Lee's right. Leaving Parke, Wright, and Ord in the lines, Grant, with Sheridan leading, started Humphreys and Warren on the morning of Wednesday the twenty-ninth.

Lee was alert to his danger, and on the thirty-first struck Warren, who was feeling for his right, a heavy blow. Meanwhile Sheridan had gained Dinwiddie Court-House, four or five miles beyond Warren, and had moved toward Five Forks on his way to the South Side Railroad, about all of the enemy's cavalry having gathered in to head him off. Lee, realizing how important it was to check Sheridan, sent Pickett and Bushrod Johnson's divisions of infantry to the aid of his cavalry, and together on the thirty-first they drove Sheridan back to Dinwiddie, winning almost a complete victory over him.

18

But threatened by Warren, who had been ordered by Grant to face about and attack their left rear, they withdrew during the night (Friday) to Five Forks, and there threw up a temporary line of entrenchments.

As soon as Lee, in the course of the forenoon of April first, Saturday, heard that Sheridan was likely to renew the offensive, he started several brigades under Anderson to Pickett's help, for at that juncture of his situation it was not only vital that Sheridan should be stayed, but also thrown back from Five Forks; but before Anderson could reach Pickett, Sheridan, reinforced by Warren, assailed him and drove him with great confusion from the field, capturing thousands of prisoners and several guns, the uncaptured Confederates fleeing northward in utter confusion through the darkness, for it was just at nightfall that they met their overwhelming defeat.

Pickett's and Fitz Lee's failure to hold that position was fatal, and offered a singular instance of Fortune's bad turn of her wheel for Lee; inasmuch as, when Sheridan made his attack, the famous, long-haired Pickett, Gettysburg's hero, and the cavalry commanders, blue and gay-eyed Fitz Lee, gigantic, high-shouldered and black-eyed Rosser, were engaged in planking shad on the north bank of Hatcher's Run, two miles or more in the rear of their resolute but greatly outnumbered troops. Although the fire was quick and heavy, it was completely smothered by the intervening timber, and notwithstanding the heroic efforts of the gallant Munford and the infantry brigade commanders, before Fitz Lee, Pickett and Rosser got to the front the day was lost; so at least the story was told to me by my friend Rosser, who lately and in honor went to his grave.

The news of this disaster did not reach Lee till about half-past seven Saturday night, whereupon he telegraphed to Longstreet, in the lines north of the James, to come to Petersburg at once with one of his divisions; while Grant, as soon as the same news reached him, — he was sitting alone before a struggling camp-fire in a thick, dripping pine wood, for it was raining hard, — ordered all the guns to open on the Petersburg lines, and the Sixth and Ninth corps to assault at daybreak.

Longstreet, in response to Lee's dispatch, started Field's division by rail, and then set off with his staff across the country for Petersburg and Lee's headquarters. To his dying day he spoke of that night's long ride. Of course, our batteries having opened in obedience to Grant's orders, theirs replied; and, as Longstreet rode on, those revengeful batteries answered each other with jarring thunder, and heavy mortar-shells rose from fort to fort, the small, trailing red lights of their burning, sputtering fuses outlining against the pitchy sky their high curving way. Sometimes one was just rising for its flight as the other, coming down with accelerated speed, exploded with surly, tremendous roar. Few men ever took a ride on a dark night toward the boom of a hundred guns, under a sky like that.

It was about dawn Sunday, April 2nd, when he reached Lee's headquarters at the Turnbull House, several miles southwest of Petersburg. Lee was still on his bed suffering from rheumatism, an ailment which had troubled him, and sometimes seriously, for years. He had Longstreet come to a seat at his bedside, explained what had happened the evening before at Five Forks, and told him to go, as soon as his troops arrived, to the support of Pickett's men, on whom he laid no blame or reproach as they had had to meet greatly superior numbers. But at that very hour, and long before Field of Longstreet's division got to Petersburg, the crisis had come; Lee's lines had been broken, and it was no longer a question of regaining Five Forks, but of holding on to Petersburg itself.

The Sixth and Ninth corps, arrayed several lines deep, their pioneers in front with axes to cut openings through the abatis, made their assaults, the former on Hill's, the latter Gordon's, just as the gray light of morning was sifting in. They carried their points of attack, a mile or so apart, valiantly, but with heavy loss, for the enemy, although greatly overmatched in numbers, defended their lines with uncommon bravery.

Not long since, toward the close of a hazy October day, I stood on the ground the Ninth corps won. The field, over which they advanced so firmly, sloped away to the east, and lay beautifully still in its autumn dream. The shadows were long, and a herd of cows at the lower edge of the pasture were feeding toward the gate, while some barefooted boys were approaching to let them go home through the bars for the evening milking. There were no flaming colors, no roar of guns or crash of bursting shells, no dead and bayoneted Confederates (for they stood to the very last), no wild cheers or trumpets pealing; but I thought I heard the mellow notes of a distant harp, and if I were asked whence they came I should guess that the harp was resting against the breast of Glory, and with swimming eyes her hands were sweeping the strings softly for the dead of both armies.

As soon as A. P. Hill heard of the Sixth corps' successful assault he left his headquarters, which was not far from Lee's, to go to his disrupted lines. Accompanied by a single courier, he came suddenly, at the edge of a wood, upon two of our men belonging to Wright's corps, who had pushed on through the breach. Hill drew his pistol and demanded their immediate surrender, whereupon they skipped behind a big tree, and, resting their guns one above the other against it, fired, killing him instantly. Soon his body was found, taken to Petersburg, and

placed in an ambulance which started for Richmond,
arriving at the south end of Mayo's Bridge about
midnight. There the ambulance had to wait an
hour or more, owing to the tide of troops and flight
of citizens pouring over the bridge out of the city.
Once across, the men drove to an undertaker's shop
whose doors had been demolished by the mob, and
after groping awhile in the darkness their hands fell
on a coffin. They washed the face of the punctilious
and ever gallant man, and on pulling off his gauntlets
found that the fatal shot had cut off the thumb of
his left hand and passed directly through his heart,
coming out at the back. Closing the lid tenderly
over him, they put the casket into the ambulance,
recrossed the bridge and wended their way up the
south side of the island-dotted, royal James; and
about two o'clock on Monday afternoon they buried
him in the old Winston family graveyard. Many
fields, as well they may, treasure his name; and
when Lee was breathing his last, Hill's image, with
Stonewall Jackson's, was in his glazing eye.

That portion of Hill's corps to the left, as they
faced their own works, of the point the Sixth corps
carried, rallied behind Gordon, who, although he
had lost the right of his lines, was holding the Ninth
corps under Parke from making further headway.
Hill's other brigades, among them Cooke's, Scales's,
Lane's, McRae's, and McGowan's, — cut off from
falling back on Petersburg by the advance of the

Sixth corps through the gate it had opened with such high valor, — followed what are known as the Cox and the River roads up the south side of the Appomattox, pursued by Miles's division of Humphreys' corps.

By ten o'clock — it was about this hour Lee sent the telegram whose receipt by Mr. Davis has already been given — all the outer lines of Petersburg, except those stubbornly held by Gordon on the north side, were in our hands.

IV

GRANT'S and Meade's movements meanwhile are given with detail in the diary of that gallant soldier and cultivated gentleman, Col. Theodore Lyman, on Meade's staff.

"April 2nd. 7.30. Dispatch that McCallister of 3d. div. 2d. corps had captured the picket line in his front — Humphreys', — a good deal of cheering from the right of the 2d. corps — Seymour of the 6th said to be on the south side track.

" 8.15 A. M. Dispatch that Ord and Hays (2d. div. 2d. corps) have taken the line in their front. (The 19th and 20th Mass. took a work with several guns and some hundreds of prisoners.) In fact the enemy were abandoning this part of the line as fast as possible, and moving to their own right. At this time the General rode off to the left, — i. e. to the west — with myself alone, so that, for some time, I wrote his orders and dispatches.

" 8.45 A. M. Sent telegraph ordering Benham to move up at once to Parke, from City Point. We found Gen. Grant in an open field, in front of Dabney's Mill, and, after a few moments of conversation, Gen. Meade kept on to the left and followed our

line of breastworks, the men of Mott's division
cheering him loudly.

"9 A. M. At the Rainie house we found Gen.
Humphreys. Miles's division, having been down the
plank, was returning, and was ordered up the Claiborne road, while the rest of Humphreys's force was
to move by the left flank and pass up the Boydton
road. It was presumed (10 A. M.) that Sheridan and
5th. corps would be moving along the Cox and River
roads, towards Petersburg, and would join our left
(Miles's div.); Sheridan, however, turned N. W.
and followed that part of the enemy that went
along the Namozine road, the 5th corps being still
detached under his orders. Meantime, Wright,
finding that no enemy lay between him and the
advancing 2d. corps, faced about and moved on
Petersburg, so that his left might swing to the Appomattox, while his right should touch the left of
the 24th corps that was reaching towards the 9th.

" Now we started for the most interesting ride
that perhaps I ever had, a ride straight up the
Boydton plank road, where hitherto none might go,
save as prisoners of war! We passed the battery,
whence came the fatal shot for poor Mills, and the
entrenched line, with its abatis. Then descended
to Hatcher's Run bridge, where our men planted
their flag at the first fight there. We crossed, rode
up the ascent and came on the wide space of open
land that surrounds the town. As we struck the

rear of the column marching onward, the men broke
into loud cheers which were continued all along.
It was grand! We halted at 12, by the Harmon
house, where Gen. Grant already was. Meantime
Parke's men were holding on gallantly to their
captures, while the enemy knew their only safety
lay in disputing to the utmost. One lunette was
retaken by them, but the rest remained with us."

All of the Confederate outer lines to the right of
Gordon having now been carried or abandoned, the
Sixth, Twenty-fourth and Twenty-fifth corps, and
two divisions of Humphreys' Second corps, began to
converge on the extreme right of the inner line of
Petersburg's defenses. About one o'clock Foster's
and Turner's divisions, under Gibbon, drew up in
front of Forts Gregg and Baldwin, the latter a
redoubt, the former an enclosed work with heavy
parapets and a deep ditch, which one of the heroic
defenders says was about fourteen feet wide, eight
feet deep and about eleven feet to the top of the
parapet. These field-works were connected by an
unfinished line of rifle-pits and surmounted a gentle
incline, which rose from a sluggish, difficult slough,
its clear slope forming a natural glacis to the brave
forts. Gregg, named for a very gallant man who
laid down his life in the previous autumn in front
of their lines north of the James, was stockaded in
the rear with loopholes for musketry, and at the
time of the assault had a section of three-inch rifled

guns, of Captain Chew's Maryland battery commanded by Lieutenant Frank McElroy of the Washington Artillery of New Orleans. These guns, it is
said, had been captured at Winchester on Lee's
march to Gettysburg in the long June days of 1863.

The garrison consisted mainly of the 12th and 16th
Mississippi of Harris' brigade, who, having been
brought over from the Bermuda Hundred front the
night before to go to the aid of Pickett at Five Forks,
in the morning, on account of Hill's lines having been
broken, were hurried back from their bivouac beyond the Turnbull house, Lee's headquarters, to the
inner line, and sent to man Gregg and Baldwin. On
reaching the forts they found some artillerymen and
squads of infantry of other commands already there,
making, in all, somewhat over three hundred men in
Gregg. How many there were in Baldwin, chiefly
Mississippians of Harris' brigade, I do not know,
but howsoever many there were or from which
soever of the southern states they hailed, they and
their comrades in Gregg made a defense as glorious
as any troops have ever made; for like two glittering
peaks their valor ended the war's mountain range
of carnage.

Gibbon moved up Foster's division to charging
distance, some four or five hundred yards from Gregg.
Osborn's brigade on the right, Dandy's and Fairchild's on the left. Turner marshalled two of his
brigades, Potter's and Curtis', in close support. And

at one P. M. that war-famous Sunday the trumpet
sounded the charge, and off with determined faces,
under leaning, rippling colors, our men dashed at
Gregg. Osborn's 39th Illinois, moving straight forward, struck the front of the fort, the 67th Ohio, the
salient to the right, the 62nd Ohio and 199th Pennsylvania that on the left. Dandy led on the 100th
New York, 10th Connecticut and 11th Maine. No
sooner had they cleared the hampering slough with
its sluggish pools and mane of willows and other
water-loving bushes, than the little garrisons opened
and from their dominating parapets poured levelled
sheets of deadly musketry and canister, for the
cannoneers, knowing what was coming, had piled
every round they had within close grasp.

By the time our men reached the moat, the glacis
that had lovingly held on its sloping bosom many a
sheaf of cradled wheat, was strewn with ripened
sheaves of Northern courage, but note, alas! the
soaked, crimson-stained uniforms and the glazing
eyes of the gallant dead. Of course, the moat was
a galling and effective obstruction. It soon filled with
men struggling frantically to clamber up the high
parapet, where they were met with pistol and bayonet, and it was only after twenty-five or thirty minutes of awful slaughter that the heroic garrison was
conquered, and Dandy says : " I forbear to describe
the scene inside that work after the surrender but I
think at least one-fourth of the entire garrison was

killed." As soon as Gregg surrendered, its guns were
turned on Baldwin and Colonel Jaynes and a number of men were made prisoners.

It appears, according to Captain A. K. Jones of
Port Gibson, Mississippi, who was one of the defenders of Gregg, that as the 12th and 16th were
filing into the forts, General Cadmus Wilcox, commanding a division of their corps, the 3rd (the body
of its spare, brilliant commander, A. P. Hill, was
hardly cold), galloped up to Captain Jones, and dis-
mounting, wanted to know who was in command.
"Colonel Duncan!" replied Jones, and then Wilcox,
mounting his horse so as to be heard, exclaimed in a
loud voice, "Men, the salvation of Lee's army is in
your keeping. Don't surrender this fort. If you can
check the enemy for two hours, Longstreet will
be here and the danger averted." Our artillery
cut short his speech. How well the Mississippians
and their brother Southerners in the fort answered
to that appeal let Gibbon's and Turner's losses tell,
— ten officers and one hundred and twelve men
killed outright, twenty-seven officers and five hundred and sixty-five men wounded. — And in the fort
clad in gray lay fifty-seven Confederate dead.
These numbers, I think, fall short of the actual
casualties.

By the time these works were carried, Field's division of Longstreet's corps, that had been delayed three
or four hours by a breakdown of the trains they were

on, arrived from the Richmond lines and under Lee's very eye moved into the inner line of defenses and our men were in neither condition or mood to tackle them.

By half-past three P. M., Miles overtook the forces fleeing westward, who, joining those that had set out to support Pickett, gave him battle at Sutherlands Station, some ten or twelve miles west of Petersburg, but were defeated at last with the loss of guns.

Lee's situation was now exceedingly grave, and although Gordon's men were responding with great steadiness, the chances were barely even that he could hold on till night; and in case he could not, it was manifestly clear that the long-dreaded hour had come when both Petersburg and Richmond would have to be given up.

And what the effects would be of Richmond's downfall its leading paper, the *Examiner*, had only a few weeks before set forth with seriousness and emphasis. "Our armies," said the able editor, "would lose the incentive inspired by a great and worthy object of defense; our military policy would be totally at sea; we should be without a hope or object, without civil or military organization; without a treasury or commissariat; without the means of keeping alive a wholesome and active public sentiment; without any of the appliances for supporting a cause depending upon a popular faith and enthusiasm; without the emblems or the semblance of nationality."

In view of the end, which we now so clearly see was inevitable, I have sometimes thought it would have been better, sparing lives and days of suffering, had Lee that afternoon asked terms then and there of Grant. For Mr. Lincoln, who, like Solomon, had " wisdom and understanding exceeding much, and largeness of heart," was at City Point, only a few miles away; and, knowing his sagacity and his longing for peace, we can be sure that he would have dealt wisely and been abundantly generous. Besides, it might have proved a stroke on Lee's part attended with far-reaching and beneficent political results, that would have stamped a fitting obverse to his military fame, inasmuch as Mr. Lincoln's terms, backed as they would have been by the honor and good faith of the veteran Army of the Potomac, might have outlined a policy so merciful and practical for bringing the states once more into harmony, that, notwithstanding his cruel and shameful death, the politicians would not have dared to repudiate it.

But, like Grant, Lee had been educated at West Point, and that stern national school so inculcates the theory of the subordination of the military to the civil authority that the thought of encroaching upon, much less assuming, the prerogative of the Confederate Congress and Executive, never entered his mind, however convinced he may have been of the lean chance of success.

And while I believe that he longed for peace with just as much holy eagerness as did Mr. Lincoln, yet we must bear in mind that, only a few months earlier, at Longstreet's suggestion he had made overtures to Grant, and that Grant's response, dictated from Washington, shut the door with a slam on everything short of unconditional surrender. Meeting such a rebuff, he had, as we all have, a natural unwillingness to beg for peace at the hands of a cold enemy; and this unwillingness was the stronger because of his belief in the righteousness of his cause.

However, is there real doubt that Mr. Lincoln would have let the South resume its rights of statehood? I think not, for he knew, as we all know, that the brains and character of a state must be intrusted with the duties of carrying it on.

But Lee did not know, nor did the bulk of Mr. Lincoln's Northern contemporaries know, the wisdom, depth, and natural warmth of Mr. Lincoln's heart; much less did they dream of the way in which he would tower above the common level of his age; so, although it might have been a stroke of large and merciful consequence for Lee to have pocketed his rebuff and asked for terms, that he did not do it is not to be wondered at, when we come to know him better. And surely not, whatsoever that estimate of Lee's nature may be, if we lift our eyes

from this misty, transitory life up to that undis-
tracted power called Fate and see her looms
all busy, their shuttles flying back and forth cease-
less till the fullness of time is come.

But let this conjecture engage attention as it may,
Lee was faced by something far removed from
airy conjecture, on the contrary and in fact with the
gravest military exigency of his life. The one he
confronted after Gettysburg, with the Potomac bank
full behind him, and the Army of the Potomac that
had just repulsed him on the point of attacking, was
black, yet its cloud fell far short of what now overhung him. Let us take a sweeping look at it, and
I am sure that the way he met the situation, will
challenge, not only the admiration of every student
of war, but of every reader who admires lofty character.

The extreme right of his line turned by Sheridan
the night before at Five Forks, Pickett and Fitz
Lee, disastrously defeated on that field, retreating
hopeless up the south bank of the Appomattox,
followed by Anderson. The men from the Hatcher's
Run line to the south and west of the point where the
Sixth and Twenty-fourth corps were pouring through
the gap the former had made in Hill's line, all cut off
from Petersburg, and threatened with destruction by
Sheridan and Miles; Hill, one of his ablest corps
commanders, dead at his feet; Longstreet's corps,
although on its way to Petersburg, yet, owing to a

breakdown of the railway, not near enough to be of
any immediate help, and Parke assaulting Gordon
desperately. Is it easy to imagine a more trying
situation? Yet, every account shows that Lee
quailed not, nor for a moment lost his balance, by
this critical turn of affairs; he sowed no seeds of
panic by rushing from place to place making passionate appeals, but, calmly and self-reliantly, rallied
what was left of Hill's forces for the defense of the
inner lines.

That he would have to abandon Petersburg, and
Richmond, was self-evident, and the only question
in his mind now, was, could he hold on till night?
But whether he could or not, in order to have his
trains out of the way, he started them on the roads
north of the Appomattox for Amelia Court-House,
where he meant to re-assemble his army, and from
there lead it on to Danville, so as to join forces
with Johnston in North Carolina.

The hours moved on, but not his lowring peril,
yet Lee rose and met it with an adamantine will,
worthy of greatness. A single incident, which illus-
trates his poise and natural tenderness, and throws
the charm of a sweet flower, a flower like that of the
eglantine, into the field of this trying hour, gives me
pleasure to record.

His young and gallant aide, Walter H. Taylor,
sought, and got permission to go to Richmond and
marry his sweetheart. Off hurried the light-hearted

youth, the marriage took place at midnight, and immediately after the ceremony he set out to rejoin the headquarters of his chief. Colonel Taylor at this writing is still vigorous, bodily and mentally, lives in Norfolk, and has a large family that with natural pride revere their honored parents. May this day, and every day to the end, be soft and sweet to the last living one of Lee's personal staff.

The arrival of Field's division of Longstreet's corps, Grant not renewing the offensive after the fall of Gregg and Baldwin, and the sturdy way Gordon held off Parke, — indeed Parke was now, two P. M., on the defensive to retain what he had gained, — laid at rest in Lee's mind the question as to whether he could hold on till night.

At or about this time, he telegraphed Ewell, " I wish you to make all preparations, quietly and rapidly, to abandon your position (Richmond) to-night. *Send back on the line of Danville railroad all supplies, ammunition, etc., that is possible.*" I have emphasized those instructions, for in them lies an explanation of weighty circumstance, that gave rise, after the war, to some bitter controversy between Mr. Davis and his critics. Later in the afternoon, Col. Walter H. Taylor, before he set off for his wedding, formulated Lee's orders for withdrawal. The artillery should pull out as soon as it was dark, followed by the infantry, first Longstreet, and then Gordon, and all to take the roads to Bevil's Bridge on the Appomattox, and from there to Amelia Court-House. The troops in the Richmond and Bermuda Hundred lines were notified to commence to withdraw at eight o'clock, pickets to stand until three A. M., and head for Goode's and Genito bridges on the Appomattox, thence to Amelia Court-House. In a dispatch to Breckenridge, Secretary of War, received at seven P. M., Lee said, " I have given all the orders to officers on both sides of the river and have taken every precaution that I can to make the movement successful. It will be a difficult operation, but I hope not impractical. The troops will all be directed to Amelia Court-House."

The delivery and promulgation of Lee's orders, at one of the posts on the James that Sunday night, well deserve mention; and may the spirit of the occasion, signalized by reverence and recognition of a Power above all powers, breathe, God willing, on this narrative to the end.

Major Stiles, commanding a battalion of artillery at Chaffin's Bluff, had stood, so he tells us in his sterling *Four Years Under Marse Robert*, a greater part of the day on the parapets of his works, listening to the guns at Petersburg. The guns he heard were on Gordon's front, for that brave man held his lines and fought Parke till the sun went down and the attack was given up. Their dull reverberations, rapid and continual, so foreboded adversity, that, before going to meet with his men for worship at nightfall, in a dimly lighted little chapel which they had built during the winter, he told his adjutant to remain in the office, and if any orders came, to bring them to him at once. " I read with the men," says the major, " the Soldier Psalm, the Ninety-first, and exhorted them in any special pressure that might come upon us in the near future, the ' terror by night ' or the ' destruction at noonday,' to abide with entire confidence in that ' stronghold,' to appropriate that ' strength.' "

The major says that, as he uttered these last words, a lad's open face with brimming eyes caught his attention and checked his speech momentarily. Just then the door opened, and there stood the adjutant with an official communication in his hand. Stiles asked him to stand for a moment where he was, and proceeded to tell the men what, he was satisfied, was the purport of the adjutant's message. The young major, for he was scarcely twenty-five years of age, then led them in prayer, imploring the " realization of what David had expressed in the psalm — for faith, for strength, for protection." After Amen had been said, all on bended knees and with heads bowed, — deep must have been its holy pause, — the major rose and read Lee's orders. Softly, at the appointed hour, for our sentinels were within speaking distance, his men stole out of their works and, leaving their hollow tents standing, took up the march. Daylight, when it broke, found them miles away in Chesterfield; and there they lay down and fell asleep in a grove. And I hope their slumber was sweet, and that the lad's eyes, if he had dreams, saw home or heaven.

By the time the dead hours of the night had come on, the Petersburg forces were well across the Appomattox and the sun was just peeping over the tree tops when the last of the Richmond troops, Gary's brigade of South Carolina cavalry, crossed Mayo's Bridge over the James.

V

THE abandonment of Richmond by the Confederate
and state authorities, and by many of its prominent
citizens, was marked by no such orderly and solemnly
uplifting detail as distinguished the conduct of
Major Stiles and his command. For some strange
reason, little or no fortitude and self-possession
were displayed. On the contrary, as soon as it was
learned that the troops were to evacuate the lines
that night, frantic with disappointment or dread,
they began to pour toward the railway stations and
the canal which, in those days, joined Richmond and
Lynchburg, following the banks of the James, packing themselves and their belongings into the cars
or on the sleepy boats, and by sundown all the roads
leading south and west into the country, then veiling
with twilight, were filled with groups of anxious
travelers, some on foot, some on horseback, and
many in vehicles, often hired at fabulous prices.

In all seriousness, how can this humiliating flight
from the doomed city be accounted for? Was it
because they feared that our troops, like some of
those of Sherman's, would turn barbarians and disgrace themselves and their country by outrages on

persons and property? If so, that fear was groundless; those who entered were under the firm hands of the mild and upright Weitzel, and carried themselves with becoming humanity and dignity. Or was it because there had been dreams of trials for treason and visions of gallows? Let the answer be what it may, the scene was not heroic, and was unbecoming in its contrast with the fame of Richmond, the desperate stand at Antietam, the glorious charge of Pickett at Gettysburg, or the dead in Holywood. Let us not forget, however, that it was a day of panic, and be charitable; above all, to the hundreds of minor officials, clerks, and employees in the various civil and military departments, drawn from all over the South. For all of them, I have nothing but pity in their distress; many were poor, far from home, and had only done their humble, tread-mill duties. But for all those who by hook or by crook had managed to keep out of the ranks, and especially for the oratorical, passion-inflaming politicians, I have nothing, and they deserve nothing, but contempt. Who knows how much of the mutual rage and cruelty of individuals in both armies — for cruelty begets cruelty — is attributable to the blistering, wounding speech, the habitual, unmitigated abuse of the entire North, accompanied by taunting sneers of that class before and during the War? In the final analysis,— let there be no mistake, — to their repeated gaffs of crowing, battle-challenging

arrogance and unmerited disdain, the South owed
the North's resolution to conquer or die.

And who can say whether, in some measure at
least, the atrocities that disgraced Sherman's march
and the spirit of vindictiveness which for a moment
swept the North after Mr. Lincoln's assassination,
may not be laid at the doors of these frenzied de-
claimers?

I offer no veiled or surreptitious excuse for our
armies in burning houses and barns of rich and poor,
or pillaging and ruthlessly destroying the homes of
those whose only offense was that their sons had
dared to fight for honestly held principles.   Nor do
I exculpate the authorities, Northern or Southern,
for the needless suffering of prisoners, or for the
lack of care and humanity which made Andersonville
and Salisbury gruesome horrors and filled row after
row of graves at Elmira, Chicago, and Rock Island.
To the very end of our country's history those
graves will be a disgrace to South and North.   No;
the class I have in mind are the shrill, rabid, tongue-
lashing, notoriety-craving and woe-breeding dema-
gogues, whether born in the Northland or the Southland, who, by their rancorous, malignant speech,
kindled the fires of our War.   Read what appeared
almost daily in the Southern press, consult the files
of Congress, and mark the provoking, snarling
poison-barbed language in the proceedings of
Abolition conventions.

So, then, fire-eaters, in dread of retributive justice
for your malicious abuse of heaven-born speech;
contractors, leeches, who had bled the poor Confederacy; and you, too, loudly-dressed hangers-on and
gamblers, who, in goodly numbers, infested the
hotels and saloons of Richmond but who had not
the manliness to shoulder a gun, — catch the departing trains if you can and disappear for good
and all! You made the evacuation of Richmond what
it was, a panicky scene of terror; and when the
Confederacy looks back, as I know it does, over those
four troubled years, its eyes do not seek, nor does
its heart yearn for you, no, but for those self-pos-
sessed men of moral life, quiet demeanor, respect-
ful speech, and honest convictions of the paramount rights of the state, and for the young men
in the ranks who stood by its colors to the end.
On them, as on the fathers and mothers whose
prayers night and morning went up for the Confederacy, will it look through the misting past, with
justly proud and affectionate eyes.

As the news of the evacuation spread, the scum
of Richmond, scenting plunder, swarmed in from
squalid suburbs and out of noisome lean-dog and
yowling-cat haunted alleys. Naturally enough,
these hungry and pitiful discards in the game of
life, gathered before the government storehouses in
the midst of the city. Their numbers swelled fast,
soon became tumultuous, and the confused police

had no more weight on that seared, ignorant and night-enshrouded mob, than so many thistle blooms; and pretty soon, crash went a window, and pillage began. The authorities, having lost their grip, made matters worse by ordering the barrels of whiskey and brandy to be rolled out of the saloons and the heads knocked in. Storehouse after storehouse was broken into. Debauch and Revelry, now cheek by jowl with Riot and the latent anarchy of the alleys, were having their day, as the scum, white and black,—the jail and penitentiary doors had been flung open, — lapped up the liquor as it ran in the gutters. " Met a band of women going hand in hand singing and carousing," says the color sergeant of the 18th Virginia in his account of the evacuation. He was on his way to report to the provost marshal, Major Carrington, in Capitol Square, with an extemporized command made up of the hospital stewards, clerks, and convalescent soldiers of Chimborazo Hospital.

Meanwhile, amid a pandemonium of shouts and yells from drunken wretches, the exploding magazines of forts and fired war vessels shaking the earth, and hurling bursting shells on flaming arcs through the midnight sky, Ewell's troops, like troubled spectres, marched through the dimly lit and liquor-fuming streets. The color sergeant, on reporting, was directed to protect property and lives and to have tobacco houses ready for burning. Toward morning, fires, incendiary and otherwise, were set, and by

seven o'clock on Monday, just as the last of the
dazed forces crossed the James, the business heart
of the city burst into flames, and the Confederate
Capitol was overhung by the black, swirling clouds
of a mad conflagration. Fortunately, by half-past
eight or nine, Weitzel's corps marched in, stacked
their guns, fought down the fire, and Richmond was
saved from complete destruction.

But what a night it had been! And what a satiric
contrast its debauch and flames offered to the torch-
light procession in its streets that April night four
years gone by when Virginia cut the tender cords
which bound her to the Union she had nursed. " A
track of transparencies gleamed from Church Hill
to the Exchange Hotel, and there was a vast crowd
which hung on the speeches of orators speaking
from balconies, imparting words of fire to the head
of the column that toiled for a mile in one of the
main thoroughfares of Richmond." Oh, wild and
passion-swept multitude! hearken not to your
inflaming orators, but to him who cried of old, " Be-
hold I will turn back the weapons of war that are
in your hands, and I myself will fight against you
with an outstretched hand and with a strong arm,
even in anger, and in fury, and in great wrath; and
I will smite the inhabitants of this city, such as for
death, to death; and such as for the sword, to the
sword; and such as for the captivity, to the captivity."

The other day, as I was loitering through the Capitol grounds at Richmond, dwelling on the contrasting nights, — the setting sun had just sunk behind the roof of St. Paul's, and golden was the west, — I happened to look up as I drew near Crawford's celebrated monument of Washington. The rearing horse, staring with such manifest terror off over Richmond to the southwest, and Washington's long outstretched forefinger pointing along the charger's neck apparently to the same terrifying object, and lo! both directly toward Appomattox, I paused involuntarily, and the query rose: What does the charger see, and what is the Great Virginian, the Father of our country, pointing to? And there came a Voice hoarse and deep from the field of Lee's surrender, saying, He is pointing to me. I said to myself, as with downcast eyes I moved on, " What a prophetic analogue! and was the spirit of Jeremiah directing Crawford's hand? "

But before we dismiss the account of the evacuation, there were two occurrences that night, which have the candles of history, and what is more, a noble human interest, burning brightly in them.

The first was at the Danville railway station: and that we may note it, I will ask the reader to fancy that together we have crowded or wormed our way through the feverish multitude, till we are close to the cars in the dim, lamp-lit station. What a sea of distressed and needlessly alarmed men and women, — children are actually crying aloud, — swarming this way and that, are we in! The train, bearing Mr. Davis, the majority of his Cabinet, a car with a small amount of specie belonging to the Confederate treasury, and several coaches filled with Congressmen, distinguished personages, a clergyman or two, — think of shepherds abandoning their flocks under such circumstances! — and a few pale, sick and wounded officers and privates, has just left.

Other trains to follow are made up, their locomotives hoarsely sputtering, bursting into an impatient roar at times that drowns the babel of voices. The sinewy, middle-aged engineer, bare-headed, is leaning out of his cab, one hand on the lever, watching for the signal to be off; the young, smooth-faced fireman is ringing the bell, — how the scene must have lasted in his eyes, — and sentinels, with bayonets fixed, are holding the eager, pressing mob back from the car-steps, letting only those enter who are properly authorized by superior officers.

But let us take a good look at that intent, flinty-faced, and sordid man, followed by a gang of slaves, who is forcing his way through the crowd into the presence of a sentinel. He represents the last of those creatures who dealt in his fellow mortals — at any rate that we have any knowledge of. Yes; take a good look at him, as at one of the wonders in an age of modern Christianity. His sorrowful-eyed slaves, male and female, left over from his last auction (I hope for humanity's sake that there was not a little black child among them, clutching nervously its mother's hand), are halted, and look around bewildered while he demands passage for himself and them.

The sentinel, a young man clad in gray, with that scornful and condemning look which the vocation of dealing in slaves naturally kindles, has brought his gun down, saying firmly as he bars approach to the cars, " Lumpkin " (for that was the dealer's name), " there is no room in these cars for you and your gang." The slave-dealer remonstrates in vain, his eyes shooting flames of anger into the face of the stern, manly youth, and, at last, shamefully muttering oaths, leads off his gang. Lumpkin having gone, — gone to this world's scrap-heap, — now scan the boy-sentinel's face well, for in the spirit of those words and that gesture he has made the last and by far the best argument before history's jury that the cause he loved and was willing to die for was not slavery. I do not know into what paths fate led him, nor the number of years that fell on him, but I will guarantee that when death overtook him, his spirit on its upward flight was met by a noble company, and that in the reveries of the Confederacy his memory is green and dear.

The other occurrence is given in *W. W. Black-*

ford's Memoirs.   And here I want to acknowledge my
deep obligation to Mr. R. C. Blackford of Lynchburg, Virginia, for authority to quote from the memoir his mother — and I have no doubt that she was
of that sweet Virginia type, a type I know well, for
my infant head rested on a Virginia mother's breast
— published privately of her distinguished husband.
And something tells me that my thanks will not
travel to their destination alone, but that along with
them will go, hand in hand, those of more than one
reader.

Blackford, an officer on duty in the War Department, was in St. Paul's and saw the delivery of the
dispatch to Mr. Davis.   On leaving the church he
hurried to the office, learned that Lee's lines were
broken and that the city was to be evacuated, and
just before sundown left Richmond to report to
Longstreet wheresoever he might find him.   " The
streets were full of scared people, ladies and gentlemen all in great distress but all powerless to accomplish anything.   I went down by Gamble's Hill.
My slave Gabe, who was hired out under Dr. Morris
in the Telegraph Department, as soon as he heard,
came to my room to know what he must do.   I
told him he was free to do what he pleased and that
he was as rich as I was; I should advise him to get
work with the Yankees as soon as they came.   He
and John Scott (another slave) did all they could
to make me comfortable.   I left John in charge of

our families and told him to come through the lines
as soon as he could and join me at Longstreet's
headquarters. Both went with me to the canal-
boat. Gabe shed tears and kissed my hand when
I told him good-bye and sent his love to his mistress
Nannie. A more honest and faithful man never
lived."

What a solemn and telling reproach there is in
this incident to the Abolitionists, who, in their
antagonism to slavery as a denial of human
rights, allowed a righteous enthusiasm to be converted into a personal, vindictive hatred of all
slaveholders, which had its culmination in John
Brown's attempt to bring about a San Domingo
massacre.

So, then, with Mr. Davis' train speeding on, and
he, from his seat beside a window, looking out into
the black night, ends Sunday at Richmond, and its
people in terror, riot and tears.

Let us turn back, back to the Army of the Potomac, and tell what happened between the capture
of Fort Gregg and sundown. Well, it was about two
o'clock when the forts fell, and for the reasons already given active operations against the inner
line at that point were not taken. But while Gibbon's
assault was going on, word came to Meade, that
Miles had overtaken and encountered the Hatcher's
Run line brigades, Cooke's, Scales', McRae's and
McGowan's, entrenched at Sutherlands Station.

Meade at once started Humphreys to the support of Miles, but before he reached him, Miles attacked, and after three trials routed his opponents, capturing a number of prisoners and two guns. The defeated Confederates fled up the river, and R. H. Anderson, Lieutenant-General, at midnight, from his headquarters at Namozine Church, sent word back to General Bushrod Johnson, that he had just received intelligence that the trains and troops ahead of his (Pickett's) were all stopped at Deep Creek by high water, and that Johnson on coming up should take the left-hand road.

Meade, late in the afternoon, issued orders to assault at daylight, and directed that at the same hour a pontoon bridge be laid over the Appomattox several miles above Petersburg for Sheridan, the Fifth and Second corps to cross upon, in case Lee stayed in his lines and the assault should fail.

When night fell it found the Army of the Potomac exultant, and there is no doubt when it lay down to rest that it slept well. The spring-time air was balmy, the peach and cherry trees were in bloom, in runs and swales the little frogs were piping, " and the turtle and the crane and the swallow were observing the time of their coming," as of old; and perhaps, who knows, through the slumbering camps, dew faintly sparkling on guns and moistening youth-tinted cheeks, guardian angels whispered to each and all, " Sleep deep and sleep well; for Victory, great and final Victory, is drawing near." At any rate, when morning broke, the Army of Northern Virginia was gone, and the bridges over which it had crossed the Appomattox were on fire.

VI

AND now, before the narrative sets off on its flight, if so I may speak of it, let me do what I can toward giving a bird's-eye view of the country that was traversed by the fleeing and the pursuing armies. And to this end, a map has been provided which I hope will be of some aid, to fix in the mind the relation of the places to each other as they are gained and left behind by the respective rapid-marching forces. A glance will show Petersburg and Richmond, from whence they started, the Army of the Potomac on the south, that of Northern Virginia on the north bank of the Appomattox, and Appomattox Court-House, where on the following Sunday, the 9th, the marching was over and the torn flags were furled. The scene of their operations, it will be observed then, begins where the Appomattox enters the stately James, and ends where it rises an hundred miles or more away to the west among tall, arching ferns, blooming laurel, dogwood and azalias, at the feet of shouldering, oak-timbered hills that greet the morning sun. I hope the reader will take a good long look at the map, inasmuch as I want him to feel at home with the roads and localities as they are mentioned. Moreover, from every clearly conceived landscape there comes, from time to time, a note which strikes the mysterious chords of our natures, and whose faint musical harmony the mind loves to be conscious of as it follows a narrative.

And first let me call attention to the railroads. The Richmond and Danville (easily followed on the map — it was by this railway that Mr. Davis' train, leading several others, fled on that Sunday night) is intersected at Burkeville by the Norfolk and Western, known as the South Side road during the war on account of its location south of the Appomattox, and which runs on by the field of the surrender to Lynchburg, and thence, having passed the beautiful Blue Ridge, winds its way through the Alleghanies to the Ohio. Burkeville is fifty-three miles from Richmond and fifty-one from Petersburg; Danville, the goal of Lee's blasted hopes, is on the river Dan, 88 miles southwest of Burkeville.

And now the country roads; those which Grant took south of the Appomattox are known as the Cox, and the River roads, leading, as will be seen, toward Amelia Court-House. Those Lee took on the north side of the river, the one nearest the Appomattox is known as the River, the others as the Hickory and Woodpecker roads. The former after awhile runs into the River road, which keeps on its way to Bevil's Bridge, the first on the river, and about thirty-five miles above Petersburg, and thence on to Amelia Court-House.   The Woodpecker wends aimlessly westward and loses itself at last in dreamy roads much like itself, which mingle, some to go to sleep at Chesterfield Court-House, some in Richmond. From Richmond there are several roads bearing southward, among them, the historic Genito, which, as the map discloses, leads finally to a bridge of that name across the Appomattox.   This is the one the bulk of Ewell's Richmond forces took.   Between Bevil's and Genito is Goode's Bridge on whose rumbling planks the Petersburg and Bermuda Hundred troops, the garrisons of the forts at Drewey's and Chaffin's Bluffs crossed the Appomattox.   These, then, are the main roads and I think they remember the two armies well.   They wind through much deep and pondering forest, cross many creeks and pleasant runs, and smile back on many old friends from clayey ridges, fields of wheat, tobacco and blading corn.

The river itself from its very start curves often, has many stretches through woods where venerable, leaning trees, some tangled with wild grape-vines, almost meet each other over the flowing stream, and a prettier sight one cannot see when the grapes are ripening, and the redbird and the kingfisher and the blue winged jay streak with their colors October's golden woof.

As the river runs on, it receives the waters, first

on this side, and then on that, of many a deep, winding, tree-roofed, wood-duck-nesting creek and many a run, some large and some small, each having its glittering ripples and sober pools, the homes of dace, minnows and chub. Finally it comes in sight of Petersburg, tumbles over some rapids between low bluffs, and then calmly enters the James. Its long narrow water-shed is truly Virginian, the home and burial place of more than one distinguished family whose venerable mansions, for generations the abode of culture and warm, hearty, engaging hospitality, look at you now with saddened, pleading eyes.

Mysteriously enough, besides the towering event on the upper Appomattox, this region witnessed another which cast the heaviest shadow that ever fell on any land, — the introduction of slavery by a Dutch man-of-war against the humane remonstrances of the first settlers at Jamestown. And lo! after two hundred and fifty years, — years of brave and high-minded effort to found a republic, and years blessed with sweet peace, prosperity, and fraternal brotherhood, — it witnessed the deadly struggle which grew mainly out of that very sordid importation forced upon it in its infancy. These two waters, the James and Appomattox, draining the country which is the scene of this narrative, saw slavery's coming, and the Appomattox saw its ending; and both rivers will tell you now that they are glad it is gone.

In view of the fact that the names of officers, Confederate and Federal, will appear and reappear so often in the course of my story, I have wondered whether or not it would be of advantage to the reader to throw a rushlight as it were upon their personalities; but most of them are of such renown, especially Grant, Lee, Meade and Sheridan, and they have all been dealt with in so much detail by numerous writers, — including myself in *The Battle of the Wilderness*, — that it would be carrying coals to Newcastle to enlarge upon them here. Moreover, I have a dread of repeating myself, and although I served with, saw, and knew most of them, I shall trust to the reader's imagination to portray them duly in the light of their deeds.

On second thought, perchance the reader, like myself, is pleased, if not aided, by having as a side-light on great deeds the distinctive features of the actor's face, and so I will devote a line or two to Gordon and Parke, who, when I digressed, were contending so fiercely.

Gordon, to whom more than to any one Lee owed the salvation of Petersburg that day, was a man of natural eminence. Above medium height, he had a soldier's port, raven-black hair, a noticeably deep scar across his left cheek, and as fierce and nearly cruelly blue eye as I ever looked into. His indomitable courage was like Humphreys', who commanded our Second corps; and if there were ever hearths on this green earth at which valor and honor felt at home, they were theirs.

Parke, a stocky built man, had smiling brown eyes, a low steep forehead, heavy jaw, wore side-whiskers, and about him was somewhat of the subdued air of scholarship, clothing his address and bearing in simple good manners.

The leaders on both sides were much older than I, but the staffs of Grant, Meade, Sheridan and the most of our corps commanders were of my generation, and many of them I knew casually, and some I knew well. Their faces, blooming with youth, hang, here and there, on memory's walls, and, in the reveries of my old age, I sit and look at them. But they nor I were more than inconsequential shrubs in the landscape of events, and so, dear as their memories are to me, I will pass on.

And now we have outlined the natural features of the narrative's channel, but before setting the pen's loom agoing to weave the story's fabric, damasked as it is with many contrasting figures, blasted hopes, and flowers of noble deeds, let us make as clear as we can the military situation of the Confederacy, so that the moves the two armies made may be fully understood.

Adversity's winds had blown so hard and chill, by the spring of 1865, the Southern cause had only two armies left where hope could find a resting place, Lee's in Virginia, Johnston's in North Carolina.

And even that hope hung on the slender chance of the immediate and rapid concentration of those two armies, as soon as the roads would allow, and then their attack with the desperation of despair on Grant or Sherman as the case might be.

That this concentration should be made and that the strategic moves to carry it out had been talked over more than once by Lee and Mr. Davis is most probable. But as Mr. Davis never had had much confidence in Johnston to accomplish anything, it is unlikely at this junction he expected him to withdraw his army safely from Sherman's front and join Lee. And I think Mr. Davis was right as to the latter, for had Johnston tried to escape, Sherman's crouching and greatly outnumbering veterans, inured to fast and long marches, would have leaped upon and torn him to pieces before he had got fairly started. So then, if the concentration was to be made, Lee would have to try to join Johnston, and that he had determined to make the attempt as soon as the state of the roads would admit, is a well known fact. His plan was to steal away from the Petersburg and Richmond lines; all the troops around Petersburg, taking roads up the south side of the Appomattox, those in the Richmond lines to unite with them by crossing the river at convenient distances above Petersburg, and all to rendezvous at Burkesville, the junction of the South Side and Richmond and Danville Railroads. That strategic point gained, the way was clear to Danville, where he hoped to find Johnston.

Having settled upon this series of moves, the only disturbing question was, would Grant anticipate them and strike before he was ready to carry them out? But whensoever Grant should take the offensive, Lee knew that he would do one of two things, either try to break through the lines and end it then and there, or extend his left and seize the South Side Railroad. Of the two the one to the left was the most probable and altogether the most to be desired, for it cut off Lee's shortest and only true line of retreat.

That Grant did not wait for the roads to settle is already known, and that after defeating Pickett at Five Forks he thrust the Fifth, Sixth and Twenty-fourth corps and all of Sheridan's cavalry across the South Side Railroad and thereby closed that line of Lee's retreat as completely as though a monster steel door had swung across it.

That being the state of affairs, Lee had no other line to take than the roads up the north bank of the Appomattox, and, as we know, them he took, directing all of his army to rendezvous at Amelia Court-House on the Richmond and Danville road, some twelve or fifteen miles this side of Burkeville. And the question was what would Grant do, follow him, or strike at once for Burkeville, up the South Side Railroad, and try to put the Army of the Potomac across his way?

And now, I hope the situation and the reason for the moves that had been made are fairly clear to the reader, and if he will go back to the Sunday night after the capture of Forts Gregg and Baldwin I will tell him again where Meade's headquarters were, namely, at Wall's house on the Boydton plank road. And that night between him and Lee's inner line lay dreaming happily, I hope, the old Army of the Potomac which he had led so long.

Lyman says, " About five in the morning heard Duane, chief of engineers on Meade's staff [the Duane mentioned in *The Battle of the Wilderness*] say outside my tent, ' They have evacuated the town; ' " and sure enough and safely enough, they had indeed.

Grant rode into Petersburg and made his headquarters at a large house owned by a Mr. Wallace, and at once sent orders for the Army of the Potomac to move with all possible dispatch toward Burkeville; Ord and the Ninth corps to follow the railroad, the Second, and Sixth corps to follow Sheridan and the Fifth on the River and Cox roads. At 10:20 A. M. he renewed his orders to Sheridan, saying, " The first object of present movement will be to intercept Lee's army, and the second to secure Burkeville. Make your movements according to this programme."

Mr. Lincoln, at City Point, hearing that Petersburg had fallen, rode up to see Grant and thanked him and his army with a full heart for the results of the last few days. Grant about noon set off to follow his troops, who were marching with all speed up the south side of the river, and for the first time in its history, as it marched by the flower-sprinkled fields and woods (violets, liverwort, trilliums, and cowslips were abloom), every one of its battle-torn colors was unfurled. And in a book called *Stories Told by Soldiers*, my friend, General Alfred A. Woodhull of Princeton, writes, "As far as the eye could reach, the curving country road was vivid with the lively but not boisterous blue and steel."

Not long ago, starting early on a beautiful October morning, I made a trip from Petersburg to Appomattox over the roads the Confederates took. As I crossed the rumbling Pocahontas Bridge a thin veil of mist hung just above the river, cows were feeding along its low banks, — one a large, creamy yellow with spreading white spots, — and in a clump of blushing willows a sparrow was singing. The road, having cleared the mild ascent to Ettricks, which overlooks Petersburg, leads on, bordered here and there by lonely, tapering cedars, its road-side fences, old and gray, masked by brushy thickets, and lit up now and then by blazing leaves of tangled vines; — on, by fields with peanuts and corn in shock, through woods and woods, and by old plantations still and solemn, the dreaming silence broken every once in a while by a cow-bell's *kling, klung, klang*, sometimes clear, sometimes faint, and by the

soft, pensively mellow notes of migrating bluebirds;
— on and on toward Bevil's Bridge the road goes,
over which the Army of Northern Virginia — our
whole country's pride now — made its last fore-
boding march that April morning, 1865. The road
crosses many runs and creeks, some of such great
beauty, that I stopped more than once and listened
as they gurgled the soft music of their solitude.

About twelve or fourteen miles from Petersburg,
a farmer, of large frame and stately manners, whose
freshly-painted white house with open door and
blooming dahlias enlivens the lonely road, told me,
in the course of a pleasant talk, that the van of the
army reached there by daybreak; that from that
time till the last one passed, his mother, with the serv-
ants, was engaged in preparing food for the hungry numbers; that the dooryard and the adjacent
young orchard and garden were full of men resting,
and that as a group of horsemen went riding by, he,
a boy of thirteen, heard the soldiers say, "There
goes Marse Robert."

And of the man whom this boy saw, Colonel Fre-
mantle of the English army, who volunteered to serve
for a time with Lee's army, says: "His [Lee's] cheeks
were ruddy and his eyes had that clear light which
indicates the presence of the calm, self-poised will.
His beard and moustache, both grown gray, he
wore short and well-trimmed, a gray uniform with
no indication of rank save the stars on his collar,

cavalry boots nearly to his knees, broad-brimmed gray, felt hat, which rested low on his forehead." Another who rode with him that morning says: "His seat in the saddle was erect and commanding, and he seemed to look forward to assured success in the critical movement which he had undertaken."

What a scene for old age to dwell upon! And, since the alembic of a boy's love and admiration is so durable and active, how meagre and blighted would be the nature that would fail in its reveries, as that morning came back, to clothe every one of those earnest, poorly-clad, and hungry soldiers, as well as the cause they fought for, in raiments of Right and Glory. Yes, as we stood by the roadside and talked, — his hound was running a fox or a rabbit in the hazy timbered bottom below, — my stately friend thought that the army he saw that morning was fighting for the right, and was one to be proud of; and as to the last I certainly agreed with him.

The forces he saw were Longstreet's valiant men. Gordon's were three or four miles to the north on the Hickory road, which, as has been said, comes into the road Longstreet was marching on some miles this side of Bevil's Bridge, where it crosses the Appomattox. The head of the column, Longstreet's, on approaching the river found it a-flood and spread away out over its sombre wooded bottoms, preventing all access to the bridge, so they had to strike for Goode's, the next above on the raging stream, which then, as always after a heavy rain, was roiled into the color of liquid brick-dust. Notwithstanding the long march and the frightful condition of the roads, — every stream, creek and run was bank-high and the mud churned into mortar by the trains, — Field's division of Longstreet's corps and Wilcox's of Hill's reached Goode's by twilight and crossed over.

Mahone, from the Bermuda Hundred lines, reached Chesterfield Court-House somewhat before 11 A. M. There at any rate Dr. Claiborne, senior surgeon of the Petersburg hospital, who under orders had left Petersburg the day before at 2 P. M., found him in line of battle. Mahone soon resumed his march and bivouacked some miles east of Goode's Bridge.

Ewell's, Kershaw's and Custis Lee's columns, after a march of twenty-four miles, camped at Tomahawk Church, away off on the Genito Road, which runs southward from Richmond, crossing the Appomattox at Clementown. Darkness overtook Pickett and Anderson, who, it will be remembered, had fled up the south side of the Appomattox, beyond Deep Creek. There before their camp-fires, weary, scantily rationed, and disheartened they sat, for the news of the abandonment of Richmond had reached them with its depressing and prophetic significance.

Lee himself bivouacked at Hebron Church, six

miles north of Goode's Bridge, and at half-past six, concerned by learning that the pontoon which he had ordered to be laid at Genito, farther up the river, for the forces from the Richmond and James River lines to cross upon, had not been laid, sent a note by a courier to Ewell giving him the situation and directing him to move toward Goode's.

This was the last unbroken night's sleep of the Army of Northern Virginia, and, as before my mind's eyes its veterans lie resting at random around scattered camp-fires, I pity them, knowing, as I do, what is to befall them.   And, reader, so would you, had you in your youth contended for victory against them on the fields of the Wilderness and Spottsylvania. A Confederate War Department clerk, who stayed in Richmond, kept a diary, and in it recorded that there were millions of stars out that night. If so, they saw the troops in bivouac as we have placed them, and the heart of Richmond a desolate, smoking ruin, its streets deserted save by Weitzel's patrols and guards, its houses dark, curtains drawn and blinds closed, their inmates some in tears and all weighed down by bitter defeat.

In contrast the stars saw New York, Philadelphia, and Boston lit up brilliantly and the streets packed with cheering multitudes.   For the War Department had proclaimed the fall of Richmond, and ordered a salute of one hundred guns to be fired at each military post in honor of the event.

The news reached Boston about eleven A. M., Monday, and Governor Andrew telegraphed to the Secretary of War, Stanton, " Our people by a common impulse abandon business to-day for thanksgiving and rejoicing." State Street was packed, the bells, including the Old North, rang for an hour at noon, and a salute was fired on the historic Common. The next day, Tuesday, a meeting was held in Faneuil Hall, and above the clock was an arch bearing the legend, " Stand by the work of your fathers." " Work of your fathers! " which suggests that when the news of Cornwallis's surrender reached Richmond in 1783, it was made known by the watchmen on their beats calling out, " Past — twelve o'clock — a starlit night — and Lord Cornwallis t-a-k-e-n! "

The Governor of Illinois, Oglesby, notified Washington: " We are firing salutes over the restoration of the Union, and the hearts of our people are throbbing in unison with the reverberation of Grant's artillery. God bless Abraham Lincoln, E. M. Stanton, U. S. Grant, W. T. Sherman, Phil Sheridan, and the soldiers of the Union."

In Philadelphia the State House bell clanged, all the fire engines came out, ringing their bells in front of Independence Hall; flags were waving, men embraced each other, courts adjourned, and schools were dismissed, and cannon boomed till night.

The theatres in all the large cities were crowded,

boxes, balconies, and the stages decorated with flags and bunting, and as the orchestras played the national airs, wild and still wilder were the cheers.

In the clubs of Boston, New York, and Philadelphia, champagne flowed like water, and men could be heard singing long after the millions of stars were out, " We'll drink stone blind." Well might they cheer over the downfall of Richmond, and excused may they be for carousing in the clubs and hotels; yet better far were the prayers of thankfulness made on bended knees by fathers and mothers in the dimly lighted homes on the farms in the North, for their country's deliverance, and for the prospect that their boys might be spared and come home.

But, Army of Northern Virginia, sleep on! Long, long the Confederacy's star will hang over the Southland, but the day is coming when your children will rejoice in the reunited country's glory. Moreover proud will it and they be of you and your valor; and, above all, in those trying times to come, of that display of willingness to lay your lives down for a political principle that is the very foundation on which our whole governmental system is based, namely, the Sovereignty of the States. Sleep on then around your smoldering fires: clanging bells of the North and sighs from home, may they not be borne to your ears through the vast hush of night, but, rather, the murmuring of the streams which flow through the fields and woods where you lie, and may you dream of Peace and see the land you love as it is to-day. And while they sleep, let us turn to the Army of the Potomac. It will be remembered that Grant at 10:20 A. M. Monday sent word to Sheridan that " the first object of the present movement will be to intercept Lee's army, and the second to secure Burkeville."

Sheridan replied, — he did not get Grant's dispatch till 1:45 P. M., — " Before receiving your dispatch I had anticipated the evacuation of Petersburg and had commenced moving west. My cavalry is nine miles beyond Namozine Creek, and is pressing the enemy's trains. I shall push on to the Danville Road as rapidly as possible."

Spurred on by their chief's contagious intensity, his cavalry dogged the retreating Confederates fiercely throughout the livelong day. At four P. M. he sent word to Grant, — Sheridan was then at Namozine Church, — " The enemy threw their ammunition on the sides of the road and into the woods, and then set fire to the fences and woods through which the shells were thrown. The woods are strewn with burning and broken-down caissons, ambulances, wagons and débris of all descriptions. Up to this hour we have taken about twelve hundred prisoners of A. P. Hill's corps, and all accounts report the woods filled with deserters and stragglers."

When night fell, that flaming and relentless soldier had his headquarters at the home of a Mrs.

Cousins on the left-hand side of the road leading to
Amelia Court-House, having covered at least half
the way to Jetersville, the point on the Richmond
and Danville railway, where he hoped to head off Lee.
His cavalry, the troopers of the valley, now joyous
and confident, were some miles in advance at Deep
Creek, a sluggish stream. Behind our cavalry lay
the Fifth corps and, stretching away behind it on
the Namozine River Road, was Humphreys with
the Second, and then the Sixth. Ord, followed by
Parke, had taken the South Side Railroad and was
bivouacking at Wilson's Station, while Grant and
Meade had pitched their headquarter tents at
Sutherlands Station, where Cooke's, Scales', McRae's
and McGowan's brigades of Hill's corps, cut off
from falling back on Petersburg, were overtaken and
overthrown Sunday afternoon by Miles of Humphreys' Second corps.

At eight o'clock, possibly about the hour Lee at
Hebron Church was wording his note to Ewell,
Sheridan was writing his orders to the unpretentious,
big-hearted Crook to move at three, and to the tall,
surly-looking, and stalking-gaited Griffin to move
at 5 A. M., for Jetersville, a station named in honor
of a celebrated Baptist clergyman, about half-way
between Burkeville and Amelia Court-House.

Such then is the first day, Monday, April 3rd, of
the retreat and the pursuit, and now let us give
Tuesday's important record.

The courier, whom Lee sent to Ewell, rode all
night but could not find him; and on regaining headquarters, the general made this postscript to the
communication, and started it on its way again: —

" April 4, 7:30 A. M. The courier has returned
with this note, having been able to hear nothing of
you. I am about to cross the river. Get to Amelia
Court-House as soon as possible, and let me hear
from you. R. E. L."

As it is not more than nine or ten miles from
Goode's Bridge to Amelia, Lee must have covered the distance by half-past eight at the latest,
and there his hopes met a staggering blow, for to
his utter consternation he found not a single ration
for man or beast. On reporting his surrender six
days later to Mr. Davis, Lee said, " Not finding the
supplies ordered to be placed there, nearly twenty-
four hours were lost in endeavoring to collect sub-
sistence for men and horses. This delay was fatal."
Lee, when he made this statement, must have had
in mind his orders to Ewell already mentioned, but
the Confederate Commissary-General, General St.
John, says that " by this time [that is, the receipt
of Ewell's instructions] it was too late for action
as all the railroad transportation had then been
taken by superior orders for the archives, bullion
and other government service then deemed of prime

importance." Lee, little dreaming of the panic
that would sweep Richmond on hearing that he was
to abandon it that night, relied on his orders to
Ewell conveying, as they did, their importance at
once to every one acquainted with the necessities
of an army. But had he a right to expect that
Ewell could comply with his orders amid the confusion incident to a hurried evacuation? There is
one thing certain, however: it would have been a
stroke of genius on Lee's part had he foreseen the
panic and ordered the supplies from Danville, whose
storehouses were crammed with them.

But the Commissary-General is not entirely
blameless — he, of all men, knew Lee's scant supply
in the trains, and when he found that he could not
send any from Richmond, he should have wired
his subordinates in Danville to start trains at once
to Lee's army. It only adds another and striking
proof of the panic which seized the authorities in
Richmond, from high to low, and leads one to suspect that each was thinking of his own personal
safety, and not of the wants of the hard-tried veterans.

After the war was over and the calamitous nature
of the consequences, due as alleged by Lee, were
realized, Mr. Davis' malignant Southern critics
tried to lay the blame on his shoulders. But in his
history of *The Rise and Fall of the Confederacy*, he
establishes beyond dispute that no orders or even

suggestions had ever come from Lee for supplies to be collected at Amelia.

Lee pitched his headquarters in the dooryard of a house occupied by a Mrs. Smith, a refugee from Alexandria, — so we are told by that gallant Confederate officer, Captain Frederick M. Colston of Baltimore.

The town itself is of the sleepy old Virginia type, its houses unpretentious and its streets unpaved, varying kinds of paling and board fences enclose the door yards, some of which are enlivened by clumps of flowers and bending rose bushes in bloom, and now and then a sweetly breathing honeysuckle clambers affectionately over a porch window.

In the centre of the little town is a square or common of uneven ground. On the east side of it stands the Court-House. Off the square is an old-fashioned, rambling stage tavern, and across the street in front of it, a row of large old oaks, some with dying tops. From the tavern's broad porch the eye can sweep surrounding farms, where here and there a man is ploughing, and flocks are grazing or resting under the shade of trees in sloping fields. The railway station is right near the tavern and about midnight, when I was there, a passenger train from Richmond came thundering by. I could see its lighted cars from my window, reminding me of Mr. Davis' flight when about that hour he left Richmond.

In the centre of the square is a Confederate monument with the inscription:

"AMELIA'S LOVING TRIBUTE TO HER HEROES OF 1861 TO 1865.

THEY BRAVELY FOUGHT,
THEY BRAVELY FELL,
THEY WORE THE GREY,
THEY WORE IT WELL.

COMRADES, WHERESOEVER YOU REST APART,
AMELIA SHRINES YOU HERE, WITHIN HER HEART."

Yes, quiet, deep quiet, reigns in the old shire town as it dreams of the days when Lee and the Army of Northern Virginia trod its streets.

When I was there last October, no troops worn down with hunger and fatigue, no jaded horses with staring eyes, drooping heads, and panting flanks, no trains, guns, or cavalry, met my eye. A saddlehorse or two stood, tied, dozing before a store, a group of little girls wended their way to school, and intermittently a mocking-bird, in a locust tree with a blasted top, trilled joyously, and the church spires looked up into a cloudless sky.

That Tuesday, April 4, 1865, must have been a long and harassing day to Lee. A drizzling rain was falling, and wet, tired, and famishing troops, cavalry, artillery, and infantry, were pouring in every hour, and all dumbfounded at not getting the supplies which they had been told would meet them there. Great was their disappointment, and grounds for complaint were abundant, but so far as I can learn there was nothing like mutiny or even fault-finding, and their conduct testifies convincingly of their deep and steadfast loyalty both to Lee and to their cause.

It was late in the afternoon before the rear of the divisions of Field, Wilcox, and Heth came up, but all with courage unshaken. Longstreet formed them in lines of battle east of the town, looking for a chance to strike the heads of our pursuing columns, which he imagined to be immediately in the rear of Mackenzie's cavalry, who were making a bold and persistent attack.

Anderson, Wise, and Pickett, were in ragged, demoralized lines along the Bevil's Bridge road east of Amelia. They had been protected in their retreat from Deep Creek by Fitz Lee's and W. H. F. Lee's cavalry, but had been attacked vigorously by Merritt and Custer capturing guns and prisoners, the roads strewn with arms and abandoned wagons and the woods full of stragglers. Mackenzie, who had crossed Deep Creek higher up, pushed back everything before him to within a mile or so of Amelia.

The positions of the troops, and the progress his

army had made in concentrating at Amelia, are indicated by a letter dated at nine o'clock P. M., which Lee wrote to Ewell, saying that he was very much gratified to learn of his, Ewell's, favorable prospect of crossing the river at Mattoax, on the railway bridge over the Appomattox; that he hoped he was safely over by that time, — the last of the column, however, did not cross till after midnight, — that Gordon, who had brought up the rear of the Petersburg forces, was at Scott's shop, which is about midway from Goode's to Amelia, and that Mahone was between Gordon and the bridge.

That had been a trying day for Lee, and it must have been late when his head touched the pillow; and whether he slept or not, it was an awful and eventful night. Let the truth, and whole truth, be known. Darkness had barely set in when the Army of Northern Virginia, the army of Gaines' Mill, Second Manassas, Antietam, Chancellorsville and Gettysburg, began to melt away. "At morning roll-call," says the historian of a Richmond battery, "a number of men did not answer to their names." "The men," says the diary of Creed T. Davis, published in the *Richmond Howitzer*, "as they leave Richmond believe that the cause is gone and desert in great numbers. At least fifteen men have left our company." Nearly a whole company of the Ninth Virginia Cavalry left the army on the night of the fourth and fifth, so it is recorded in the regi-

ment's history; and there is but little doubt that
all through the lone hours, singly, and in squads,
men were shoaling away toward home that Tuesday
night. A member of Fitzhugh Lee's division of
cavalry tells us that, on reaching the village the
following morning, Wednesday, " I beheld the first
signs of dissolution of that grand army which had
endured every hardship of march and camp with
unshaken fortitude, when looking over the hills I
saw swarms of stragglers moving in every direction."

The main reason for this abandonment of the
colors is not far to seek. With the fall of Richmond,
hunger and want, which had long been the grim companions of the army, were joined by two figures
that had dogged it from the Wilderness, and whose
footsteps had been heard growing nearer and nearer
since leaving Petersburg. Suddenly, as the sense
came over them that the cause was lost, the poorly
clad and half-starved veterans found themselves
looking into the hard, glaring eyes of the Inevitable
and the Inexorable; and that look for many was de-
cisive. There were other reasons, too, the cries from
home, cries that grew louder and keener at every
step they took bearing them farther away.

Reader, if you and I, worn out, spirits low from
want of sleep and food, and convinced of certain
defeat and probable imprisonment, had been in
their places, I wonder what we should have done.
Would it have been Duty's call or the cry from home

that would have determined our course? Well, it might have been the former; if so, God bless you, and here is my hand; but it might have been the latter too, for, like yourself, they were brave men. So let us be charitable to those who through the dark, mist-shrouded fields and woods stole away, and whose guns were found, some standing upright in the field with bayonets thrust into the rain-soaked ground, some leaning against fences, others against the trunks of trees. The haversacks and equipments which these men had borne with great valor on many a field were scattered here, there, and everywhere; now and then one was left dangling on a bough, in testimony of the wearer's affection. It was told me that a cavalryman or cannoneer, — I have forgotten which, — after leaving his horse that night, stumbled on a shock of fodder, picked up an armful and carried it back to his dumb companion, and when death came, not as a toil but as a high privilege, I suspect, the horses drew his hearse, for he had been kind to one of their race. But how about those who stood faithful? Garlands, garlands, for every one of them, say I.

When the morning of the second day of the pursuit (Tuesday) broke, Meade took the road Sheridan was on, and Grant went with Ord, who was aiming for Burkeville. It was a heavily overcast and drizzling day, the rain at times breaking into showers, drenching men, fields, and woods. I am inclined to think that that day, and the day which followed it, were the crucial days of the campaign. Speed now was everything, but the streams rose and had to be bridged, the water stood in pools in the low places and tussocky swales, and the mud in the road deepened, so that the wheels were up to the hub, and it was almost impossible to move the trains, which in their hurry had doubled up, the poor exhausted, floundering animals blocking the way. Miles and miles had to be corduroyed for them; but on, regardless of weather, the water spurting from their shoes at every step, and rain dripping from the soaked brims of their hats, went the gallant infantry. Never, never did coming events so breathe on an army as on the Army of the Potomac that day. Some time about noon the news came that Richmond had fallen, that the stars and stripes were waving over the capitol, and the columns broke into long and mighty cheers, that rang through woods and fields.

Sheridan, meanwhile, was hastening the brave, simple-hearted Crook on to Jetersville, the most important strategic point of the whole campaign. It is a station on the Danville railroad about midway between Burkeville and Amelia. Lee had to pass through Jetersville if his plans were to succeed. Crook reached there about three in the afternoon, and threw his division across the road, interrupting a stream of men, hungry and low-spirited, fleeing homeward from Lee's army. In seizing the station Crook captured telegraphic dispatches from Lee's chief commissary at Amelia, ordering 200,000 rations to be sent there from Danville, also dispatches for forage, etc. Sheridan, himself, joined his able division commander about five P. M., and by the time the sun was setting, Griffin, lean and grim as an old eagle, having marched nearly thirty miles, came in sight, taking position on the right and left of the cavalry, and at once went to work throwing up a line of breastworks.

While these moves of Sheridan, so fatal to Lee, were being made, Mackenzie, Merritt, and Custer, my friends of cadet days, all now asleep, God bless their ashes, were crowding Anderson, Pickett, Wise, Heth and Fitzhugh Lee back with such vigor on Amelia that Lee thought that all the infantry of the Army of the Potomac was right behind them, and, as already told, arrayed his forces, under the valiant Longstreet, to meet them, losing thereby most valuable time.

Meanwhile Meade's and Ord's columns were pushing on, Meade's following Sheridan, Ord's the road to Burkeville. At seven o'clock P. M., the storm had passed, and while the glittering constellations were marching into the overarching dome, Sheridan wrote to Meade, from Jetersville:

"The rebel army is in my front, three miles distant, with all its trains. If the Sixth corps can hurry

up we will have sufficient strength. I will hold my
ground unless I am driven from it. I understand
that Humphreys is just after the Fifth corps. My
men are out of rations, and some rations should
follow quickly. Please notify General Grant.

" P. S. The enemy are moving from Amelia
Court-House via Jetersville and Burke's Station to
Danville. Jeff Davis passed over this railroad yester-
day to Danville."

At the same time he sent orders for Merritt, then
off confronting Anderson and Pickett on the Bevil's
Bridge road, to come in all haste to Jetersville.
Merritt arrived there the next morning at seven A. M.

Sheridan's dispatch reached Meade's headquarters
at the house of a Mr. Jones, on the east side of Deep
Run. He was quite unwell, and after it had been
read to him he retired, but soon sent for Sheridan's
staff officer, the brave Colonel Newhall, who had
brought the dispatch, and asked him as to the situation and what Sheridan said about it. In effect
Newhall's report was that Lee could be balked, and
if Meade would forsake everything but arms and
ammunition and at any sacrifice hurry forward and
join Sheridan, Lee would have to surrender. Meade
at quarter of eleven forwarded Sheridan's dispatch
to Grant, who was in camp at Wilson's Station
on the South Side Road, with Ord, telling him that
Humphreys was partly across the run, that his men
were out of rations, had been moving, working on

the roads, and standing for fourteen hours, — the cavalry on the right had cut across to the left, intercepting his march during the afternoon, — but that in a general order for Humphreys and all the troops to move at three A. M. he had said, —

" The Major-General commanding feels he has but to recall to the Army of the Potomac the glorious success of the oft-repeated gallant contests with the Army of Northern Virginia, and when he assures the army that, in the opinion of so distinguished an officer as General Sheridan, it only requires these sacrifices to try and bring the long and desperate conflict to a triumphant issue, the men of this army will show that they are willing to die of fatigue and starvation as they have ever shown themselves ready to fall by the bullets of the enemy."

When, after midnight, the tired, wet, and hungry men were aroused by the pealing bugles and heard Meade's order, they broke into cheers and took up the line of march. And that on this narrative may fall the glow of the spirit of the army, and for the sake of the chords of sympathy which bind us all, let it be told that men whose shoes had given out wrapped cloths around them and, smiling over their own appearance, at the command, " Forward! " stepped off with their comrades. Others, who were wounded, refused to stay in the hospitals, and rejoined their regiments, nursing their wounds only when the troops halted. We cannot account for this inspiring zeal and fortitude unless we realize that up and down the high valleys of the mind God's heralds were blowing their trumpets; trumpets that stir the hearts of men and have been heard down the ages, and lo! the generations had prophets, religion, literature, poetry, and glory. And here ends Tuesday, the second day of the pursuit.

In view of the fact that the safety of the Confederate Army depended on its line of retreat remaining unobstructed, Sheridan fully expected Lee would spring at him as soon as the news reached him that the pursuit had reached Jetersville; but, morning having broken, the sun mounting upward on its way and Lee still not moving, Sheridan determined to find out what his famous and dangerous adversary was up to, and sent Davies' brigade of cavalry on a reconnaissance to Lee's right.

At Paineville, five or six miles west of Amelia, Davies struck a train, several miles long, of wagons and artillery headed toward Farmville. He attacked it impetuously, destroying several hundred wagons, capturing five pieces of artillery, eleven battle flags, and a number of prisoners. This train of Custis Lee's division had crossed the Appomattox at Clementown, and was the only one in the retreating army fully equipped with supplies of all kinds. Fitzhugh Lee, Dearing, Rosser and Gary fell on Davies as he withdrew, striking him with desperation, but Sheridan sent several brigades of cavalry to Davies' aid and he was able to bring in about all of his telltale captures, but in doing so lost some of his best men, among them the young, heroic Colonel Janeway of New Jersey; the Confederates lost a number of very brave officers, too.

Shortly after the return of Davies a negro was intercepted, bearing a brief note given him by a Confederate officer, and was taken to Sheridan. The letter ran as follows, —

> "AMELIA COURT HOUSE,
> "April 5, 1865.
>
> "DEAR MAMMA: Our army is ruined, I fear. We are all safe as yet. Shyron left us sick. John Taylor is well; saw him yesterday. We are in line of battle this evening. General Robert Lee is in the field near us. My trust is still in the justice of our cause and that of God. General Hill is killed. I saw Murray a few moments since. Bernard Terry [he] said was taken prisoner, but may get out. I send this by a negro I see passing up railroad to Mecklenburg. Love to all.
>
> "Your devoted son,
> "WM. B. TAYLOR,
> "Colonel."

Out of the abundance of the heart the mouth speaketh, and it is easy to read in this letter the despair that had come over the Army of Northern Virginia.

While Davies was on his way to Paineville, Lee, desiring to free himself of the burden of the surplus artillery, ordered the destruction of nearly a hundred caissons and directed the pieces to take the road to Farmville, the column being under the command of Gen. Lindsay Walker.

It was not until one o'clock Wednesday, the 5th, that Lee moved; then, with Longstreet by his side, he put himself at the head of the infantry — Ewell's and Custis Lee's columns had not yet reported — and started for Jetersville determined to clear the road of what he supposed to be a brigade or at most a division of cavalry. Jetersville is some eight or ten miles southwest of Amelia. The highway and railway which connect the towns run side by side, first one and then the other crossing each other. Both, for the most of the way, run through old, slumbering woods of pine and oak with sunshiny open spots where the solitary pokeweed spreads its branches and scattered purple asters bloom, the speaking heralds of autumn's dreams.

W. H. F. Lee's division of Confederate cavalry preceded the infantry, which, on approaching Jetersville, found itself plump up against Sheridan's breastworks, and over them they could see the colors of the Fifth corps flying. Of course the Confederate cavalry was not long in finding out that if the road was to be cleared, the infantry would have to do it, so Longstreet came up and formed Field's, Wilcox's

and Heth's divisions for assault. But no one sent
to reconnoitre Sheridan's lines brought back a single
hope of carrying them; they were too grimly strong,
and, moreover, the stiff bearing on the part of the
skirmishers in front of them told the story of what
the attacking soldiers would meet from the men behind them; in other words, that Sheridan was ready
to play the desperate game of battle. Sheridan in his
report of the campaign says, " It seems to me that
this was the only chance the Army of Northern
Virginia had to save itself, which might have been
done had General Lee promptly attacked and driven
back the comparatively small force opposed to him
and pursued his march to Burkeville Junction." If
all of Lee's army had been there, I have no doubt he
would have assaulted.

Alexander says that a long conference was held
between Lee and his son, W. H. F., and Longstreet.
I suspect the question to have been, whether or not
the whole of the Army of the Potomac was before
them, and that Lee could not conceive it possible
that it should be there; but he did not know what a
spirit of resistance to fatigue and hunger inspired
the Army of the Potomac now that the end was near.
As a matter of fact, Humphreys at that very hour
was going into line at the right and left of Griffin,
but the Sixth corps was four or five miles away,
though coming on at full speed.

At last Lee's fighting spirit had to yield and he

decided to take the only course that was left, namely, to move during the night toward Rice's Station on the Lynchburg road, nine miles west of Burkeville. The baffling of his plans he owed to Sheridan, who that day, and on to Appomattox, was the lion in his way.

Longstreet tells us that " no orders came, the afternoon was passing, further delay seemed perilous, I drew the command off and filed to the right to cross Flat Run to march to Farmville. The infantry, trains, and artillery followed, and kept the march up until a late hour."

Lee turned Traveller back and bivouacked at Amelia Springs. I do not know how the great man felt that night, — there was reason for gloom: no rations at Amelia Court-House! Grant squarely across his way to Burkeville! — and I have wondered if as he gazed into his camp-fire he heard the knell of his hopes. But I trust his tent was pitched in an open oak wood, that the ground sloped away gently, that now and then through the tree tops he caught sight of friendly stars, that every south wind breathed sweetly, and that sleep fell softly and kindly over his thwarted, troubled mind.

Let us turn to his pursuers on that Wednesday, the 5th. Humphreys' Second corps, that had bivouacked on the west bank of Deep Creek, moved between one and two o'clock A. M., and without food; Meade's orders were to march at three A. M. Wright's,

on the road, in rear of Humphreys, left their burned
down camp-fires as soon as Humphreys' bugles to
resume the march were heard, and at seven A. M.,
about the hour the sun was clearing the tree tops,
got to Deep Creek.

Humphreys, although delayed by Merritt's division of cavalry on its way to report to Sheridan,
reached Jetersville at half-past three, as we already
know, while Lee was debating with himself whether
to attack or not.

About six P. M. the advance of the ever gallant
Sixth corps with flags unfurled which it had carried
on so many fields, bore up to Jetersville, marching
strongly.

Meade, although still unwell from cough and fever,
pushed ahead of Humphreys and Wright and rode
out to see Sheridan and Griffin. The former, when
Meade arrived, was with his cavalry helping to
drive back the enemy which had pursued and attacked Davies so viciously. On Sheridan's return
about half-past six, Meade dined with him at his
headquarters, the Childres house, and later in the evening ordered a general attack at six A. M. the next
morning.

Grant had accompanied Ord, who was following
the railroad to Burkeville, and at five P. M., about the
hour probably when Longstreet started his trains
and artillery toward Rice's Station, notified Meade
as follows:

" Ord has covered fifteen miles to-day to reach here [Nottaway Court-House] and is going on. He will probably reach Burkeville to-night. My headquarters will be with the advance.

" U. S. GRANT,

" Lieutenant General."

At three o'clock Sheridan sent a dispatch to Grant, reporting Davies's operations, adding, " I wish you were here yourself. I feel confident of capturing the Army of Northern Virginia if we exert ourselves. I see no escape for Lee." With this dispatch he enclosed the captured letter from Col. Wm. B. Taylor, already given.

Toward sundown Sheridan's intrepid and more-than-once-tried scout, Campbell, wearing the uniform of a Confederate officer, his horse in a lather, emerged from the woods on the right of Ord's marching column and, on being taken to Grant, handed him Sheridan's dispatch, written on tissue paper and rolled up in a pellet covered with tinfoil. Grant as soon as he read it dismounted — he was riding " Jeff Davis," a middle-sized, stocky, black pony; those who served at headquarters will remember the fast-pacing little fellow well — and, with the saddle for a rest, wrote a message to Ord. He then mounted Cincinnati, his high, thoroughbred bay, — how proudly he stood, ears alert, that first day at Spottsylvania when his rider and all headquarters were under fire, — and, with Campbell in the lead, set off for Sheridan, now through dark, tangled woods, now up narrow lanes, now across fields by lone barns, on past unlighted houses where the watch dog alone was awake, and, once more, across gray, night-mantled fields for Jetersville. " I wish you were here yourself," Sheridan had said, and that was enough; no distance, fatigue, or darkness could be so great or so deep as to stay the quiet and mighty-hearted Grant from answering the call.

It was well past ten o'clock when he reached Sheridan at the Childres house near the railroad, and, after hearing how things stood, sent a note to Meade saying, " I would go over to see you this evening but I have ridden a long distance to-day. Your orders directing an attack to-morrow morning will hold in the absence of others, but it is my impression that Lee will retreat during the night and, if so, we will pursue with vigor."

That Lee withdrew as Grant predicted, we already know. And now we hope that after all that day's work was done, this modest, true, magnanimous man had, as well as Lee and Griffin, a bed under towering oaks; that sleep, sweet sleep, came to him as I trust it came to them, and that every night wind breathed of the days to come, and he saw visions of his country moving upward in splendor and glory.

VII

THE road from Amelia Springs by which the weary, sleep-longing, hungry, yet dauntless Confederate army moved toward Rice's Station and Farmville is narrow, winding, and lonely; one that never before that fatal day had seen a battle-flag, heard the clattering march of cavalry or felt the heavy tread and jar of thundering guns. Nor had it ever dreamed of the sounds it was to hear before the sun went down; hear amid the terrible din of battle the shriek of disemboweled horses, the piercing cries of the wounded, and the faint, intermittent, muttering, delirious speech of the dying. No, it had heard the voices of Peace only: care-free negroes singing in adjacent fields as they ploughed, hoed, and stacked the ripened grain (oh, sweet and long are the shadows when the sheaves of wheat are shocked). Wagons chuckling happily under their loads, tobacco and cotton to the market, wheat and corn to the mill; carriages rolling softly to and from the country churches, and now and then the natural glee of a light-hearted, whistling boy. It is bordered for long reaches by unfenced woods of soothing pines and brushy oaks, which rise above a dense undergrowth. On leaving Amelia Springs it shuns the frequent tributaries of Flat Creek by swerving around their swampy heads up among billowing, cultivated uplands creased by many ravines, the cradles of living streams, along whose thickety banks wild plums and azaleas bloom and redbirds build their nests.

The soaking rains of a few days past had made the road very soft, and the heavy trains and cavalry soon so cut up the low places that they were almost impassable. It is tiresome enough to march all night on good broad roads, but from marching over a narrow one like this, crowded with stalled trains, and packed with men whose hearts are bowed down, spare us, spare us, good Lord!

So, through fields alternating with woods, the road goes on, and after a while comes to Deatonsville, a hamlet of three or four houses. There, after crossing the historic Genito Road, one of Virginia's oldest highways, it loiters along as before till it gets well over a shallow sandy creek flowing northward, when it bends southwestward. About a mile and a half this side of Sailor's Creek, another road — I have called it Gordon's for reasons that will appear later — sets off to the right, running northwest, skirting the creek's wavering valley until almost within sight of the Appomattox, when it turns abruptly toward the setting sun and, plunging down into the valley, crosses the creek at a bridge and several fords.

The main road, after Gordon's leaves it, changes
a little more to the westward and soon, through its
bordering woods, catches the light of Captain
Hillsman's Plantation, which slopes into the narrow
valley of Sailor's Creek. The Captain, by the way,
a quiet, pleasing man, was in the 44th Virginia and
captured when we carried the Bloody Angle of
Spottsylvania. Just before reaching the house, the
road passes on the left hand, and I think reveren-
tially, the old graveyard where lie the gallant Captain's ancestors under moaning pines, then by the
dooryard it goes down into the creek's shelving,
scored-out valley, which, from bluff to bluff, if the
shouldering sides may be called bluffs, is six or eight
hundred yards wide. The stream itself is at the
extreme western side of the narrow valley and is not
large or deep, but has very miry banks planted
densely with willow, wild rose, and alder, cowslips
in spring-time gilding its margins richly. At the
time of the retreat it was high and well out of its
treacherous banks.

The road crosses it on a low, rickety, pole bridge
opposite the mouth of a considerable ravine which
reaches up to the timber on the west side, the birthplace of a cherished little brook that comes singing
down to the creek. The road, having crossed, turns
to the left, and at once begins to mount diagonally
the long, sharply rising left bank; scattered on
each side are wild plums and young pines whose roots

are beneath quilts of daisies and broom grass, which were stained that afternoon by much rare and gallant blood.

If you look backward over your shoulder as you mount the bank, the valley of the creek, and the old Hillsman homestead, with its big chimney and venerable dooryard, evergreens, and all the sloping fields of the plantation, greet your eye. Having gained the top of the ridge, the road wanders on in a forest stippled with dogwoods and now and then blazing with an azalea, to Rice's Station, some four or five miles away.

Before reaching the station it crosses another Sailor's Creek, called the Big Sailor, and then winds around the heads of many deep, black gulches which, Captain Hillsman told me, as we drove by them, are known as the Devil's Tavern. A road from Gill's Mill, on the creek above Captain Hillsman's, comes into the Rice's Station road several miles west of Hillsman's. Wood and plantation roads, some leading to Vaughn's below Hillsman's and some off toward High Bridge on the Appomattox, take their departure from time to time from the Rice's Station road.

Perhaps we have dwelt with too much particularity and too long on this road. But that was a crucial day of the war, and on this road as a whole, and for the last time, marched the Army of Northern Virginia. Here, too, as the sun was going down, the Confederacy, under Sheridan's mortal wounds, sighed out its last hope. Moreover, this was the scene of much valor and much suffering; and I think, dear friend, were you to sit down beside it, and in the silence of its loneliness, let your mind dwell upon the past, the old road would unburden itself to you as it did to me; for I know right well that you are a true, kind-hearted man, one to whom old roads like this, church-spires, and battle-fields would love to tell their memories and talk with you, as the evening shadows deepen around, of life's strange, immortal, and fruitful mysteries.

Well, then, such is the general character of the road Lee's army took, hoping to pass around Grant's left on Thursday, the sixth. It is probable that Longstreet got back to it from Sheridan's and Meade's fronts at Jetersville before midnight.

Lee rose early that morning and sent the following letter to Gordon:

"AMELIA SPRINGS, April 6, 1865 — 4 A. M.
"(GENERAL GORDON:)
"GENERAL: I have seen the dispatches (intercepted) you sent me. It was from my expectation of an attack being made from Jetersville that I was anxious that the rear of the column should reach Deatonsville as soon as possible. I hope the rear will get out of harm's way, and I rely greatly upon your exertions and good judgment for its safety.

I know that men and animals are much exhausted, but it is necessary to tax their strength. I wish after the cavalry crosses the bridge at Flat Creek that it be thoroughly destroyed so as to prevent pursuit in that direction. The bridge over the same stream on the road to Jetersville I have had destroyed. By holding the position at Amelia Springs with our cavalry, which can retire by Deatonsville or up the road toward Paineville, we can secure the rear of the column from interruption. About two miles from Amelia Springs on the Deatonsville road, a road leads off to the right to Chapman's into the Ligontown road, by which Farmville may be reached provided there is a bridge over the Appomattox at Ligontown. I hear there is none, therefore I see no way of relieving the column of the wagons, and they must be brought along. You must, of course, keep everything ahead of you, wagons, stragglers, &c. I will try to get the head of the column on, and to get provisions at Rice's Station or Farmville.

"Very respectfully, &c.,

"R. E. Lee,

"General."

He then left his camp at Amelia Springs to join Longstreet, well on his way to Rice's Station, nine miles west of Burkeville. Alexander, Longstreet's chief of artillery, and a man of courage, rare spirit, and mild bearing, says that the troops halted for a short rest just before dawn, that Longstreet and his staff went on to Rice's Station; and that he himself, as morning was breaking, selected a line of battle which they were to occupy on arrival.

Field, Wilcox and Heth were in the lead of the moving army. Mahone's division came next, followed by Anderson with the forces he had brought up the south side of the Appomattox, that is, the remnants of Pickett's and Bushrod Johnson's divisions, Pickett in advance. Ewell's troops came next, first Custis Lee's division, and then Kershaw's. Ewell had been marching and halting all the livelong night and did not reach Amelia Springs from the vicinity of Amelia Court-House, until 8 A. M. Thursday. They had covered eight or nine miles only, owing to the congested state of the road, packed with their own and Anderson's troops and trains, and obstructed by half-burned and abandoned wagons, the havoc of Davies's raid. Bringing up the rear was heroic Gordon, and it was after nine o'clock as he rose above the hill west of Amelia Springs.

After sunrise there was a heavy April shower, but by this time, nine o'clock, the sky was free and the sun was warm. And now that the rain has stopped and all the column is under way let the pee-wee sing near his home under the bridge, the bluebird warble in the old orchard, and the larks flute in the meadows; yes, let all the fields and fresh-leaved woods rejoice;

on and on by them all, with their songs of happiness
and carrying suggestions of home, went the Army of
Northern Virginia, weak for want of food and sleep,
and low at heart. Toil on, veteran heroes; a few
days more and it will all be over, and loving hearts in
days to come will testify their admiration in monuments of bronze and marble. And if, among the
readers of this page, there be a worshiper of Mammon, to him I say firmly but in all kindness, stand
back! stand back! for, not, not was their spirit or
their ideals like yours. They saw not and cared not
for the gods and the temple you worship in, they saw
through the eyes of faith, a God above all gods, and
neither gold nor script conveyed to them what it
conveys to you. In other words, they heard the
heart's high music, and although they met defeat they
gained glory; and, as a member of that old army
which contested victory with them on so many fields,
I say to you worshipers of Mammon who this day
belittle our country, stand back, stand back as
that old Army of Virginia toils on. But hark! from
the east comes the quick boom of guns: the Army
of the Potomac is afoot and has finally struck Gordon's rear guard.

The Army of the Potomac, strangely enough, did
not know of Lee's retreat till it moved in battle
array from its works at Jetersville at 6 A. M., Thursday, to engage him: Griffin on the right, Humphreys
on the left, the Sixth corps under Wright in reserve.

They soon found out, however, that Lee had gone;
the corps then broke from line into columns, taking
the roads toward Amelia Court-House, from which
the enemy had approached their position at Jetersville. On reaching Flat Creek near Amelia Springs,
Humphreys' advance, the Twenty-sixth Michigan,
spied across the open country, a mile or more away
to the northwest, the rear of Gordon's division. It
was then about half-past ten.

The news was sent to Meade, and at once Humphreys and Griffin were turned to the left, and Wright
was brought back to Jetersville and told to follow
Sheridan, who, with Crook in advance, had set out
to strike the road at Deatonsville. Griffin swung
wide, circling to the left, clear around to the right
and north of the retreating column, but Humphreys
at once sent the Second corps after Gordon, who on
every rise threw his rear guard across the road and,
supported by Macon's battery, made such a resolute
stand as to compel Humphreys' leading brigades,
one on the right and one on the left of the road, to
form line of battle before yielding the positions.
Gordon never displayed more of his sterling qualities
as a soldier than that day and fully justified Lee's
confidence in him as expressed in the letter of 4 A. M.
given above, " I rely greatly upon your exertions
and good judgment for its safety," namely, the rear
of the retreating army.

While Gordon is thus guarding the rear from harm,

allowing the column packing the road ahead of him to make all the speed they could, let us turn to Sheridan.

As before mentioned, when the infantry under Meade left Jetersville, moving toward Amelia Court-House, Sheridan, with Crook in advance, took roads leading toward Deatonsville, convinced that that would be Lee's line of retreat.

About noon, he gained a position not far from Sandy Creek, several miles west of Deatonsville, from which through a gap in the woods he descried the retreating column and threw Crook against it. But Ewell and Anderson, as soon as he began to threaten, faced their divisions to the left and flung him back while the trains filed by. Sheridan, seeing Crook's repulse, brought up Merritt, but soon made up his mind not to try again for the trains at that point, and sent him, Crook and Custer farther along to the left with orders to look for a weaker spot, keeping by him a brigade of cavalry for effect. Sheridan then sent a dispatch to Grant, — it was dated 12:10 P. M., — " The trains and army (Confederate) were moving all last night and are very short of provisions and very tired, indeed. I think now is the time to attack them with all your infantry. They are reported to have begged provisions from the people of the country all along the road as they passed. I am working around farther to the left." As a matter of fact, they had only a few grains of parched corn, and one officer in his diary recorded that he that day traded his necktie with a poor family for a bit of corn-bread. Sheridan then rode to the top of a hill and scanned the uplifted silent country. Off on a sun-bathed ridge, that rose to the northeast beyond several miles of intervening timber, his eye fell on Gordon's skirmishers slowly falling back before Humphreys. He then, accompanied by Miller's battery and Stagg's brigade of cavalry, followed the path of Merritt and Crook until he reached another overlooking point and discovered on a parallel ridge the Confederate trains in full view, hurrying with all speed, and flanked by infantry and cavalry. Miller at once opened on them, and Stagg was ordered to charge them, Sheridan's aim being to check these forces till Crook, Custer, and Merritt had reached a position to strike the road ahead of them.

Stagg's Michigan men charged gallantly but were signally repulsed. The point at which Sheridan made his drive was vital, for it was where the road, which has already been referred to as Gordon's and which the harassed trains were gladly taking, breaks off northward, a mile or more east of Capt. Hillsman's plantation. Ewell says that Sheridan's demonstrations continued at that point from 11 A. M. till 2 P. M., and that he retained his troops in position to cover the passage of the trains and that as soon as they were out of the way he followed Anderson. Wright, of the Sixth corps, reports that he turned into the road leading up to the scene of Stagg's attack, Miller's guns quickening his march, and on nearing Stagg's position put his leading divisions into line, gained the road, and then turned to the left toward Sailor's Creek.

While Sheridan was attacking and Wright was hurrying from Jetersville (his corps did not get back to their morning starting place till noon was approaching), Mahone, Pickett, and Bushrod Johnson's divisions had reached Sailor's Creek. There they halted to rest from their all night and forenoon march. Mahone, who was across the creek and not under Anderson's orders, after tarrying a while, moved on without notifying Pickett, next in line. Pickett, seeing Mahone going on, asked Anderson for authority to resume the march, but Anderson sent word to him that his orders were to wait for Ewell. Meanwhile Custer, having made the detour of Gill's Mill, was heading for the gap between Pickett and Mahone.

About half-past three or four Ewell came up, and had barely crossed the creek with Custis Lee's division, — Kershaw was bringing up the rear with Humphreys' Mississippi brigade through the Hillsman plantation, — when Anderson sent word back to Ewell to come to his aid, for Custer and the rest of the cavalry had broken in ahead of him. Loyally, Ewell, the maimed, venerable old fellow, started with Custis Lee's division to help Anderson. A Confederate officer in the *Southern Historical Papers* writes that he rode up to Ewell just at that moment and heard him say to some one of his party, "Yes, tomatoes are good. I wish I had some." Readers of *The Battle of the Wilderness* will recall that as that famous two days' engagement was about to begin Ewell was delivering a dissertation on deviling turkey legs to Major Stiles. Ewell had hardly got under way before Kershaw notified him that the whole of the Sixth corps, Wright's, was at his heels, which made it necessary for Ewell to halt and look after his own rear.

Kershaw having been driven across the creek, Ewell faced Custis Lee about and formed along the open brow of the sassafras- and pine-tufted hill, Kershaw on the right, and Lee on the left; the ravine scored out of the face of the hill was about the centre of his line. There, without a single piece of artillery to support them, with flags over them, they lay, from the road down into the ravine and up its northern bank, and every man in that line knew that a crisis was coming. For Anderson, behind them to the west, was engaged — Custer, Crook and Merritt were all plunging at him — and, in full view on the valley's eastern brink, the Sixth corps was massing rapidly. They could see the regiments pouring into the fields at double quick, the battle lines, blooming with colors, growing longer and deeper at every moment, and batteries at a gallop coming into action front. They knew what it all meant; they had been on the fields of Antietam, Gettysburg, and Spottsylvania.

While Seymour's division was forming on the right of the road, and Wheaton's on the left, preparatory to move to the attack of Ewell, Wright ordered intrepid Cowan to bring up his battalion of batteries, the 1st Rhode Island, 1st New Jersey and 1st New York. He posted them to the right and left of the Hillsman house and opened on Ewell's line a rapid, and terribly destructive fire.

Hyde, commanding a brigade of Getty's division of Wright's corps, says that, as he passed him, Sheridan " was fuming and raging that he could not do all himself." Just about this time Edwards, with Wheaton's Third brigade, reported to Sheridan. Sheridan said to him, " The enemy are there " (pointing across the creek). " I want you to form your brigade in one line, cross the creek, and carry the heights," indicating the left of Custis Lee's position. " I asked him," says Edwards, " if my flanks would be covered." Sheridan gritted out, " Never mind your flanks. Go through them. They are as demoralized as hell."

The historian of the 37th Mass., in Edwards' brigade, has this to say of their reaching Sheridan's position at Hillsman's: " The 37th had already marched more than 20 miles on the sandy, rolling,

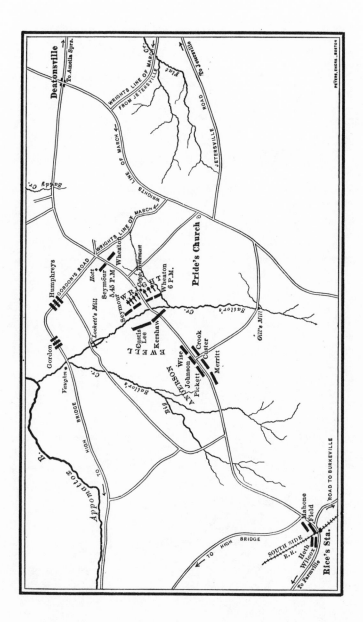

pine-covered country on that warm 6th of April when the desultory artillery fire (it was probably Miller's at the time of Stagg's attack) which had been heard, assumed that steadiness (they were hearing Cowan's guns) which proclaimed to the toiling infantry that their services would be called for. Dashing the sweat from their faces, the enthusiastic fellows began to fill the magazines of their rifles (they were armed with Spencers) and to cast aside knapsacks, blankets and superfluous clothing. The men were ready to break into a run when the order to double-quick was received, and for three miles they went forward at a pace which nothing but the intense excitement of the occasion could have enabled them to maintain." So the men from the Berkshire Hills came on the field. Let us dwell for a moment on the scene.

The sun is sinking down, and the oak and pine woods crowning the hill are laying evening's peaceful shadows on Ewell's line; on Sheridan's its long afternoon beams tinge the hot billowing smoke of Cowan's guns, and sparkle on the steel barrels of the shouldered arms of the moving infantry, for they are all under way. Sheridan's battle-flag, which has waved on many good fields, is fluttering behind him; his horse Rienzi, as usual, is champing the bit, trumpeters are ready to sound the charge, and before her mighty harp, War's stern musician is ready to sweep the iron strings. And now while Seymour's and Wheaton's divisions are approaching the creek, let us hurry over to Ewell's lines, to a spot on the bare, rounded, eastward-sloping knoll, where under Cowan's awful fire lies Major Stiles's battalion. We shall remember that when we saw them last they were listening to him as he read the soldier psalm, and that then they knelt with him as he led them in prayer in the dimly-lighted little chapel on the banks of the James, and we shall not forget that there was one boy, as he read, who met his look with swimming eyes.

They are all lying down, loaded guns in their hands, and the major, that young, rare, transparent gentleman, is walking behind them, talking softly, familiarly, and encouragingly, warning them not to expose themselves, for the batteries' fire is accurate and frightfully deadly.

It is no place, reader, for you or me. Let the major tell the story. "A good many had been wounded and several killed when a twenty-pounder Parrott shell struck immediately in my front on the line, nearly severing a man in twain, and hurling him bodily over my head, his arms hanging down and his hands almost slapping me in the face as they passed. In that awful moment I distinctly recognized young Blount, who had gazed into my face so intently Sunday night."

Reader, excuse the oath, but, by God! this narrative must break; for my pen halts as my heart bleeds. Those tears in that poor boy's yearning eyes touched it deeply, and I had so hoped that he would be spared. Sing on, Valley of Sailor's Creek, sing on to the memory of that tender-hearted hero; and oh, Peace, blessed Peace! come and save the world from the sacrifice of youths like this.

And now to go on with the bitter action: — Until our infantry had crossed the creek the artillery's fire had been fast and dreadfully fatal; then the guns ceased firing, and all was still as the grave, as the men made their way through the thickety banks and formed on the farther side. I'll not try to give all of the details of the bloody engagement, but Stiles's men under his orders reserved their fire till our lines were close up. Then they let go a crashing volley, — their execution was frightful, — and at once Ewell's centre charged our centre with fury, and drove it back in confusion across the creek.

But, meanwhile, our troops on the left and right had gained the top of the hill, and overlapping their opponent's flanks, crowded them into the bowl-like hollow of the ravine's head. There the Thirty-seventh Massachusetts, most of whom were from the laurel-blooming hills of Berkshire, had one of the fiercest, most hand-to-hand and literally savage encounters of the war, with the remnant of Stiles's battalion and that of the marines from the Confederate ships which had lain in the James. They clubbed their muskets, fired pistols into each other's faces, and used the bayonet savagely.

At the reunions of the Thirty-seventh Massachusetts, I used to see one of the Berkshire men who had been pinned to the ground by a bayonet thrust clean through his breast, coming out near his spine; this brave fellow, Samuel E. Eddy of Company D, "notwithstanding his awful situation," says the historian of the regiment, "succeeded in throwing another cartridge into his rifle, the bullet from which was next moment sent through the heart of his antagonist. The Confederate fell across the prostrate Unionist," who threw aside the body, withdrew the bayonet from his own horrible wound, rose to his feet, and walked to the rear.

And yet, looking at him, you would have seen a quiet, self-respecting, high-minded man; and I think that some of those beautiful, blue-tinted Berkshire Hills glory in the spot that holds his gallant clay.

Keifer, who commanded one of Wright's brigades, chiefly of Ohio men, — and the state is proud of him and them, — says, "One week after the battle I revisited the field," — he was on his way back from Appomattox, — "and could then have walked on Confederate dead for many successive rods along the face of the heights held by the enemy when the battle opened."

These men were put in a trench, and Mrs. Hillsman told me that a mother, one of unmistakable breeding, who lived in Savannah, shortly after the battle came there to look for her son. A deluging rain had swept the shallow covering of earth away, and among the festering bodies she found that of her boy by a ring still circling his ashy, shrunken finger.

On my trip to the field last October, I stood alone on the bank of the trench; it was in a little cradling ravine, green grass carpeted it, and an open-eyed daisy lifted its innocent face to the sky, its gaze perhaps following the track of those upward-gone spirits; all around was still, a white cloud or two floated in the east, and the day was done. I paused a while; the mood was deep, and soft and tender were the murmurs that floated down about me.

The end of the carnage came quickly; for our cavalry, having torn and scattered Anderson, Pickett and Johnson, charged down on poor old Ewell; and he, seeing that all was lost, surrendered himself and his command. The captives amounted to thousands.

A Confederate officer in the *Southern Historical Papers* says, " When the infantry which we had so recently repulsed came up to us again it was with smiling faces. They commenced opening their haversacks, offering to share their hardtack with us, which in our famished condition we most eagerly and gratefully accepted. They moreover complimented us on the gallant fight we had made. In this connection I will add that we were always treated with every consideration by the veterans at the front. It was only when we fell into the hands of the provost-guard that any harshness was shown."

The gap between Mahone and Anderson proved to be the key of that fatal day, which for Lee was like that which floated before the vision-seeing eye of Zephaniah, " a day of trouble and distress, a day of wasteness and desolation, a day of darkness and gloominess."

Custer struck the gap just as Col. Frank Huger's battalion of artillery was trying to cross, capturing his West Point friend Huger and most of the guns, and supported by Crook on the right and Merritt on the left, broke down Anderson's stubborn attempt to clear the road, taking Corse and Hunton of Pickett's division prisoners, Pickett himself, Fitz Lee and Anderson escaping by the speed of their horses. Bushrod Johnson fled up the road in the midst of a panicky swarm of soldiers and teamsters toward Rice's Station, pursued by Merritt.

And now as to Gordon. He got up to the road, which I have called by his name, about 6 o'clock and, thinking the rest of the troops had gone that way, turned into it. Humphreys, of course, followed him and about dusk struck Gordon's rear-guard as it was crossing the creek at Vaughn's, capturing two guns, a considerable number of prisoners and two hundred wagons that were in a great mass across the approach to the bridge over Sailor's Creek.

Gordon took a position on the height beyond the creek with artillery, but night soon put an end of his trials for that day, and later he moved on toward High Bridge and went into bivouac. At this time it may be well, as a note of the progress of events, to say that Humphreys at 4:20 P. M. was about three miles west of Deatonsville and said in a dispatch to Meade, " The road is literally lined with their tents, baggage and cooking utensils. We have taken one gun." He reported his final and successful blow at Gordon's rear guard from the east bank of Sailor's Creek at 7:30 P. M.

Night came on before Ord could get his troops in line ready to assault Longstreet's position at Rice's, and perhaps it was just as well, for he might not have carried it: the men that were in those works were the veterans of Gettysburg and Chickamauga. Meanwhile, Anderson and Ewell not reporting with their divisions at Rice's, Lee became concerned, and as the afternoon was waning, sent his aide, Col. Venable, to find what was the trouble.

When Venable got back from his mission, Lee was talking to Mahone, and the aide asked his chief if he had received his message. Lee replied he had not. When Venable told him that our cavalry had captured the wagon trains at Sailor's Creek, Lee exclaimed, " Where is Anderson? Where is Ewell? It is strange I can't hear from them." Convinced of some disaster, he ordered Mahone to retrace his steps and see what was the matter. Lee rode with Mahone, and presently they came to the south bank of Big Sailor's Creek. Mahone says, " The disaster which had overtaken our army was in full view and the scene beggars description — hurrying teamsters with their teams and dangling traces (no wagons), retreating infantry without guns, many without hats, a harmless mob." What they saw were men from Anderson's, Johnson's, and Pickett's divisions pursued by Merritt; the sun was setting. " Lee, at the sight of the spectacle," so says Mahone, " straightened himself in his saddle and exclaimed, as if talking to himself, ' My God! has the army dissolved ? ' " Mahone put an end to the cavalry's pursuit mighty quickly.

As soon as the battle was over, Sheridan started an aide to Grant with a dispatch saying: " Up to the present time we have captured Generals Ewell, Kershaw, Barton, Corse, Hunton, Dubose and Custis Lee, several thousand prisoners (it turned out that there were five or six thousand), fourteen pieces of artillery and a large number of wagons. If the thing is pressed, I think Lee will surrender."

That dispatch brings to an end the story of the day's activities, which I wish I could have arrayed with more life and skill, but the armies moving as they did before daylight, and covering so much ground, it is hard to keep all that was going on clearly before the eye. The only way that could

be done, would be to imagine ourselves up on the
gray shady porch of some overhanging pinnacled
and bastioned cloud; then all the field would be
below us, and we could watch hour by hour the
moving, bannered forces. But reader, let that be
as it may. I have done the best I could for
you. Well, the sun had gone down red, signalling
rain; night had fallen, and the last shot had
been fired; Merritt had withdrawn from Mahone's
stern front at Big Sailor, and Sheridan's camp-fire
on his victorious field was lit. "He is lying," so
reports Newhall, and although I never saw this
man but once or twice that I remember, yet I wish
I had known him well, for he must have been a rare
companion, " he is lying on the broad of his back on
a blanket, with his feet to the fire, in a condition of
sleepy wakefulness. Clustered about are blue uniforms and gray in equal numbers, and immediately
around his camp-fire are most of the Confederate
generals. Ewell is sitting on the ground hugging his
knees " (one flesh and blood, the other lifeless wood),
" his face bent down between his arms."

Ewell's brave old heart was beating low: neither he
nor any of his comrades was in a mood to talk, yet
sadly he told Wright, who invited him to share his
headquarters, that their cause was gone, and that
Lee should surrender so that no more lives be wasted.
Before closing his eyes in sleep, with his natural
love and affection, he sent for Stiles, and in the

presence of a half-dozen generals complimented him on the conduct of his battalion.

General Kershaw, Colonel Frank Huger, and several other Confederate officers were guests of Custer. Huger and Custer had been fellow cadets in the same company, D, at West Point. Huger, as well as Kershaw, was from South Carolina, and of distinguished Huguenot birth, to which his look and bearing bore daily witness. Custer was from Ohio and was then about twenty-six years old, of heavy build and full of natural joy. After his promotion to a generalcy, Custer dressed fantastically in olive corduroy, wore his yellow hair long, and supported a flaming scarlet flannel necktie whose loose ends the wind fluttered across his breast as, with uplifted sabre, he charged at the head of his brigade, followed by his equally reckless troopers, who, in loving imitation, wore neckties like his own.

He was always a boy, and absolutely free from harboring a spirit of malice, hatred, or revenge. Whenever fortune made any of his West Point friends prisoners, he hunted them up, grasped their hands, with his happy smile, and, before parting, tendered generous proffers of aid.

While Sheridan, Wright, and Humphreys were pursuing, and finally wreaking such signal disaster upon Lee's retreating forces, Grant and Meade had remained near Jetersville. Close by was a house that had an upper piazza from which toward noon, across the country and three or four miles away, Lyman says, they caught sight of a bare knoll over which the Confederate trains were passing, Gordon and Humphreys having a running fight at their rear. No news from the front of any great importance arrived till Sheridan's dispatch dated 12:20 P. M. (already given), to which Meade responded by renewed orders to Wright and Humphreys for action and pursuit more vigorous than ever, if possible.

Toward sundown, and still unaware of the day's good fortune, Grant and Meade separated; Grant set out for Burkeville, and Meade took the road to Deatonsville, and about half-past eight came to the bivouac by the roadside which Lyman, having galloped ahead, had selected some two miles beyond the village. He had barely ridden into camp when up came Sheridan's aide riding fast with his dispatch to Grant — Sheridan thinking he was with Meade — announcing his Sailor's Creek victory. Meade, as usual in such cases, and by Grant's instructions, read it, exclaiming with surprise and impatience, " Where was Wright? " Had Wright been one of the smooth, keen, foxy men of the world, he would have started an aide to Meade before the smoke had lifted from the victorious field that his troops had helped to win; but he was of that other class of old-time West Point men, men who did not boast, and who shunned newspaper fame. But very soon Meade heard from him and Humphreys direct, and was comforted.

Grant at Burkeville did not get Sheridan's dispatch till midnight and at once wrote to Meade, " Every moment now is important to us," and ordered Griffin, in bivouac near Ligontown to the right of Humphreys and near the Appomattox, to start by the most direct road without delay for Prince Edward Court-House, seven miles south of Farmville; adding that Mackenzie's cavalry, then with Ord, confronting Longstreet at Rice's Station, had been ordered to the same place and would be under way by 2 A. M. That these moves were made to head off Lee from reaching Danville is clearly obvious. The movement of Griffin to Ligontown was singularly futile, contributing nothing toward the results of the day. Had he been brought back early in the morning with the Sixth corps and been thrown against the left of Lee's long marching column, Lee's disaster would in all probability have been complete.

During the evening, while at Burkeville and before Grant had heard of Sheridan's success, he had had a long talk with a prisoner, an old army surgeon, a Doctor Smith, a Virginian, who had resigned at the breaking out of the war. The doctor in the course of his interview repeated what Ewell, his relative, had said to him at some time in the course of the previous winter, to the effect that he thought the cause was surely to be lost in the end, and that the South ought to ask for peace.

I think I can see Grant's old friend at perfect ease during this talk and looking with kindliness into Grant's steady mild blue eyes, for his old army friends always met him with frankness and trust whether he was in sunshine or shadow; and I think I can hear Grant responding with his unaffected, low voice, one of noticeable purity and pleasingly vibrant. As will be seen, the interview had its fruit.

So ends the chronicle of Thursday, the fourth day of the pursuit, and, as in my mind's eye I contemplate that entire field, the overcast sky with night drawing on, I can see the camp-fires twinkling, can hear Sailor's Creek murmuring in tones of lament, can see the spirit of the old fields and woods along the road from Amelia Springs standing aghast in sleepless wonder, and you, too, little roadside wild flowers, full of pity and shuddering in terror over war's dead and dying victims; yes, I see you all and it may be weak in me to feel as I do, but a young soldier lying alone dead on a field always evoked a haunting and deep sorrow.

VIII

GRANT and Meade had the lulling of victory to go
to sleep on, but not so Lee. The day had gone fear-
fully against him, and with it had gone, too, about
all hope of reaching Danville. But Lynchburg,
with its line of works and abundant supplies, seeing
his baffled, dismal plight, beckoned to him, and he
gave orders to fall back on Farmville, the first stage
thitherward. According to Mahone, he was somewhat disturbed as to how to get away from their
immediate position at Rice's Station, and asked his
advice. Mahone, who knew the country, suggested
that Longstreet should take the river road to Farmville, about nine miles west on the railway, while he
would strike across country to High Bridge, where
the river is crossed by a country road bridge, whose
roadbed, after traversing a little crescent intervale
on the north bank of the Appomattox, comes to the
feet of heaving, leaning fields with a background of
timber, lifting a crown of green up against the remote
and mute horizon line.

This roadway bridge is four or five miles from
Farmville, and just below the railway bridge known
as High Bridge, an airy structure on piers that at

the centre are nearly a hundred feet high. The
valley of the Appomattox at that point is narrow and
its banks are willow-fringed. Ord early in the morning of Thursday sent a small force of infantry and
cavalry from Burkeville to destroy this bridge, but
it was attacked when nearing its aim by Fitz Lee's,
Rosser's and Munford's cavalry, and after a very
desperate encounter was completely overcome and
captured. In this engagement my classmate, James
Dearing, commanding a brigade of Confederate
cavalry, was mortally wounded, and I never see the
name "High Bridge," that his handsome, cheery
face does not come back to me and I hear again his
happy voice. Dearing was taken to his home in
Lynchburg and when in the next week Mackenzie of
our class was entering Lynchburg with his division,
Dearing's surgeons sent word to him and asked that
the occupation of the city might be made as quietly
as circumstances would allow. Mackenzie at once
gave orders to that effect and went to inquire for
Dearing. The attendant at the door told him that
Dearing was very low and that the surgeons had
forbidden any one to see him. Mackenzie expressed his sorrow and asked a surgeon who then
appeared to give his love to his old classmate. Dearing heard and recognized Mackenzie's voice and
against his surgeon's protest insisted on seeing him.
When Mackenzie entered the room, Dearing reached
out his paling hand. Mackenzie took it in both of

his and knelt by Dearing's bed; his eyes were shedding tears, for he saw that Death was not far away. Dearing asked after a number of his class and sent his love to all of us. In a few days his spirit mounted, accompanied for awhile on its heavenly way by those of the fields, woods and brooks he loved, for I am fain to believe they go with us for the sake of old friendship on the first stages of that last journey. His clay now rests within sight of the Blue Ridge whose azure sky-line was so familiar to his open, nobly beaming eyes.

Lee adopted Mahone's suggestions as to withdrawing from their position at Rice's Station, and Latrobe, Longstreet's adjutant-general, in his orders, written by candle-light and issued about nine o'clock, directed that the trains and such batteries in position as were not necessary should be started at once for Farmville; that Field's division should retire first, followed by Heth and Wilcox; that the sharpshooters should be withdrawn an hour after the troops had marched; and that Rosser's cavalry should bring up the rear; closing the orders with the injunction, " Every effort must be made to get up all stragglers and all such men as have fallen asleep by the campfires or by the wayside."

Meanwhile, Wallace, Wise, Moody, Ransom, the remnants of Bushrod Johnson's and Pickett's and Anderson's divisions were shoaling to High Bridge and crossed it about 11 P. M. Gordon, to whom

Lee's orders had been communicated, aroused his men after a few hours' rest, resumed the march, and was over the river before daylight. Mahone reached the bridge just after Gordon had cleared it, but the sun was up as his rear-guard was crossing.

According to Col. John S. Wise, a son of the General Henry A. Wise, Lee himself did not leave the vicinity of Rice's Station till late in the night, for he says, " It was after midnight when I found General Lee. He was in an open field north of Rice's Station. A camp-fire of fence-rails was burning low and Colonel Marshall [Lee's adjutant-general] sat in an ambulance with a lantern and lap-desk, and Lee, with one hand on a wheel, his foot on a log, was dictating orders."

And this is how it happened that the distinguished author of *The End of an Era*, then a boy of twenty years, reached the army.

Mr. Davis was at Danville. Three full days had gone by, and not a word from Lee. Anxiety grew, and keener and keener was the longing of the President of the Confederacy to know how it had gone with the Army of Northern Virginia. Midnight of the third day was approaching, and the spare, sleepless Mr. Davis, with his pathetically channeled face, could stand the suspense no longer. He telegraphed to a General Walker, commanding the troops nearest to the army to send some one out to see and get the news. For this signal duty young Wise was chosen.

After stirring adventures Wise got to Farmville late Thursday evening, a few hours after the blow at Sailor's Creek, and from there he threaded the shattered, retreating forces to Lee's headquarters. More anon of this visit of Wise, but first let us follow the events of the night.

Longstreet's troops were moving by twelve, and Alexander says, "I remember the night as peculiarly uncomfortable. The road was crowded with disorganized men, and deep in mud; we were moving all night and scarcely made six miles." In one of the Southern diaries we read, referring to that same night, "The march now assumed every appearance of a rout, soldiers from every command were straggling all over the country, and our once grand army was rapidly melting away." The diarist's battery, the Richmond Howitzers, reached High Bridge at a late hour and remained there till daylight, then crossed the river and moved toward Farmville.

Of all these unhappy nights — and bear in mind that they had marched practically every one except the first since they set out on the retreat — I think this must have been about the dismalest. Hope had parted company with them, defeat had laid its hand heavily on them, it was pitch-dark and drizzling, — the rain had come that the red setting sun had foretold, — the famishing horses were falling, the men were sleepy, wet, and hungry. Yet through mud, up hill and down, listening to the call of duty, they went, till many out of pure weakness, no longer able to drag one foot after another, reeled into the woods, dropped limply down, and laying their cheeks on the drenched leaves, went to sleep, some to the very long, long sleep. Those whose strength held out plodded on and on, wondering at every step they took how much farther it was to Farmville. When morning broke, Friday the 7th, the fields and woods by the roadside were dotted with squads of men tired, sick at heart, and moving as in a dream.

Now mark the contrast. At that very hour, sunrise, Friday the 7th, our troops were all under way in pursuit, and the historian of one of the regiments in the Sixth corps says, " The men were singing, laughing, joking, and apparently happy. Along the road were evidences of the rapid retreat of the enemy, all sorts of ammunition strewn around loose, dead horses lying where they dropped, others abandoned because they could no longer carry their riders, and here and there a dead soldier, lying in the road where he had halted for the last time, with every appearance of having died from hunger and exhaustion."

" Soon," says one of Humphreys's corps, in the track of Gordon, " we began to come upon whole packs of wagons burned as they stood, artillery ammunition scattered by the roadside, and caissons partially destroyed." In fact, there was scarcely a rod of the way that did not have its mute witnesses to the demoralization of the retreating forces.

Of course, all these signs of distress only quickened our advance, and soon brought Humphreys to the vicinity of High Bridge. The Nineteenth Maine, a regiment that in the Wilderness won great honor for its far-away Pine Tree State, now leading its valiant corps, carried the approaches to the burning wagon-road bridge, which Mahone had set fire to, as well as to the lofty railroad structure, after crossing.

The tall woodsmen from Maine rushed down and, by one means and another, put out the fast-creeping blaze, all the time under severe fire from Mahone's rear-guard. For the spare, little, blue-eyed, cool, ambitious man, witnessing the efforts to save the bridges, started a brigade back to drive our men away till the fire could do its work, but the Nineteenth Maine, its courage drawn from the timbered reaches of the Penobscot and Kennebec, stood its ground till help came, and then, in turn, drove Mahone's brigade back across the intervale up to the hills, forcing them to abandon ten guns.

By nine o'clock the whole Second corps was over, and Humphreys, on reporting the fact to Meade, said he could see a column of the enemy's infantry some two miles distant moving northwestward. What he saw were Gordon's and Mahone's columns on what is known as the Cumberland Church Road, a road which comes into the Appomattox Court-House and Lynchburg road about three or four miles above Farmville. So much for Humphreys, Gordon, and Mahone.

Sheridan started Crook from Sailor's Creek battle-field — imagine an open-faced, blue-eyed man with a splaying, tawny beard and an aquiline nose — early toward High Bridge; while he, accompanied by Merritt's and Custer's divisions of cavalry, set out for Prince Edward Court-House by way of Rice's. Prince Edward Court-House is on the main road leading south from Farmville, and was to Lee's plans, if he had any left of going to Danville, what Jetersville was to him at Amelia Court-House.

As Custer rode by the Confederate prisoners and recognized Kershaw and Huger, his guests of the night before, he lifted his hat to them. Kershaw lifted his and exclaimed, " There goes a chivalrous fellow, let's give him three cheers; " to which Custer responded by ordering the band just behind him to strike up the Confederate tune " The Bonny Blue Flag," and the prisoners screamed their fierce "rebel " yell with delight.

Crook on approaching High Bridge ran up against Humphreys, pulled his left bridle-rein and struck across the country, and presently fell in at the head of Ord's troops on the trail of Longstreet's column from Rice's Station. At Bush River, which is but little more than a good-sized creek, about half-way from Rice's Station to Farmville, Crook's advance came up with Longstreet's rear-guard, Scales' brigade of infantry, Rosser's and Fitz Lee's people lining its opposite bank.

But by the time Crook got ready to attack, Ord's advance, who had actually marched as fast as the mounted force, — so fleet were they now, hearing the call of the end, — hurried to his ranks, and together they charged across and swept the enemy's cavalry away from the ridge. Then, with Dandy's brigade of infantry, Crook pushed on after them.

Wright, who had started from Sailor's Creek, had by noon only got as far as Sandy Creek, an easterly tributary of Bush River, and reported to Meade that Griffin himself, on his way to Prince Edward Court-House, was there, and the head of his column drawing near. It will be remembered that Grant had given Griffin orders for this move while at Burkeville.

Meade, who was still unwell, took the road to High Bridge, reached there at eleven o'clock and established his headquarters.

Grant left Burkeville about seven and overtook Wright's corps, that was following Ord's, the troops cheering him well as he rode through them. Keifer, under Wright, in his *Four Years of War* says, " The roads were muddy and much cut up by the Confederate army. Grant was dressed to all appearances in a tarpaulin suit," — it was still raining a little, — "and he was even to his whiskers so bespattered with mud, fresh and dried, as to almost prevent recognition. He, then as always, was quiet, modest, and undemonstrative. A close look showed an expression of deep anxiety." And now having all of Grant's army in motion on that Friday morning, let us turn to Lee's. Here is what my friend Alexander, says, who only last autumn crossed that other great river, and when I shall cross, too, I hope some one, preferably he who saw the vision on the Isle of Patmos, will lead me to him, for he was good, soothing, and winsome company.

"About sunrise, we got to Farmville and crossed the river on a bridge to the north side of the Appomattox, and here we received a small supply of rations. Four railroad trains had been sent down from Lynchburg.

"Here we found General Lee. While we were getting breakfast, he sent for me and, taking out his map, showed me that the enemy had taken a highway bridge across the Appomattox near the High Bridge, were crossing on it, and would come in upon our road about three miles ahead. He directed me to send artillery there to cover our passage and, meanwhile, to take personal charge of the two bridges at Farmville (the railroad and the highway), prepare them for burning, see that they were not fired too soon, so as to cut off our own men, or so late that the enemy might save them.

" While he explained, my eyes ran over the map and I saw another road to Lynchburg than the one we were taking. This other kept the south side of the river and was the straighter of the two, our road joining it near Appomattox Court-House. I pointed this out, and he asked if I could find some one whom he might question. I had seen at a house near by an intelligent man, whom I brought up, and who confirmed the map. The Federals would have the shortest road to Appomattox Station, a common point a little beyond Appomattox Court - House. Saying that there would be time enough to look after that, the general folded up his map and I went to look after the bridges.

" As the enemy [Crook and Dandy] were already in sight, I set fire to the railroad bridge at once, and, having well prepared the highway bridge, I left my aide, Lieutenant Mason, to fire it on a signal from me. It also was successfully burned. In *The End of an Era*, by John S. Wise, he has described an interview occurring between his father, General Wise, and General Lee, at Farmville at this time, which I quote: —

" ' We found General Lee on the rear portico of the house I have mentioned. He had washed his face in a tin basin and stood drying his beard with a coarse towel as we approached. " General Lee,"

exclaimed my father, " my poor brave men are lying
on yonder hill more dead than alive. For more than
a week they have been fighting day and night,
without food, and, by God! sir, they shall not move
another step until somebody gives them something
to eat."

" ' " Come in, General," said General Lee, sooth-
ingly. " They deserve something to eat and shall
have it; and, meanwhile, you shall share my breakfast." He disarmed everything like defiance by his
kindness. . . . General Lee inquired what he thought
of the situation. " Situation? " said the bold old
man. " There is no situation. Nothing remains,
General Lee, but to put your poor men on your poor
mules and send them home in time for the spring
ploughing. This army is hopelessly whipped, and
is fast becoming demoralized. These men have
already endured more than I believed flesh and blood
could stand, and I say to you, sir, emphatically,
that to prolong the struggle is murder, and the blood
of every man who is killed from this time forth is
on your head, General Lee."

" ' This last expression seemed to cause General
Lee great pain. With a gesture of remonstrance,
and even of impatience, he protested. " Oh, General,
do not talk so wildly! My burdens are heavy enough!
What would the country think of me, if I did what
you suggest? " ' " Lee must have had in mind Pemberton, whom the South had execrated for surrender-

ing Vicksburg to Grant a few years before; in fact while Lee was at Gettysburg.

" ' " Country be damned," was the quick reply. " There is no country. There has been no country, General, for a year or more. You are the country to these men. They have fought for you. They have shivered through a long winter for you. Without pay or clothes or care of any sort, their devotion to you and faith in you have been the only things that have held this army together. If you demand the sacrifice, there are still left thousands of us who will die for you. You know the game is desperate beyond redemption, and that, if you so announce, no man, or government, or people, will gainsay your decision. That is why I repeat that the blood of any man killed hereafter is on your head." General Lee stood for some time at an open window looking out at the throng now surging by upon the roads and in the fields, and made no response.' "

Well might Lee say, " My burdens are heavy enough! " and Alexander adds that General Wise had in no way exaggerated them.

This heart-sick, volcano-like eruption of Governor Wise — he was then aged, and Lyman describes him, when, two days later and after the surrender, he came to see his brother-in-law, General Meade, as " an old man, with spectacles and a short white beard, a stooping sickly figure with his legs tied round with gray blankets " — shoots up once more into the clear light of national events, recalling the conditions and passions of my youth, and if for a moment I dwell on them, it is because out of them I saw the tragedy of the war burst upon us all.

It was Wise's fortune to be the Governor of Virginia (the Old Dominion had not then been dismembered) when the trial and execution of John Brown for murder at Harper's Ferry took place, in the autumn of 1859. The event startled the country from shore to shore and lifted Wise and Brown into flaming notoriety; and they two, predestined actors in one of Fate's dramas, held the stage for months. Wise, as governor, went to Charleston, West Virginia, where Brown was incarcerated, and had an interview with him just before he was led out to the gallows, and was deeply impressed by the tall, roughly-framed, cool, shock-haired, blue-eyed man, secure against any shake of Fortune, whose utterances showed that he had thought profoundly on life's mysteries. More, the governor saw clearly that Brown was fortified with a virtue upon which he, Wise, prided himself: indomitable courage.

And now, because I lived through it all, — my room-mate at West Point was a Southerner and intimate friends from the South were all around me, and I know how much Brown's attempt had to do with bringing on the war, — allow me to make a few reflections on this interview, and to confess, moreover, that I am prone thereto for the sake of the narrative, whose life and worth depends on the shadowed depths of its background.

Reader, let me tell you that that meeting of Governor Henry A. Wise of Virginia and John Brown of fadeless history was a meeting face to face of the representatives of two mutually antagonistic forces which, from the dawn of civilization, let peace have bloomed or sung as it may, have never laid down their arms. One feeding in spirit on the idea of the brotherhood of man and contemplating with lonely rapture, as he toiled, the laying down of his life, if need be, for the freedom of his brother-toilers, black or white; and the other, born into the purple, the Gates of Opportunity wide open in front of him, ambition leaping freely and clutching highest honors, musing, not on the humanities, but on the priceless idea of democracy, till he, also, contemplated with a noble rapture the laying of his life down, if need be, for that basic principle which in his mind, as in that of all mankind, is just as dear as freedom itself: that is, the right of a people to govern themselves.

There they stood, looking keenly into each other's face, each trying to read to the bottom the other's heart, John Brown and Henry A. Wise, living, breathing types of two old and mutually distrusting forces; Wise in a broad sense a child of Fortune and sipping the wine of Success, John Brown, in God's providence, a son of Toil and drinking to the lees

the distillations of obscurity and failure; and before
the grass had matted over Brown's grave their
political embodiments rushed at each other and
clenched in a deadly struggle, for the fullness of
time had come.

In vain the North protested Brown's bloody
intent, involving as it did a universal massacre and
causing the South to shudder as it recalled the frightful butcheries of San Domingo. Unfortunately the
unscrupulous among the Southern fire-eaters trans-
lated Brown's demoniacal attempt as duly expressing the real and true feelings of the entire North; and
their orators, after Mr. Lincoln's election as President, lashed themselves into delirium and clamored
for secession, with its inevitable war. Finally the
challenge was thrown down with wild screams of
defiance by the original secessionists, and the thousands who had clung to the Union were swept as by a
tempest into a war which many had prayed God to
avert.

The challenge was accepted, the tragedy began;
slavery, as an institution for the South to fight for,
disappeared in a twinkling, and in the North the
question whether one state or a dozen states could
drag the country itself from its natural, yes, predestined orbit, became the inspiring, living issue.

Well, well! But, as St. Juliana said, " All *is* well
and all *shall* be well ;" yet how little did Governor
Wise dream that day in Charleston that in less than

six years he would be on the hills above Farmville in the hopeless wreck of the last fighting force of the South. But so it had come to pass, and I pity the old man, with spectacles and gray beard, who, under the awful disappointment of defeat, and worn out with worry and hunger, unbolted the door of his heart. He has long since gone to his grave on the eastern shore of his beloved Chesapeake, and I am sure he sleeps quietly, for I have heard the lulling of the waves on those long sandy beaches myself.

While the interview between Wise and Lee was going on, that Friday morning, some of Longstreet's trains were hurriedly replenishing their supplies from the cars sent down from Lynchburg; but, before they had filled their wagons, Crook's cavalry and Dandy's brigade of Ord's corps appeared in the high fields to the south of and overlooking the attractive little village of Farmville. One of their batteries, Elder's I believe, opened; the railway trains, apprehensive of just that danger, fled back toward Lynchburg, and the swarming Confederates, infantry and cavalry, scampered across the bridges up on to the bare, high sloping fields, above Farmville. Rosser's cavalry, when Crook charged down into the town, — the bridges by that time were burning, — had to seek a ford several miles up the river. Ord's advance got into Farmville about two P. M.; Wright with the Sixth corps, somewhat later.

Gordon and Mahone reached Cumberland Church

about ten o'clock, halted and entrenched. The road their works spanned soon enters the Lynchburg pike, which runs north from Farmville and then turns west for Appomattox, about twenty-five miles away. It is nearly paralleled by a road known as the Plank as far as New Store, not quite half way to Appomattox Court-House. These were the roads Lee, who had his quarters where the Cumberland Church road comes into the Lynchburg pike, meant to take, and it was necessary to hold that point until the trains and artillery could get a start out of the way of the infantry. Longstreet was in line with a number of batteries ready to check any advance from Farmville, and that Gordon and Mahone might hold their own against Humphreys, Colonel Poague's battalion of artillery, which played such havoc with the same corps, then under Hancock at the Wilderness, was sent to the Cumberland Church lines.

The sky cleared about noon and every old white- and pink-blooming apple tree, the fields and woods sprinkled with flowers, yellow, white, and blue dogwood, and blazing azalea, began to rejoice.

But not so those weary, hunger-feeble, Confederate veterans, throwing up a line of works across the road above Farmville to stay the inexorable Humphreys until the famishing horses dragging artillery and trains could get a little start for Appomattox. No, there was no rejoicing among them, let the fields, sky, and brooks smile and gurgle as they might; and I have no doubt that more than one of the tired men, their heads bowed down, envied the dead in Cumberland churchyard. Yet their courage rang like an anvil when Humphreys struck at them late in the afternoon.

Humphreys came up about two o'clock, and after a survey reported to Meade that he had the whole Confederate army in his front, and apparently full of fight. Whereupon Meade sent orders to Wright, who he supposed had reached Farmville, to cross and attack at once. Wright, however, could not obey this order immediately, for he had to wait until Peter Michie, chief engineer on Ord's staff and my dear friend of West Point days, could bring up his pontoon train to bridge the river; as a matter of fact it was growing dark before the bridge was ready for Wright.

Crook's division forded the Appomattox above the village about four o'clock, and his advance brigade, Gregg's, catching sight of retreating trains, attacked; but Rosser and Munford turned on him so savagely that Gregg was captured and his troops driven back on to the rest in confusion. The other brigades of the division had to take the defensive, and later received orders from Grant to recross and join Sheridan, who, after lunching at Prince Edward Court-House under spreading oaks, sent Mackenzie's division of cavalry to Prospect Station, eleven miles west of Farmville on the Lynchburg Railroad, and then followed after him with the other two divisions, Merritt's and Custer's.

Humphreys, that man of steely courage, hearing Crook's guns and thinking they were Wright's advance, assaulted, selecting his most determined division-commander, Miles, to deliver the blow. Lee, however, apprised of Humphreys' threatening attitude, hurried Longstreet to the spot, who on arriving sent G. T. Anderson's and Bratton's brigades of Field's division to Mahone, who in turn directed them through a woodland to Miles' right and repulsed him with heavy loss. By this time it was almost dark.

In the course of the afternoon, Wright, while waiting for Michie's bridge to be built, told Ord and Gibbon, who had already reached Farmville and been joined by Grant, what Ewell had said to him the night before at Sailor's Creek, namely, of Lee's duty, in view of what had happened that day, to stop the shedding of any more blood. Wright repeated the same story to Grant, thus confirming what Doctor Smith had told him; then Grant talked over with these officers the propriety of sending a note to Lee suggesting the surrender of his army.

There is no record of what Wright, Gibbon, or Ord said at this interview; but knowing that Ord had tried through his old army and fellow West Point friend, Longstreet, to bring about an interview between Grant and Lee the previous winter

with a view to ending the war, I have no doubt that
he urged it warmly. But perhaps what decided the
matter in Grant's mind was that he knew from
Sheridan's position that he would soon be across
Lee's way at Appomattox as at Jetersville, and that
Lee would then have to surrender. Hence he wrote
to him as follows: —

> " HEADQUARTERS,
> " ARMIES OF THE UNITED STATES,
> " April 7, 1865 — 5 P. M.
>
> " GENERAL R. E. LEE,
> " Commanding C. S. Army:
> " GENERAL: The result of the last week must con-
> vince you of the hopelessness of further resistance
> on the part of the Army of Northern Virginia in this
> struggle. I feel that it is so, and regard it as my
> duty to shift from myself the responsibility of any
> further effusion of blood by asking of you the sur-
> render of that portion of the C. S. Army known as
> the Army of Northern Virginia.
>
> " Very respectfully,
> " Your obedient servant,
> " U. S. GRANT,
> " Lieutenant-General, Commanding
> " Armies of the United States."

Surely this momentous note could not have been
pitched in a better key to still the sea of passion or

turn the mind toward the paths of peace; and I am free to confess that whenever I ponder on this campaign there always emerges from its background of providential results, results so vast and beneficent, a vision of the country's good angel standing by Grant's side guiding his pen, what time soever he took it up to address Lee.

Meanwhile Sheridan was pushing on from Prince Edward Court-House to Prospect Station; he arrived there about sundown and notified Grant that one of his scouts had reported that eight supply trains were at Appomattox Station for Lee's army, and that he would move his cavalry column thither. Grant in response told him to go ahead and that the Fifth corps, at that hour, seven P. M., going into bivouac at Prince Edward, and the Twenty-fourth, then in Farmville, would push after him.

Grant sent word by Newhall, who had brought Sheridan's dispatch, that he had addressed Lee as to surrendering his army. Sheridan, however, put no faith in Lee paying any heed whatsoever to Grant's proposal, and gave orders for an early march to Appomattox Station. Crook reached Sheridan's bivouac about midnight, Friday.

While Grant's peace-breathing letter is on its way to Lee, let me bring forward two complemental circumstances, both prophetic and freighted with historic interest, for they reveal how the trials of the last few days had breached the walls of the hitherto

invincible confidence of final success that distinguished the Army of Northern Virginia. The in-
cidents referred to are these; first:

About the very hour that Lee received Grant's
letter, the regimental officers of the 11th North
Carolina, McRae's brigade, held a conference, and
Captain Ralph Edward Outlaw was charged to see
that the battle-frayed colors, come weal, come woe,
should not be parted with. Accordingly he took
them from the staff, replaced their water-proof
cover, and carried them in his breast.   When,
thirty-six hours later, Lee rode through the lines
to meet Grant, the officers of the regiment retired
to a thicket, raked together a pile of leaves, and
committed the flag that had been carried on so
many fields of glory to the flames.

This speaks in unmistakable terms of how the
coming crisis was felt through the line of the army.
Now, as to the general officers.

Sometime during the morning after the arrival of
the army at Farmville, Gordon and a number of
leading division and brigade commanders, Pickett
among them, as I have every reason to believe, met
and held a conference. After discussing the situation, they came to the conclusion that the days of
the Confederacy were numbered, and that some one
should go to Lee and tell him so; and, if odium
there were for asking terms of Grant, it should be
allowed to fall on them alone for first making the

suggestion. They delegated Gordon to lay the matter before Pendleton, — Lee's chief of artillery and a West Point boyhood friend whose relations with his commander were as intimate as Lee's nature permitted any one's to be, — and further instructed Gordon to ask Pendleton, provided he felt as they did, to be the bearer of their message to Lee. Pendleton's account of his interview with Gordon is as follows:

"Fighting was going on, but not very severely, so that conversation was practicable [it was in the afternoon and they were on the hills above Farmville]. General Gordon had with me an interview, told me of discouraging intelligence from the South, and of a conference which had been held between other responsible officers and himself, and announced their joint wish that, if my views agreed with theirs, I should convey to General Longstreet, as second in command, and then, if he agreed, to General Lee, our united judgment that the cause had become so hopeless we thought it wrong to be having men killed on either side, and not right, moreover, that our beloved commander should be left to bear the entire trial of initiating the idea of terms with the enemy. My judgment not conflicting with those expressed, it seemed to me my duty to convey them to General Lee. At first General Longstreet dissented, but on second thought preferred that he should be represented with the rest."

The significance of the foregoing incident, not to be matched in purport by anything which occurred on that fateful march, leads me to ask the reader to let me interrupt Pendleton's account with a comment or two.

Can any better proof be offered of the desperateness and hopelessness of Lee's situation? For were not Gordon and every one of his fellows at that conference perfectly familiar with the Articles of War, which provided that even to hint at surrender in the presence of an enemy was the most despicable sin a soldier could commit, that it was a military crime and called mutiny, carrying a death penalty which, if executed, is forever tainted by disgrace? No graduate of West Point and no one who ever wore a sword in time of war will fail to be impressed by the seriousness of what they did. Yet in the face of this dread danger, unshaken, they took that grandly moral, perilous step, but in taking it they rose to the level of the truly great.

In one sense, Gordon and Pickett and every one involved could afford to take it, for the scars they bore and the records of the days of battle when they led, shamed out of sight all suspicion that the fires of their courage and loyalty had ceased to burn. The thought that these virtues failed them now would be an outrage to their memories. And moreover, as the calm light of the present falls on the scene of their conference, lo, Reason and Humanity stand

there ready to establish that their courage was of
the very highest type, a type loftier than Gordon's
at Spottsylvania when he spurred his horse across
Traveller's front, seized his bridle-rein and checked
him, shouting to General Lee above the roar of the
musketry at the Bloody Angle, "You must go to
the rear!" or Pickett's when he set out with a
cheery face to storm the lines at Gettysburg.

And now let me tell you a strange fact, and one
that I wish my eye had not fallen upon. When
Gordon wrote his *Reminiscences* he disclaimed being
present at the conference; and even brave old Longstreet, whose last years were made so pitifully miserable by venomous attacks from brother soldiers
with whom he had worn the gray, in his military
Life says that he turned on Pendleton and inquired,
"if he did not know that the Articles of War provided that officers and soldiers who asked their
commanding officers to surrender should be shot?"

Let it be observed that, when Gordon and Longstreet wrote their accounts of that conference, poor
Pendleton and Lee were in their graves and the
pæan to Lee and the steadfastness of the Army of
Northern Virginia was ringing loud. Oh, pale
Retractions withering breath! and how weak we
are, and how often we cringe before public opinion, abandoning and dismantling the strong works
built by those royal engineers, the inward senses
of Right and Duty!

Whom, then, shall we believe? All I have to say is, that Pendleton was a gentleman and so was Gordon and so was Longstreet, and now they are across the river in a land beyond domineering opinion, where all earthly glories seem dim, and controversy never breathes. Green, forever green, I hope, will rest their laurels: they served the Confederacy well, they won a place by their manliness and valor in the hearts of North and South, they won a place, too, in the heart of Peace by that conference; and when she passes their graves or that of any one who said, " Let the odium fall on me," she whispers to her angelic companions, " Here lies the clay of a valiant man; he was a friend of mine on the hills of Farmville."

But what was the nature of the discouraging intelligence from the South that Gordon had spoken of to Pendleton, and how had it come to Gordon's ears, in view of the fact that all telegraph lines were cut? There are but two sources whence it could have come, namely, either through John S. Wise, who, so far as there is any record, was the only bearer of dispatches, and his were verbal, who reached Lee's army from the time it left Petersburg till it surrendered; or through the commissary officers in charge of the trains that had come down to Farmville from Lynchburg. But how the discouraging intelligence was brought, is not so material as the character of the news itself. That it must have been weighty, causing Gordon and the conference to suggest the surrender of the Army of Northern Virginia, goes without saying. What was it? At first, I thought it had to do with Johnston's army, but I am now convinced it was the capture of Selma, Alabama, on the 2nd of April, the Sunday when Lee evacuated Petersburg, by my life-long friend, Gen. James H. Wilson. Selma was the last of the South's main arsenals and depots of supplies, and its capture, accompanied, as it was, by the hitherto invincible Forrest's absolute defeat, forbade all hope of stopping Wilson from sweeping, as he did, through the very heart of Alabama and Georgia, breaking up and destroying the railroads, completing Sherman's devastating work and leaving the South a mere frail and hollow shell doomed to be crushed, for there were no troops that could possibly be gathered to check him.

Situated as the South then was, Johnston helpless in the presence of Sherman now reinforced by Scho-field, and Lee's army a mere shadow of its former self after the defeat of the day before at Sailor's Creek, Wilson's success, I believe, was paramount; it was the finishing blow to the Confederacy and made it only a matter of days, or weeks at farthest, when Lee and Johnston would have to lay down their arms.

Such then, Wilson's fateful campaign and capture

of Selma, was, in my opinion, the discouraging intelligence referred to by Pendleton. It is possible that
news of the fall of Selma might have reached Wise
before he set out on his journey. In that case, when,
on his way to Lee's headquarters from Farmville,
he met, as he says he did, two general officers whom
he knew, both very much cast down, declaring that
all hope was gone, is it not probable that, learning
whence he came, they asked him for the latest
news from the South? And is it not likely that he
told them all he knew? For who ever met one of
that Wise blood yet, young or old, and did not find
him a frank, transparent gentleman and courageously
truthful, besides being mightily interesting and companionable?

After explaining his mission to Lee and being told
by him that it was unsafe to send any written communication to Mr. Davis on account of the danger
of capture, and that he himself should be governed
by each day's developments, young Wise caught a
little sleep, went back to Farmville, saw his father,
and then was off for Danville.

Suppose, on the other hand, the news of the capture of Selma and discomfiture of Forrest was brought
down from Lynchburg by the quartermaster or commissary officers in charge of the railway trains, how
quickly it would have spread! for who ever met a
quartermaster or a commissary anywhere in the rear
during a campaign, that did not find him a fountain

charged to the very brim with mysterious news and
army gossip? Of course to have the fountain open
freely you must treat him as a man of great importance.

Well, howsoever the "discouraging intelligence from
the South " found its way to Farmville, you may rest
assured it soon reached Gordon's ears and through
him Breckinridge, the Confederate Secretary of
War, who left Richmond, the burning capital, with
Ewell. Now he and Gordon knew, and I think liked
each other very well; they had shared together
Early's disastrous campaign in the valley, each
resenting Early's official report of the part their
divisions had played, and, under these circumstances
is it not reasonable to suppose that they discussed the
situation in the light of Wilson's victory and opened
their hearts to each other? May not Breckinridge
casually have dropped the remark that Lee might
just as well see Grant first as last now that Scho-
field had united with Sherman and that there was
not one chance in fifty of Lee being able, with his
army in its then enfeebled condition, to accomplish
anything against Sherman even if he did circum-
vent Grant?

It is true, there is no evidence that Breckinridge
had any knowledge of the " discouraging intelligence," or that he said a word to any one who was at
the conference, but I cannot believe for a moment
that Gordon and his fellows were influenced to take

the step they did by mere camp rumors. The South's grave situation as a whole must have been talked over, and no one knew its hopelessness better than the Secretary of War, and I cannot resist the conclusion that, before the officers took the step they did, somebody in authority like a cabinet officer — the astute Secretary of State, Benjamin, was with Breckinridge also — had expressed an opinion which justified their action.

Well, whether Breckinridge said a word or not to his old campaign friends, he left the army early that Friday morning for the Roanoke, and on the following day sent a dispatch from Red House to Mr. Davis saying, " I left General Lee at Farmville yesterday morning, where he was passing the main body across the river for temporary relief. . . . The straggling has been great, and the situation is not favorable."

IX

Now, to go back and take up the thread once more: Grant's note to Lee was given to Seth Williams, the Adjutant-General of the Army of the Potomac; and a more lovable and rarer man never walked the plain of old West Point as a boy, or as a man wore the army uniform. Moreover, when Lee was superintendent of the Academy, Williams had been his adjutant.

Williams, having to go around by High Bridge, it was about half-past eight when he reached Humphreys in front of Gordon's Cumberland Church works. Passing through the skirmish line (it was then quite dark and no moon), he was soon challenged by a member of the City Light Guards of Columbus, Georgia, in Sorrel's brigade, then under command of Colonel Tayloe. The gallant Sorrel was absent recovering from a desperate wound.

The Confederate officer to whom the challenging picket reported the presence of the flag of truce that Friday night was Lieutenant G. J. Peacock of the Guards, who at once notified his superior officer, Major Moffett. The major came to the picket, and advancing in the darkness some thirty paces, called out, "What is wanted?" "Important dispatches from General Grant to General Lee," answered Williams. "Stand where you are till I communicate," came back the response.

A messenger was then sent to the brigade headquarters, and the adjutant-general, A. H. Perry of Mahone's division, was directed to go and receive the note. This officer says that he buckled on his revolver, passed some fifty yards beyond their pickets, halted, and called for the flag. It was then about nine o'clock, and scattered about in the starless woods were many of our dead and wounded, for it was the ground Miles had fought over. Williams answered the call; Perry came forward and "met," he says, "a very handsomely-dressed Federal officer. We stopped in front of each other, about seven or eight feet apart." Williams spoke first, announcing his name as of General Grant's staff; Perry then in turn made known who he was; whereupon Williams put his hand in his breast-pocket, as Perry supposed feeling for a document; instead of which he produced a silver-mounted flask and hoped that Perry would not think it unsoldierly courtesy if he were to offer him some fine brandy. Perry austerely declined the civility; Williams begged his pardon, and without comment replaced the flask.

If ever there was one occasion in this world when brandy had a heaven-born mission, that was the time, and I think Perry made a mighty big mistake, and he thought so, too, before he died.

Under the circumstances, however (they were gloomy enough), he felt that to take a drink with an enemy would be undignified. But I don't believe that would have hampered you, reader, at all, for I have a notion that, besides being companionable, you are also a chivalrous sort of fellow. Off would have gone your hat, and out would have gone your hand — and lifting the flask, you would have said, " Here's to you, with my best respects! " and taken a good long pull. And had Perry done as you would have done, I have no doubt Williams would have exclaimed with beaming face, for he always looked as if he carried a harp in his breast, " Thank you, colonel, thank you, and drink right heartily, my soldier friend! "

Perry having rather haughtily declined the proffered courtesy, Williams produced the dispatch, expressing the hope that it would be delivered promptly to General Lee. Then they bowed profoundly and parted. Within a few paces Williams met a member of Miles's staff in search of a friend among the wounded. Being told that this officer had several letters and family pictures found in Mahone's personal baggage, captured that afternoon, which he wished to return, Williams called back to Perry and asked him if he would meet the officer. Perry answered " Yes," and retracing his steps, took Mahone's effects, and offered to do, and did, something for our wounded. Williams, meanwhile, made the best of his way to Humphreys' headquarters.

The dispatch was forwarded promptly to Lee, who was not far off, and alone with Longstreet, who, by the way, had not yet seen Pendleton. After reading it Lee, without referring to its contents, handed it to Longstreet, who read it, and as he returned the note made the sole remark, "Not yet."

Without consulting Longstreet further, Lee responded to Grant as follows: —

"April 7, 1865.

" GENERAL, —

"I have received your note of this date. Though not entertaining the opinion you express on the hopelessness of further resistance on the part of the Army of Northern Virginia, I reciprocate your desire to avoid the useless effusion of blood, and therefore, before considering your proposition, ask the terms you will offer on condition of its surrender.

"R. E. LEE, General.

"Lieutenant-General U. S. GRANT."

Within an hour Lee's reply was received at Humphreys' headquarters, and Williams started with it to Grant; but having to take the circuitous route by way of High Bridge, he did not reach Grant at Farmville till midnight.

Meanwhile, without waiting for Grant's answer to his question as to terms, Lee consolidated his army into two corps, Longstreet's and Gordon's, and I have authority for saying that about this time he directed that orders be issued dismissing Pickett, Anderson and others. Fortunately the order was withheld, but Anderson left the army that night. By ten o'clock Lee's men were moving toward Appomattox, and in the light of this fact, is there anything plainer than that, when he asked Grant as to the character of the terms he would give, he had no intention whatsoever of accepting them, let them be what they might? His answer was a parry pure and simple. But his enforced delay at Farmville to enable his trains to get out of the way, made it utterly impossible for him to realize his hopes.

And yet I can hear a student of war, whose whole life is devoted to reassembling the bones of dead campaigns, ask sternly, " Why did Lee not concentrate every soldier and attack Humphreys? neither Wright nor any of the troops at Farmville could have come to his help in time to have served him." Well, proud Gentleman of the Sword, if you ever go through a war like that which this narrative is dealing with, and after four years of it you should make a retreat like that from Petersburg, I will, to use the language of Izaak Walton, go you twenty to

one that you will not press the question. For so
well will you learn that there is so much to be taken
into account in actual warfare, of which experience
alone can give any idea, that to ask why this or
that was done will never enter your mind.

But little, little does it matter now, Student of
War, what Lee might have done that day on the
hills above Farmville. Doom was throwing the
last shovelfuls out of the grave of the Confederacy;
and Slavery's inveterate enemies, Humanity and
Freedom, were standing there looking down into
it and demanding that it be dug sufficiently deep.

But lift your eyes: there on the Future's dawning
sky is the flush of better days to come, days of peace,
days without lament and full of national splendor.
So, let the Army of Northern Virginia have been
called upon to do this or that, nothing could stay
God's march of events on this our church-spired
world.

Therefore let us not speculate on what Lee might
have done, but go on with the narrative; for it is
toward midnight and his army is moving again,
moving silently away from its fainting camp-fires.
The cavalry, who are to bring up the rear, are
mounting their gaunt horses, and the division officers of the day are withdrawing the pickets. Far
in the lead is Lindsay Walker's column of surplus
artillery, that had reached Lee's position at
Farmville from Amelia by way of Cumberland

Court - House early that Friday morning and taken the road to Appomattox Court - House, camping that night at New Store. In this column were, among others, Hardaway's, Lightfoot's, Stribling's, Leyden's and John Lane's battalions. Lane, I knew very well at West Point. He was large, slow, good-natured, and had dull black eyes. His father was a United States Senator from Oregon and ran for Vice-President with Breckinridge on the ticket of the Southern wing of the Democratic party against Mr. Lincoln. Lane's classmates sometimes called him the Senator, and the " Senator " dearly loved the atmosphere of the " Immortals," the men at the foot of West Point classes, many of whom, like Custer and Sheridan, became truly Immortals.

In Stribling's battalion, originally the 38th Virginia, commanded by Dearing until he was promoted to a brigadier generalcy, is Blount's battery, first known as Latham's, organized at Lynchburg on the breaking out of the war. Blount was in my class, from Georgia, and a sweeter, more lovable boy I never met. He was scarcely medium height, had such a modest, earnest, sincere face, such naturally kind eyes, — they were open and dark, — and a heart that never knew any other beat than that of friendship and good will. " Joe " — his name was Joseph R. — and I lived on the same floor in the " Angle " at West Point, and night after night, and day after day, we visited back and forth. My room mate was John Asbury West, another Georgian — oh, God, bless his memory — and when the war came on and they left the Academy to go with their state, tender, tender was the parting with "Joe" and John.

Blount's battery is in the lead of Walker's column, Bushrod Johnson's division, assigned to Gordon and composed of Wise's, Wallace's, and Moody's brigades, is behind Walker, and then comes Gordon's old corps, followed by Longstreet's, Fitz Lee's cavalry bringing up the rear. They are on two roads, the Stage and the Plank, which meet at New Store about half-way to Appomattox. Both are bad, very bad in some places, and at a certain point Lee's headquarters wagons are being lightened by the destruction of letters and papers — a significant portent. And now, leaving them to trudge on, let us turn to the Army of the Potomac.

While Lee's troops, weary, sleepy, and heavy-hearted, were picking up their guns and leaving their little camp-fires to take the road for Appomattox, Wright's Sixth corps was marching through the village of Farmville to the bridge across the river. On their way they spied Grant observing them from the piazza of the hotel, and my life-long and brilliant friend, Horace Porter, of his staff, says, " Bonfires were lighted on the sides of the streets, the men seized straw and pine-knots and impro-

vised torches, cheers arose from throats already
hoarse with shouts of victory, bands played, banners
waved. The night march had become a grand review, with Grant as the reviewing officer."

Army of Northern Virginia, what a contrast!
But march on! you, too, are passing in review, —
passing in review before History, who, with tablet
and pen in hand, stands between the lofty columns
of her porch, and Valor with moistening eyes is
by her side. That other figure standing deep in the
shadow is Fate.

Meanwhile Ord's troops are in bivouac at Farmville, Sheridan's in and about Prospect Station, and
the Fifth corps, under tall, hollow-cheeked Griffin, is
at Prince Edward Court - House resting after its
twenty-eight-mile march.

One of Sheridan's regimental surgeons, in giving
an account of overtaking his command that night,
after having attended, as I assume, some of the
wounded at Sailor's Creek, says that the camp-fires
of the encampments of artillery and infantry reddened the sky in every direction; that of those along
the roadside, some burned brightly, some faintly,
but every one had its group of weary men seeking,
and I hope finding, refreshment and rest. "As the
light played over the forms and faces of these men,"
says Surgeon Rockwell, " and those that were sleeping, with here and there a blood-stained bandage;
and as it reflected from the stacked arms, and pene-

trated woody recesses revealing still other groups of blue-coated soldiers, scenes were presented well worthy to be reproduced upon canvas." To this vivid picture should be added the indistinct forms of the drowsing horses.

Yet, reader, for loneliness — and every aide who like myself has carried dispatches will bear witness to the truth of what I say — give me a park of army-wagons in some wan old field wrapt in darkness at the dead hours of a moonless night, men and mules asleep, camp-fires breathing their last, and the beams of day, which wander in the night, resting ghost-like on the arched and mildewed canvas covers.

Lee's army, meanwhile, was marching as fast as their condition, weakened by hunger, would allow. Apparently each man and organization grew indifferent to what happened to others; and when any of the wagons or caissons got mired, or the faltering teams gave out, they did not stop to extricate them, but after cutting down the wheels of the artillery and setting fire to the supply-trains, went on. Lee himself passed through the village of Curdsville about midnight, and dawn Saturday morning found him and his weary army well away from Farmville.

Yet let them make the best time they could, demoralization was growing and spreading with equal speed. A Confederate surgeon, John Herbert Claiborne of Petersburg, says of the march after daylight,

that there were abundant signs of disintegration all
along the road; that whole trains were abandoned,
ammunition and baggage dumped out, and everywhere muskets thrown away or, with their bayonets
fixed, stuck deep in the ground. Soldiers who, he
knew, had been men of steadiness and courage,
straggled unarmed, or lay down and slept apparently
unconcerned. He says also that he saw officers of
the line as well as colonels and distinguished generals
doing the same thing; a staff officer of one of the
latter dismounted and threw himself down, uttering
an oath that he never would draw his sword from
its scabbard again.

About noon, the doctor met Lee's inspector-
general, Colonel Peyton, posting some men, not
over a hundred of them, on a knoll from whose bare
top they could see in the distance off to the left some
of Sheridan's cavalry then hastening to Appomattox
Station.

Claiborne asked Colonel Peyton what command he
was posting, and the response came back slowly and
sadly, " That is what is left of the First Virginia."
It belonged to Pickett's celebrated Gettysburg division, a mere remnant, for it had been nearly an-
nihilated at Five Forks.

" Does General Lee know how few of his soldiers
are left? " asked the doctor, " or to what extremities
they are reduced? " " I don't believe he does," replied Peyton. " Then whose business is it to tell

him if not his inspector-general's?" blurted out Claiborne; and here we see again how the spirit of the night before had spread. Peyton with sad emphasis answered, "I cannot, I cannot;" and I have no doubt that to the end of his days he was glad of the decision he came to. For this world loves the man who stands by his captain till the ship goes down.

It may have been that Pendleton at that very hour was conveying to his chief the message Gordon had asked him to carry. Here at any rate is what Pendleton says in reference to its delivery:

"General Lee was lying down resting at the base of a large pine tree. I approached and sat by him. To a statement of the case he quietly listened, and then, courteously expressing his thanks for the consideration of his subordinates in daring to relieve him in part of the existing burdens, spoke in about these words: 'I trust it has not come to that; we certainly have too many brave men to think of laying down our arms. They still fight with great spirit, whereas the enemy does not. And besides, if I were to intimate to General Grant that I would listen to terms, he would at once regard it as such evidence of weakness that he would demand unconditional surrender, and sooner than that I am resolved to die. Indeed, we must all be determined to die at our posts.'

"My reply could only be that every man would

no doubt cheerfully meet death with him in discharge of duty, and that we were perfectly willing that he should decide the question."

Let me make one comment on Pendleton's statement. He says that Lee declared that our army did not fight with spirit. This is astonishing. In view of Five Forks with its heavy losses on both sides, the assaults on his works around Petersburg, which were carried only by the most desperate resolution and gallantry, — indeed, it may be said, with slaughter unparalleled during the war, — the stubborn cavalry engagements at Jetersville and High Bridge, the sanguinary field of Sailor's Creek, in view of all these combats is it not inconceivable that Lee should have said that our men lacked spirit? Go ask any living veteran of the Army of Northern Virginia whether our troops quailed from the day the campaign began till their general, Cox, fired the last volley at Appomattox. No, no, General Pendleton, you certainly misunderstood General Lee, or General Lee was amazingly misinformed: never, never, did the old Army of the Potomac show more spirit.

But that Lee said he would never submit to unconditional surrender is no doubt true, for he knew how the South rebelled at the thought of Buckner submitting to Grant's terms of unconditional surrender of Fort Donelson and in what universal scorn and resentment it held Pemberton for sub-

mitting to Grant's terms at Vicksburg; and rather
than follow in the steps of either Buckner or Pemberton he would lay his life down. Pendleton, after
discharging his delicate mission, rode for a while with
Alexander and told him of his interview. Alexander
says that he got the impression from his manner that
he had been snubbed by Lee. I hope, however, he
was entirely mistaken.

But let us proceed with the march, the Confederate army's last. Walker's command of sixty-odd
guns, accompanied by a guard of two artillery
companies equipped as infantry, reached the vicinity of Appomattox Station by three P. M., and
there, in supposed security, unharnessed, and started
little fires to cook what they had foraged on the
march, all looking forward gladly to several hours
of refreshing rest.

Wallace's, leading brigade of Gordon's corps,
and next in line to the surplus artillery, went into
camp about sundown, within a mile or so of Appomattox Court-House; the rest of the corps lay between
Wallace and New Hope Church. McIntosh's battalion of batteries, and that of Haskell's, were on the
banks of Rocky Run, the bordering fields and road-
sides packed with guns, wagons and ambulances.
Except the batteries, the column of trains had lost
all semblance of organization.

Longstreet, bringing up the rear, Fitzhugh Lee's
cavalry between him and Humphreys' advance,

gained Holiday's Creek, six or seven miles east of
New Hope Church, about sunset, but he did not go
into bivouac till near eleven P. M., and before his
men closed their eyes they threw a heavy line of
entrenchments across the road.

It had been a pleasant day, the sun had shone
brightly, and, from time to time, soft refreshing
breezes had blown; and I have no doubt that the
sunshine and fresh breezes were made sweeter by
the fact that it was the first day since the Army
of Northern Virginia crossed the Appomattox at
Goode's Bridge that it had been free from harassing attacks by our cavalry.

Lee camped in the open wood on the top of the
first ridge beyond the Appomattox, and on the east
side of the road, a hundred yards or so from it on
gently rising ground. Near by, and towering high
over his camp-fire, was a large white oak. So, then,
having established the weary, supperless men in their
bivouacs, let us leave them to their sleep, which I
know came quickly, for they were tired. Night and
the listening fields and woods, which as soon as darkness falls always becomes suddenly vast, reflectively
conscious personalities, were around them; over
them were fast-moving, patchy, sinister clouds
dimming the Milky Way, that starry bivouac of the
heavens' marching systems. Gaunt care, I have no
doubt, drove sleep away from more than one officer
and man. For were they to be subjected to harsh

terms at the surrender which something told them was coming, and then to a march of humiliation through the cities of the North, to Point Lookout, Fort Delaware, Elmira, and Johnson's Island, as prisoners of war? What months of confinement and agonies of body and mind were in store for them? These were hovering, living questions. But veterans, looking with thoughtful eyes into your camp-fires and dreading the future, none, none of those bitter experiences will come to you; on the contrary, you will receive kind terms, and chaplets will be yours at last. For this country will feel a glorious national pride in your fortitude, your soul-stirring valor, and your loyalty to her when the storm of war shall be over. Who, who are to be the heroes of the Army of Northern Virginia, then, if not you — you who, like gold tried in the furnace, stood by colors and cause to the end?

X

And now let me say a word of the lay of the land where Lee's camp-fires glittered along the Lynch-burg road. Following the road that bears north-eastward from the Appomattox, lone and bushy ravine-scored fields tilt up for a mile, at least, to a timbered ridge circling southwestward around the birthplace of the river. The challenging note of a chanticleer perched in the old village on a November starlit night, with the wind from the south or the east, can be heard, I think, clear to the ferny tips of the river's source.

This ridge, where it is crossed by the old road, is flattish, crowned with woods, and about half a mile wide, breaking down sharply on its northern side into the bed of Rocky Run, a pleasant brook that goes gurgling around the ridge's base and falls into the Appomattox about a mile below the Court-House. Beyond the run the ground begins at once to rise in a long commanding incline to the top of a higher ridge. As you follow the road upward, on each side are beautiful, leaning and dipping fields, and when I was there last October, in one of them on the right lay a flock of Southdown sheep, and opposite, amid venerable trees and somewhat away from the road, was an old brick mansion house, called Pleasant Retreat masked by dooryard trees, overlooking dreamily the generous plantation.

At the top of the second ridge, the divide between the Appomattox and James, the road enters woods and then sweeps directly to the east by New Hope Church on toward New Store and Farmville. The prevailing timber through which it bears its course, leaving a track almost as red as brick, is oak, and roamed by wild turkeys. The other day, as I was following it, a half-grown one scurried across it ahead of me and disappeared in the leafy silence. I halted when I came to the spot, but could neither see nor hear him; may he live to grow to a ripe old age, a stately, fleet, and beautiful ornament of the woods' sun-dappled loneliness.

The Appomattox, whose murmur can almost be heard at the old Court-House hamlet, is nothing more than a good-sized willow-fringed run, that an ordinary coatless country boy, with even a short start, can clear from bank to bank, landing on the turf with the usual sense of having performed a feat; a sense to which I can testify, for more than once, bareheaded and barefooted, I leaped a run of about the same size that wanders through the fields of the old home farm; and I hope that, as I write, the elecampane and ironweed are blooming golden and

purple there as in my youth, and that off on the gray
stake-and-ridered fence which runs by the old wild-
cherry tree, the last of the primeval forest of my child-
hood, a bob-white sings to his mate mothering her
covey in the clover-field.

The rivers' birthplaces are at the feet of shouldering knobs, covered with monarch oak, and from
any one of them you can overlook the old Court-
House village, and all the scene of the last
struggle.

And now, before telling you, reader, of the movements of the Army of the Potomac on that same Saturday, April 8, let me first say that Grant on the
evening of the seventh, after sending his first note
to Lee, issued orders for Humphreys and Wright to
pursue the enemy with vigor in the morning on whatsoever roads he might take, and for Ord's command
to follow Sheridan up the railroad toward Appomattox Station, since it was obvious that, to gain
Lynchburg, Lee, confined to the narrow divide between the Appomattox and the James, would have to
cross there at its outlet. It is quite clear that these
orders, all issued before receiving a reply to his letter,
show that Grant did not expect Lee to halt in his
tracks and surrender at once.

Before leaving Farmville Saturday morning, the
8th, Grant replied to Lee's inquiries which he had
made in his letter, already given, as to terms, and as
will be seen they were quite explicit.

"April 8, 1865.

"GENERAL, — Your note of last evening, in reply to mine of the same date, asking the condition on which I will accept the surrender of the Army of Northern Virginia, is just received. In reply, I would say that peace being my great desire, there is but one condition I would insist upon, namely: that the men and officers surrendered shall be disqualified for taking up arms again against the Government of the United States until properly exchanged. I will meet you, or will designate officers to meet any officers you might name for the same purpose, at any point agreeable to you, for the purpose of arranging definitely the terms upon which the surrender of the Army of Northern Virginia will be received.

"U. S. GRANT, Lieutenant-General.
"General R. E. LEE."

This letter was direct, candid, and generous, and brought the issue squarely to Lee, inasmuch as, where or whensoever it might reach him, he would have to make up his mind to one of two courses: to yield to the inevitable, a spectre that had been haunting him for many a day, or to take his chances to escape from it by further retreat and battle. He chose the latter.

This important communication, like the first, was put into the hands of Seth Williams for delivery.

In due time that sunny-hearted man, who rode through Humphreys' troops, came up with the enemy's rear-guard of cavalry, and, although he was displaying a flag, was fired on, and his orderly wounded. He had to make several approaches to the line, and at last gained the attention of an officer of some sense, who ordered his ill-trained men to desist from firing on the flag of truce. Williams, on handing him Grant's letter, asked to have it forwarded promptly to Lee, and to make it clear to his immediately superior officer that hostilities would not be suspended on account of the communication he had given him.

But before Williams started on this mission from Farmville, day had broken pleasantly, and to the call of the bugles all of Humphreys' and Wright's troops had stepped off briskly in pursuit of Lee. All, did you say? All of the Army of the Potomac?

No, not quite all. Up where Miles had made his resolute assault at Cumberland Church, just as the sun was setting the night before, were many in blue and gray whom no earthly bugle could wake; there, boys of twenty were sleeping on, waiting in peace for that other trumpet, the one at the lips of an angel who, on resurrection's morning, shall sound for us all. Poor fellows, Northern and Southern, had your lives lasted but two days more, you would have heard the bands at Appomattox playing " Home, Sweet Home."

Humphreys, with Miles in the lead, had taken the

Stage road, Wright the Plank, for New Store. Humphreys did not get to New Store till about five P. M. At that hour Wright was at Curdsville, about seven miles from New Store. Humphreys sent word to Meade that the enemy were reported as about four miles ahead, and asked if he should halt to let the rear close up (that is, Wright's Sixth corps) and have rations issued. After resting a little while, and without waiting to hear from Meade, he renewed the march till half-past six, and by that time Miles with the advance was near Holiday's Creek.

At 6:55, just after the sun had set and Humphreys had gone into camp, Meade's reply to his dispatch came, saying, " Push on to-night until you come up with the enemy. No attack is ordered, but it is desirable to have the army up to him." — " Have the army up to him! " In that command I hear the ring of the iron in the blood of old George Gordon Meade.

Humphreys in reply said that, although it was against his judgment, he would obey the order, but that the men were exhausted and without rations. In a postscript he added that Miles at that moment sent word that the enemy, Longstreet's corps, were encamped on the first high ground in front of him, and that he had directed him to push forward his skirmishers and feel them.

Before this order could be executed, the enemy had moved on, but the corps, tired as it was, resumed its

march in the falling darkness. The men had to
yield at last, however, to fatigue and hunger, and
at ten o'clock the leading division went into bivouac. The head of the rear division did not reach the
halting-place till four A. M. Sunday. Nearly twenty-
five miles had been covered and the day had been
warm; they deserved and I hope enjoyed a night of
sweet rest. The camp-fires of some of them were
on the banks of Holiday's Creek, and as their eyes
were closing to its murmurs the dull boom of guns
away to the southwest went floating by. Boom!
boom! boom! and Wonder asked sleepily, " What
is that? " It was Sheridan, at Appomattox Station,
planting himself squarely across the road to Lynchburg.

Meade, setting out from camp at High Bridge,
overtook Humphreys about eight o'clock A. M., just
after Williams with Grant's second letter had gone
forward, and Lyman says that as they kept along
the road they came on General Williams returning
from the front. Meade, at eleven-thirty, had got
to the house of a Mr. Elam, where they rested the
horses for a spell, and then over a wide road full of
boulders and holes they came to Crutes, a large
white house on the left side of the road. Just before
reaching there Grant overtook them and said to
Meade, " How are you, old fellow? " As will be
remembered, Meade had not been at all well for
three or four days. That night, Saturday, the

eighth they both made their headquarters at Crutes.

Now let us turn to Sheridan and Ord, and not forget that this is Saturday morning.

While the dew was still sparkling and the feet of grazing cows and quick nibbling sheep trailed the pastures, Sheridan's cavalry poured out of the fields and woods around Prospect Station, and with Custer in advance set off up the railroad for Appomattox Station, which is about two or three miles south of the Court-House. Behind the cavalry came Ord's infantry from Farmville, Turner's division of Gibbon's Twenty-fourth corps leading them, and then Griffin from Prince Edward Court-House, with Chamberlain of Maine, that hero and scholar, at the head. For the sake of the memory of the night when I rode with Warren on our way from the Wilderness, where this corps had left so many of its gallant men, I wish that I could have seen them march by on that sunshiny morning, — not only the Fifth corps, but all of that column.

Reader and friend, on second thought I have something to propose to you, and, much as it will delay the narrative, I hope it will strike you pleasantly. Let us find some suitable spot by the roadside from which we can see those veterans go by; for before the sun sets to-morrow their marching will be over and the old Army of the Potomac, that I served with as a boy, will pass through the Gates of Peace and enter the Land of Dreams. I want you to see them, too, for I believe you feel a pride in the glory their courage has brought the country. I marched with them on many campaigns, — Chancellorsville, Gettysburg, the Wilderness, and thence through the bloody fields of Spottsylvania and Cold Harbor to the James. Do you wonder then that I long to look once more at the regiments and batteries, and lift my hat to those brave men whose oft-repeated display of valor made my heart beat? And if, when some dear old friend goes by, you should see tears dropping from my eyes, never mind, never mind, — the sight will bring back such appealing memories.

Break off that spray of budding laurel and bring it along. It will indicate that what is in your heart is in your hand, that you would like if you could to wreathe it around the brows of more than one of those boys. For they are only boys, after all; their average age is under twenty-one.

I wish we could find a good, overlooking spot. How will that little elevation down there in the valley answer; that rises like an old-fashioned bee-hive on the left of the road and has a brotherhood of four or five big-limbed oaks crowning it, one of them leaning somewhat? Admirably! We are lucky as usual: here is a pair of bars, and we shall not have to climb this old Virginia rail-fence; but let us be sure to put the bars up, for nothing is more provoking, nothing shows worse breeding, than to

leave a farmer's gates open or his bars down. Well,
here we are: oaks spreading above us, at our feet
violets, liverwort, and spring beauties scattered
among acorn hulls, dead leaves, and clustered
grass. What a reviewing stand, and so near the
road that we shall be able to distinguish faces!
Truly we have chosen a pleasant spot; let us sit
down and enjoy it till they come.

How graciously the road greets us as it emerges
from those thick primeval woods yonder to our right
and how cool and fresh its earthy track looks as it
comes gliding down between the fields toward us!
Why, it almost sings, — I'm a brother of the morning and my sweetheart is the dawn.

And is not this leaning valley in front of us sweet?
How the wavering fences and the heaving fields en-
tice the eye farther and farther up and off northward, until at last it rests on distant woods and the
peace of vast solitary, traveling clouds! Do you
know that under those very clouds the Army of
Northern Virginia is marching at this very moment?
How peacefully beneficent they look! I wonder if
heaven in her sympathy has not set them a-sailing
so that their shadows may comfort our enemies, —
for the day is warm and their hearts are low. I
wish we could review them also, for perhaps I might
see some old West Point friend, and I think he would
speak to me, and I should like to slip a sandwich into
his hand, for I know he is hungry. But whether I

should see one or not, I know I would wave the laurel
to more than one of those Confederate regiments.

But upon my soul we could not have found a
better place had we looked for weeks. Note how
the road climbs up athwart the open hill at our left
beyond this lusty, blessed run, the gurgling child of
the valley before us; and I'll warrant you that there
are minnows, dace, and, maybe, shiners in some of
its pools, and that I could find a cardinal's or a cat-
bird's nest somewhere along its willow- and alder-
covered banks. Those master songsters, like the
thrush, love quiet places like this. And do you note
the regular, intermittent pauses in the beat of the
wings of that bird, which is coming from the woods
to the oaks? It's a flicker, for I know his undulating
flight right well. And do you hear that meadow-
lark? He is up there in that shouldered pasture where
you see a few sumacs near a settlement of big boulders, travelers from ages gone by that are resting a
while; and as he sings to his golden-breasted mate,
who knows if his song does not set the stern travelers
dreaming of the world's first morning, just as the
thrush's sets the fields dreaming of its first evening?
But, like the flicker, what a naturally wild bird is
the lark!

Surely the old road hears many a wild trilling
song and runs by many a pleasant scene, but not one
is sweeter than this or more suited to serve an innocent purpose like ours. For we can see the troops

coming and going, and follow them as they climb the hill, until banners and men disappear beyond its pastured crest. But here they come!

The cavalry brigade at the head of the column this morning is Pennington's, of Custer's division, and when its commander rides by I will point him out to you, for he is a friend, and as was said of Sir George Beaumont, the intimate of Wordsworth and Coleridge, he is inherently a gentleman. The regiment that is now approaching in the advance is the Second New York, and that behind it is the Third New Jersey. The colonel of the former is Alanson M. Randol, and when he rides by, you will see that he has thin, straight, light red hair, blue eyes and a spare face; and I wish that you could hear him sing, for he has a fine tenor voice, which on many a summer night at West Point I heard rising high and clear as he led a group of his fellow cadets, who used to gather at the head of some company street during encampment, and, seated in a circle on camp-stools in their gray fatigue jackets and white trousers, sing the evening away. It is this regiment that will capture the four trains at Appomattox to-night, and then, with the rest of the brigade and division, at last, and notwithstanding musketry, canister, and darkness, will gain the Lynchburg road, and force the surrender of Lee to-morrow.

Bless my heart! Here comes Custer now, and riding by his side are Pennington and Randol;

Custer, a major-general, Pennington, a brigadier, and not one of the three has yet seen his twenty-seventh birthday. They were all fellow cadets, and I will wager you that this very moment they are talking about those old West Point days; for no matter when or where we graduates meet, soon, very soon, we are back at that beautiful spot on the Hudson and living over the days of our youth.

But do look at Custer, for he was one of my close friends and we passed many a happy hour together. Did you ever in all your life see any man more spectacularly dressed? That broad upturned sombrero, those long yellow locks, that olive-green corduroy suit tinseled lavishly with gold braid, those huge roweled spurs, and that long, flowing scarlet necktie! Just look, too, at the length of the sabre scabbard and the gold knots dangling from the sword's hilt, and note also those pistols in his high cavalry boots.

But don't misjudge him: Custer is only a great big jolly boy, and no one ever had a better friend, and no foe an antagonist with more generosity of spirit. I wish you could catch his mischievous smile and hear his merry laugh.

I declare I believe he sees us. He does. — " Hello, Morris! Hello, ' Old Shoaf ' ! " Yes, yes, I hear you, Custer, Pennington, and Randol. Yes, I hear you, but my heart is too full to answer; I can only murmur as the tears fall, " God bless each of you! " Wave, wave your laurel, reader, and keep on waving it till the mist clears away from my swimming eyes. And, if some one should ever ask you, " Why did they call him ' Old Shoaf ' ? " tell them it was a nickname he got at West Point.

That regiment now passing is the First Connecticut, and I wish to call your attention to its major, Goodwin; and near him is Lieutenant Lanfare. Those two brave officers each captured a gun at Five Forks, only a few days ago, when after repeated charges, with Pennington at the head, the brigade carried the enemy's breastworks. There goes the Second Ohio. I have a pride in my native state; let us lift our hats to the Second, and to them all.

That man at the head of the Fifteenth New York is Colonel Coppinger, and when I saw him first he was an aide, I believe, on Sheridan's staff. He is one of several young Irish gentlemen who came over and offered their services to our country, and braver or wittier men never graced a camp.

The lieutenant-colonel, on the white horse, is Augustus I. Root, and to-night, at the very end of the battle, he will charge into the village of Appomattox Court-House and there meet a volley from Wallace's Confederate brigade and fall dead from his charger; and to-morrow morning a tender-hearted Confederate lady, before whose house he has fallen, will have his body brought from the road and buried in her yard. And when, after the war is over, his family shall come to take his body home, do you know, she will gather some flowers from the garden to deck his coffin!

" Who is that colored woman riding in state in that old-fashioned family coach, drawn by two mules, among the headquarter wagons and led horses bringing up the rear of Custer's division? "

Well, my friend, — I might address you as Stranger, but I think you are closer to me than that, — that's Eliza, Custer's cook. He picked her up near the Blue Ridge on one of his campaigns in that lovely region. I don't know where he laid his hands on the coach. But this I know, that, at the fierce battle of Trevilian last summer, Eliza and all of Custer's and Pennington's private baggage were captured. That night, after the brigade had got out of a very tight place and gone into bivouac, Custer and Pennington, while lounging before their camp-fires, heard cheering up the road. Pretty soon the cheering broke out again, but this time it was stronger and nearer. " What does that mean? " they asked each other; and when they went out to learn the cause, there came Eliza, the men lining the road and cheering her at every step.

It seems that her mounted captors, while marching her off the field, told her to throw down a high fence in their way; but instead of beginning at the top rail she pulled out a low one, bolted through, took to her heels among young pines, and then with native shrewdness struck off in the direction she thought our troops had taken; and there she was, ready to get Custer's breakfast as usual. Of all the Army of the Potomac to-day, Eliza is the only one riding in state, and I've no doubt that at this very moment she is canvassing in her mind whether the coffee and sugar amid the trumpery with which her mud-spattered vehicle is loaded, will hold out till the campaign is over. It will; don't worry about it, Eliza; ride on without a care.

But what a contrast is that old coach with its family memories to that column of cavalry now doubled up and riding four abreast, — horses bay, sorrel, white, black, and roan, guidons and colors waving, and each trooper armed with carbine, sabre and pistol! The old carriage is not going to church or to a wedding this morning.

The division following Custer's is Merritt's, Wesley Merritt's, one of the most popular men at West Point in my day. He has smiling blue eyes and has led this division in many a charge. Moreover he is naturally modest, can write inspiring English, and is an addition always to the good company he loves. I think that Sheridan relies on him more than on any one of his division commanders, and to-morrow he will be one of three selected by Grant to receive the surrender of Lee's army.

That brigade just passing is the famous Michigan brigade; you notice that every one has a flaming scarlet necktie like Custer's; they were his first

command, and they love him. I wish that I could
dwell on some of their exploits with him at their
head. You do not know how the sight of those
cavalrymen brings back to me that night after the
two awful days in the Wilderness, when, with Warren
in advance, I rode by them to Todd's Tavern, where
they had fought so bravely for the Brock Road,
without which Grant's move to Spottsylvania would
have been seriously baffled.

And here come Merritt's second brigade under
Charley Fitzhugh. Wave your laurel, for he is
another of my fellow cadets. He has brown eyes,
and in that robust figure is a warm and gallant heart.

And now passes the Reserve Brigade. At its head
is the Second Massachusetts under Colonel Forbes,
who bears a name which the Blue Hills of Milton
cherish with pride. Its young colonel, Lowell, was
killed last autumn in the valley, and his sword
brought much added lustre to a family already distinguished.

The troopers and those grim old sergeants with
grizzled moustaches and imperials, who sit their
horses so firmly, belong to the First, Fifth, and Sixth
Regulars; and, companion, my heart swells at the
sight of them again, for I, too, was a Regular.

And here comes Crook's division. I have already
told you what kind of a looking man he is, and how
he is beloved. I wish I could point out all whom
I know and who have rendered great services, but

I am afraid of being tedious. That regiment just passing, its guidons flirting so cheerily, is the First Maine. At its head is Colonel Cilley, and when all is still to-night, he with his regiment will be standing guard across the Lynchburg Pike, just this side of the little graveyard at Appomattox, and within hearing of the enemy's bivouac down in the old, weary-looking hamlet.

And here comes Sheridan, — Sheridan! he to whom the country to-morrow, and as long as it lives, will owe more than to any one in the Army of the Potomac for its final victory over what is called the Great Rebellion, inasmuch as, had it not been for his inflaming activity, the pursuit would not have been so rigorous, and Lee, instead of being where he is to-day, at the very verge of complete overthrow, would be, I fear, well on his way to the Roanoke.

Sheridan is mounted on Rienzi. Look at man and horse, for they are both of the same spirit and temper. It was Rienzi who with flaming nostrils carried Sheridan to the field of Cedar Creek, " twenty miles away;" and on the field of Five Forks, the battle which broke Lee's line and let disaster in. Before the final charge there, the horse became as impatient as his rider, kicking, plunging, tossing his head, pulling at the bit, while foam flecked his black breast. Sheridan gave him his head, when he saw that Ayres, at the point of the bayonet, was going to carry the day; off sprang Rienzi and with a leap bounded over the enemy's works and landed Sheridan among the mob of prisoners and fighting troops. In the oncoming infantry that will soon appear you will see Ayres and that very division; and I have no doubt that you will look on them with admiration when I tell you of their exploits, for I have been with them and seen them under fire.

Well, Rienzi, to-morrow you will bear your distinguished rider to the McLean house, and there you will see General Lee coming up on Traveller, a horse with a better temper than yours, and soon thereafter Grant will ride up on high-bred Cincinnati, and you three horses will go down to history together; and Grant to the day of his death will say that your rider, little Phil Sheridan, was the one great corps commander of the war.

As you see, Sheridan is cased in the uniform of his grade; he has on a double-breasted frock-coat, the brass buttons in groups of three; his trousers are outside of his boots and strapped down; and, slightly tipping on his big round head, is a low-crowned, soft felt hat, concealing his close-cropped black hair. He is the very embodiment of vital energy, and in addition to his natural force and courage he is supported by an extraordinary, clear and quick comprehension of the phases of battle. Were you to get close to him, you would not fail to note his set jaw, his rather high, solid cheekbones, quick blazing eyes, and all the impulsive characteristics of his determined nature mingling in his weather-bronzed face; and perchance it would make you think of a living anvil. His voice is naturally low, and on one occasion, amid all the tension and din of battle, an aide came galloping up and began to scream out some bad news, whereupon Sheridan, with set teeth and low measured tones, said, "Damn you, sir, don't yell at me!" Great as will his honors be, he never will have any affectations, but will ring true to the end.

Those threescore or more unfurled Confederate colors carried behind him and his brilliant staff, "Tony" and "Sandy" Forsythe, Newhall, and Gillespie, were captured at Sailor's Creek; and could anything equal the sight of those flags in stirring the hearts of his men to renewed daring?

And now the rear of the cavalry is passing, the head of the column has long since disappeared over the open crest. Sheridan is near the top of the hill and I can still make out his blue headquarters flag.

In the momentary pause between cavalry and infantry, goes by a little squad with bandaged heads and limbs, hurrying along, some on mules and some on horses. They are wounded cavalrymen who have slipped away from the field hospitals of Sailor's Creek and Farmville, and are bound to be with their regiments.

. "What has that hatless man with the bandage across his brow dismounted for? Where? There at

the run." Watch him and you will see. He is filling
the canteens of his comrades. And how eagerly
the feverish fellows drink! He has had to fill one
canteen a second time; the contents of the first
has been poured over a bandaged arm. Oh, fine
is the spirit in the Army of the Potomac to-day!

"But why are you smiling?" Oh, because I
know those fellows well, and except that obviously
broken down, abandoned old mule, and that woe-
begone, bald-faced chestnut horse which they have
picked up, the chances are ten to one that those
young rascals have stolen every mount they have.

Now they are off, and the infantry is just issuing
from the woods, and Turner's division of Ord's
command is in the lead. Those troops, some from
Illinois, some from Ohio, West Virginia, and far-
away Massachusetts, were in the lines north of the
James when the campaign began, and have covered
more miles than any other in the army. Note the
swing of Harris's brigade as they pass by, for they
mean to keep up with the cavalry.

They are all from West Virginia, the 10th, 11th
and 15th Regiments, and have marched in and out,
over and around their wood-clad native mountains,
until they are all pedestrian athletes. "Down on the
James," says my friend General Woodhull, "I have
seen them after a fair march throw off their coats and
organize running and jumping matches for sheer
amusement when other troops were lying at rest."

Woodward's, the third brigade of what was Birney's division of colored troops, is with Turner also.

Behind them is Foster's division, and with it is Doubleday's brigade of colored troops. Do you know, my friend, that these earnest black men recall some vivid memories? For I sat on the parapet of one of our batteries and saw Ferrero's division — they were all negroes officered by white men — move to the attack, when the mine was exploded at Petersburg. Up to that day thousands of us doubted the colored man's courage, and for fear these negroes would falter, a division of white troops was assigned to lead the assault. But such heroism as they displayed I never saw surpassed on any field. Their advance up the incline was in full view, and you should have seen their steadiness in the face of a most deadly front-and-flank fire. Their flags began to fall as soon as they cleared our works, but up they would come boldly and on they would go. I cannot tell you how my breath shortened as the ground was strewn with their dead and wounded. Let us uncover; they have shown that they can be loyal and true to their masters, and they have shown that they can stand undaunted the final test of battle. Full of pathos are their songs and their fate for me, and I sometimes wonder if marble and bronze are not waiting for the hand of genius to express nature's deep feeling in their behalf.

That spare man with iron gray hair and moustache

is Ord, the senior officer of all this column of cavalry
and infantry hastening on to head off Lee. He graduated at West Point the year Grant entered, and
his eyes are bluish-gray and kindly. In company he
is an easy but not a loquacious talker, and never is
known to be angry or excited; in other words, reader,
he is a man of good breeding. His voice, which is
naturally clear, has a tinge of persuasiveness or
solicitation in its tones. It was he who tried to bring
about an interview between Grant and Lee before
this final campaign began, for he felt sure that if
they could meet they would bring the war to an end.
Longstreet joined with him in this merciful and patri-
otic design, but as soon as it was heard of in Washington, Grant got peremptory orders to have no communication with Lee on questions of a political
nature.

All in all, I am glad that Ord's scheme failed, but,
nevertheless, it tells what kind of man he is, and
Peace at the last great day will beckon to him, you
may rest assured, to come and sit down by her side.

That young man, in fact almost a boy, among his
staff, is Alfred A. Woodhull, an assistant surgeon
in the army; and when Ord went to see Longstreet
on his peace mission, he took Woodhull with him.

And now there is another pause, for some of Ord's
wagons are stalled at the run and block the way, but
the officers and drivers are using the vigorous terms
which the mule understands, and soon the road will

be cleared. Yes, even now, for look, look! there comes
the old Fifth corps. See how the sun glints on the
leaning gun-barrels! Griffin is at its head, and behind
him floats the Maltese cross. What fields the sight
of that flag evokes! Gaines's Mill, Glendale, Mal-
vern Hill, Manassas, Fredericksburg, Gettysburg,
the Wilderness, Spottsylvania, Cold Harbor, Five
Forks! Blood of the Fifth corps reddened, and in
some cases almost deluged, every one of them. And,
upon my soul, I hear the volleys again, and once more
I see their colors crossing the old Sanders field in
the Wilderness and wavering up toward the orchard
on the Spindle farm at Spottsylvania! Come on,
you that are left! Come on! I was young once, too,
and shared those bitter days with you. God bless
you, come on with those tattered banners! Griffin
is on his little chestnut mare, Sally, and day after
to-morrow he will sell her to Captain Fowler of his
staff for $350. — And there among his staff is my
friend Winne.

Leading the first brigade is Chamberlain of
Maine, and for the sake of Round Top, the key of
Gettysburg, which at the sword's tip he helped to
save, and for the sake of his gentleness and knightli-
ness, for he will bring that division to a salute when
the Army of Northern Virginia marches by to lay
down their arms, wave your laurel for Chamberlain.

There go Coulter, Bartlett, and Baxter; they do
not know me, but I know them; and when I saw

Bartlett last in the Wilderness, blood was streaming down his face. And here comes Crawford, neat and trim as usual; and behind him is Kellogg leading all that is left of the Iron Brigade of the West, the Sixth and Seventh Wisconsin; for the sake of that first day at Gettysburg, let us rise and uncover.

And here comes the sturdy old Regular, Ayres, with his division fresh from Five Forks. Look at those shredded and bullet-riddled colors! In their lacerated bands of red and white, and in those ripped, star-decked fields of blue, is written the visible history of the Army of the Potomac. Oh, let us be grateful for that breeze which has set them a-rippling. They seem to be rejoicing. And who has told the west wind that peace is coming?

There go the One Hundred and Fortieth, One Hundred and Forty-sixth New York, the One Hundred and Fifty-fifth Pennsylvania, and the Maryland Brigade. All hail! but oh, brave fellows, are you all that are left? Reader, if you should ever visit the field of Spottsylvania, I wish you would go to where a stone bears this legend: —

FARTHEST ADVANCE ON THIS FRONT

THE MARYLAND BRIGADE

" Never mind bullets, never mind cannon, but press on and clear the road "

That was the order they got from Warren that Sunday morning, and I saw them try to obey it. "Can I easily find it?" Yes; and it will be glad to see you, and as you stand beside it in its loneliness and recall what it commemorates, you will feel how gently persuasive is the peace of the arching sky.

And now that they have all gone by and are mounting the hill, I feel sorry that I directed your eye to a few only of those brave officers and men. But perhaps I have delayed the narrative already too long. Would that I could keep right on with the story, and that I did not so often forget that the majority of my fellow men have no particular interest in the mysteriously suffusing lights which haunt the background of heroic deeds, but are concerned rather in the deeds themselves.

XI

Sheridan, starting from Prospect Station with Custer's and Merritt's divisions, took the road nearest the river, the one that leads by way of Walker's Church, leaving orders for Crook to keep on that which runs along the railroad, notifying him that he, Crook, would be followed by the infantry.

Newhall says that Sheridan only halted once for rest and water, and, while waiting, sent a regiment to Cutbank Ford on the Appomattox to see if any of the enemy were heading for the south side of the river. The regiment he dispatched was the Second New York, under the command of Colonel A. M. Randol. It was against this reconnoitering party that Lee's inspector-general, Peyton, was posting the last of the First Virginia when Colonel Claiborne asked him the question, "Does General Lee know how few of his soldiers are left, or to what extremities they are reduced?"

Sheridan tells us that on the previous evening his scouts reported to him the presence of four railroad trains with supplies for Lee's army at Appomattox Station, and I have no doubt they did; but scouts were, as a rule, such infernal liars, that I doubt very much if he felt absolutely sure of the truth of their story. At any rate, the other afternoon, as we looked off on the sea at Gloucester, Massachusetts, General Pennington told me that, after Randol had returned from his scout, he and Custer and Randol were dismounted and lay resting under the shade of some trees by the roadside a mile or more from Appomattox Station, when the whistle of a locomotive was borne to them. The sun was about an hour high. Custer jumped to his feet, exclaiming, " By George! there's a train; let's go for it! " and sprang into his saddle. Randol says his regiment set off at a trot, and that Custer rode up and, laying his hand on his shoulder, said, " Go in, old fellow, don't let anything stop you: now is the chance for your stars; whoop 'em up and I'll be after you."

Randol, followed by Pennington, at once struck into a gallop. The leading troopers, catching sight of the trains at the station just getting under way, for they had taken alarm, circled ahead of them, and, spurring up alongside the engines, covered the engineers with their revolvers and told them to throw the levers and stop; which orders they wisely obeyed. Randol then called for men to man the trains, when old firemen and engineers gladly threw themselves off their horses and, mounting the cabs, started the trains toward Farmville, with bells ringing and whistles blowing.

Randol then pushed out from the station over the

several roads which radiated from it through the thick growths of jack-oak and scrub-pine to the Lynchburg Pike, a mile or more away. By this time twilight was about to give way to night.

It will be recalled that Walker's column of sixty-odd pieces of reserve artillery had bivouacked in supposed security in the open fields along the pike; but to their amazement they heard Randol's men engaging some of their stray flankers, and at once rushed to their guns. But the horses were barely hitched when the cavalry were on them. The cannon-eers, however, had had time to load their pieces with canister, and companies of artillery whose guns had been abandoned and who had equipped themselves as infantry were able also to get into line, and to-gether they met our men with a destructive fire which swept them back into the woods.

Pennington came on at a gallop with the rest of the brigade, but so dense were the scrub-pines and oaks, and so stubbornly did the enemy hold their ground, that he could not budge them. Custer hurried to the field with the other brigade and sent them in with his usual vehemence, but owing to the darkness and his ignorance of the lay of the land, he made no headway. But the fighting kept on.

In the midst of the din Randol ran across Custer, who, now wild with desperation, was dashing here and there, his bugle sounding the charge, trying to push his men up against the enemy's line, although

he was guided alone by the flash of their guns.
Randol screamed to him that if he would let him get
his regiment together he believed he could break
through; but Custer exclaimed, " Never mind your
regiment, take anything and everything you can find:
we must get hold of that road to-night; " and then
roared out to his adjutant-general, " Go tell the men
that those guns must be taken in five minutes."   Off
went the adjutant-general, and the woods rang
with the cheers of the cavalrymen as they heard
him shouting Custer's words through the black
night. Almost simultaneously his trooper charged in
among the batteries, and the day and the road were
theirs.

Meanwhile Sheridan had come up and sent
Devin of Merritt's division to Custer's right; but
before they could get ready to attack, the victory
had been won and the uncaptured guns and wagons
were fleeing, — a few westward and out of danger
toward Lynchburg (Blount's battery escaped), but
the bulk backward and downward toward the Court-
House, pursued by the Fifteenth New York Cavalry. At the head of this regiment was Colonel
Root on a white horse, whose wild speed soon carried
him to the edge of the village. There he met a
volley from Wallace's brigade, which, as soon as
the retreating mob of men, batteries, and wagons
would allow, had formed across the road. Root
fell dead in the street, and his horse wheeled madly

and dashed out of the withering fire which our men were glad to run from.

It was now nine o'clock and after, and that was the end of the day's operations on Lynchburg Pike; Custer captured twenty-five pieces of artillery, over two hundred wagons, and many prisoners, and Lee's last chance was gone. By their triumph, every one will agree, Sheridan's cavalry had earned the country's gratitude.

It may be interesting to repeat in substance what Doctor Claiborne and General Pendleton, already quoted, have to say of their experiences in this spirited combat. Both happened to be with Walker when Randol's bugles sounding a charge were heard, and, says Pendleton in his report, " to avert immediate disaster, demanded the exercise of all our abilities." The infantry and artillery were prompt and resolute, as we know, in repulsing Randol at first; and Pendleton, concluding the affair was over and receiving a message that he was wanted at Lee's headquarters, left Walker and had got within a short distance of the Court-House when — this is his language — " the enemy's cavalry came rushing along, firing upon all in the road, and I only escaped being shot or captured by leaping my horse over the fence and skirting for some distance along the left of the road toward our column, then advancing, until I reached a point where the enemy's charge was checked."

He must have skirted pretty widely, for he did not get to Lee's headquarters till one A. M., and from where he leaped the fence it could not have been more than two miles. But the country was very rough and new to him; besides, he had to find some place to cross the river. The old general, what with having to carry the unpleasant resolve of the council to Lee, and then being hustled so suddenly, unexpectedly, and disagreeably, by Sheridan's cavalry, had certainly had a bad day.

Doctor Claiborne and his two companions, Doctors Field and Smith, had unsaddled their horses near Walker's command, and with the saddles for their pillows were enjoying some sleep, when Claiborne's attendant, Burkhardt, a soldier Quaker, leaning over, shook the doctor rudely by the shoulder and cried, "Doctor! The Yankees be upon thee!" It is not necessary to say that there was no delay in waking up or disappearing in the black jack-oaks. The Yankee cavalry charging with yells and clanking sabres in every direction, the doctors made good time, as doctors should when suddenly called upon in any emergency. They rambled round till the fight was over, and then raked some leaves together and bivouacked in the corner of a fence. I do not know what there is about doctors, unless it is their cheerful way of assuring us that we will soon recover after taking their vile tasting nostrums, accompanied by an air of native fastidiousness on their part, that always impresses me as humorous; and now as in my mind's eye I see three of them in that fence corner, waking and eyeing each other after that night's experiences, I cannot resist a smile. Well, they had barely left their bed of leaves when in the mist loomed one of our cavalry videttes, who pulled a heavy revolver, and they were soon taken to the rear as prisoners.

That night Sheridan made his headquarters in a little frame house not far from Appomattox Station, and, stretched out on a bench in the cheerful parlor lighted by a bright wood fire, dictated a dispatch to Grant. It was dated 9:20 P. M., and after telling Grant what had been accomplished, it ended, "If General Gibbon and the Fifth corps can get up to-night we will perhaps finish the job in the morning. I do not think Lee means to surrender until compelled to do so." At an earlier hour Sheridan had sent back word to Ord that he was across Lee's front, and urged him to bring up the infantry with all speed, for he felt sure that Lee would try to break through. Ord communicated the news to Gibbon and Griffin, and they continued the march till well on toward midnight; and on halting, the men were so tired by their march of nearly thirty miles, that they did not stop to make coffee, but sank down beside their gun-racks and fell asleep.

As soon as Crook came up, Sheridan had him join his right to Devin's left and establish a line squarely across the road; Custer's men being occupied meanwhile in clearing the field of their captures, regaining their organizations, finding and caring for their stricken comrades. Custer, before going into bivouac, rode to the hospital and visited his wounded. "Had it been daylight," says Tremain, "he would have seen green saplings, about which his men so valiantly and successfully fought, bent and split by canister from the artillery. The trees and artillery carriages in the park were perforated with bullet-holes; horses wallowed in the bloody mud, and the first dawn of the day upon the spot would tell any observer of the deadly character of that evening's contest. Surgeons of wide experience in the cavalry remarked that they never treated so many extreme cases in so short a fight."

It was toward one o'clock when the videttes of the First Maine Cavalry, under Colonel Cilley, Crook's division, took their position across the road at a point within three quarters of a mile of the Court-House. The colonel, after posting them, attracted by the noises which came through the darkness from the Confederate artillery camping in the valley below him, dismounted and passed through his line. He approached near enough to hear distinctly the angry exclamations of the drivers and teamsters at their poor, famished horses, and then, returning, sat at the foot of a chestnut tree where he had planted the standard of his regiment.

Up to him, as he sat there drowsing, were borne the confused sounds of the enemy's camp, and over him, and over friend and foe, bivouacking or moving, fleets of clouds were drifting mid pools of starry light. And now, while the hours draw on, let us turn and see what was transpiring, first at Grant's and then at Lee's headquarters, that Saturday night.

Grant's, as well as Meade's, were at J. I. Crute's, a large white house on the stage road about two and a half miles south of Curdsville. The plantation was called Clifton. Grant had accompanied Meade, so that he would be in quick reach of Lee's reply to his second letter, which he had good reason to believe would be answered promptly; but the afternoon and half the night passed before the expected response came to hand.

In the afternoon Grant was taken with one of his severe headaches, and at night threw himself on a sofa in the room to the left of the hall. Unfortunately for his comfort, there was a piano in the opposite room, about which after supper the young officers of the respective staffs gathered, caroling and bellowing out choruses. Grant with his usual forbearance bore the racket for quite a while, hoping the youngsters would soon tire out; at last, satisfied that they had no intention of ending the nuisance, he sent word asking them to stop; and I think I can see them tiptoeing away from the dumfounded old piano that had never been called on for anything but hymns, "Nearer my God to Thee," "The Bonnie Blue Flag," and "Dixie."

For some reason or other, it seems that Lee did not receive Grant's letter till a late hour, and I am perfectly free to confess that there is something unaccountable in the delay, for it entered Lee's lines before eleven o'clock A. M., and an aide ought to have overtaken him in two and a half hours at most. Fitz Lee, on whose lines Williams delivered the letter, shortly after its receipt sent a flag back asking Humphreys if the contents of the dispatch to General Lee was intended to interrupt the operations of the day. Humphreys replied that the letter was sealed and its contents unknown, but he did know that the operations of the day were not to be interrupted.

I suspect Fitz Lee's curiosity grew out of his already premeditated and probably declared intention to strike off with the cavalry in case surrender was imminent, a resolution he tried to carry out the next day. But on the receipt of Humphreys's reply he was as much in the dark as ever, and I suspect that the foxy Fitz intimated to the aide entrusted with Grant's dispatch not to be in too big a hurry to find the general. Let the explanation be what it may, Alexander says it was answered by the roadside, late in the afternoon, and that Lee's reply was delivered to Humphreys after sundown. But it must have been considerably after sundown, for Major Mason of Fitz Lee's staff brought it to Colonel Egbert's line of skirmishers, One Hundred and Eighty-third Pennsylvania, who were not put in the advance till after eight o'clock — and whenever it reached Humphreys after that hour, it did not reach Grant till about twelve o'clock. Up to that time, on account of his headache, he had not been able to get much sleep. Rawlins took the dispatch to him; after making a few comments, — probably to the effect that Sheridan was right, that Lee did not mean to surrender till he was forced to do so, — he lay down on the sofa again. Here is the letter.

"April 8, 1865.

" GENERAL, — I received at a late hour your note of to-day. In mine of yesterday I did not intend to propose the surrender of the Army of Northern Virginia, but to ask the terms of your proposition. To be frank, I do not think the emergency has arisen to call for the surrender of this army, but, as the restoration of peace should be the object of all, I desire to know whether your proposals would lead to that end. I cannot therefore meet you with a view to surrender the Army of Northern Virginia, but as far as your proposal may affect the Confederate States' forces under my command, and tend to the restoration of peace, I should be pleased to meet you at ten A. M. to-morrow on the old stage road to Richmond, between the picket-lines of the two armies.

"R. E. LEE, Gen."

Just where Lee was when he wrote this letter I do not know, but he soon bivouacked, and his camp-fire was started, the last that should blaze ere the flames of his hope were quenched; for before the next was kindled he had drunk the bitter cup of defeat and the end had come.

It was on a golden October afternoon that, in my ramblings over the field of Appomattox, I came to Lee's last camp, and gentle, gentle was the hour I sat there on a long since fallen tree around whose shrivelling trunk nature was lovingly weaving a mossy green shroud. Rooted in the camp-fire's ashes a simple white-fringed daisy on a crooked leaning stalk was blooming; over them and amid the tawny rug of leaves that covered them, lay here and there a black gum's waxy, scarlet leaf blazing like a living coal of that last old camp-fire itself. From the intermingling limbs above me, russet oak and yellowing chestnut leaves from time to time came silently twirling down, and off in the still surrounding woods, a bird fluted a soft pensive farewell note.

Yes, gentle was the afternoon I sat on that fallen tree, and I sometimes wonder if hours and scenes like that are not the emblem of the soul's peace at last; for surely, the consciousness of sin, the modern accumulating blight of natural joy in this sweet, brook-singing world, had no dominion there.

Well, early in the evening, and doubtless on account of hearing Walker's guns pouring their rapid fire into Custer, Lee, from that camp-fire, sent orders for the cavalry to be moved to the front, and its commander, Fitz Lee, to report to him in person, inasmuch as he had decided to hold a council of war with his three corps commanders. For the boom of that artillery was ominous, and, figuratively, he was like the captain of a ship on a tempestuous night, who is feeling his way to a harbor and suddenly hears the breakers thundering on the bar.

When Fitz Lee arrived at headquarters, which had neither chairs, tents, nor camp-stools about it, he found Longstreet there sitting on a log, his arm in a sling, and smoking a pipe; and soon after Gordon appeared. And then, before the low-burning camp-fire darkly over-arched by leafy trees, — there was no moon, and the sky was heavily patched with high fast-drifting surly clouds, — they sat down on blankets and saddles and listened to Lee.

Longstreet says that the great Confederate, with clouded face but in complete command of himself, opened the conference. It is not probable that he dwelt with particularity on what had happened since they left Petersburg: that the Capitol had fallen, that the chance to consult Mr. Davis and his Cabinet were gone, that the supplies were gone, that thousands and thousands of weak and disheartened soldiers were gone, and that their enemy's cavalry was ahead of them on the Lynchburg road, for all those facts were common knowledge. But the correspondence he had had with Grant in reference to the surrender of the army, *that* they did not know definitely, and he proceeded to read it to them. And the question then was, what next?

And now, reader, before the momentous question is discussed in all of its phases by the council and then answered, I beg for a pause. For we have reached one of those solemn hours when the hand of the Inevitable is on the wheel of Fortune, one of those hours, indeed, so fatal to institutions that are sham, inhumane, corrupt, and sordid in this world, as well as to states and conditions which have had their day of shutting out ideals with the smoke of sacrifices on the altars of Mammon, involving the just and the unjust: an hour when nations, with all their ties, aspiration, and glory, begin to pass away like a mist of the morning and are gone.

And now that same mighty, fatal wheel is about to turn again and crush a cause which God has been implored to bless, and for which many a life has been laid down. Let us not say who is right or who is wrong, for this is not the time to stir the ashes of dead fires, but put yourself in the place of that group and forget not the dooming hour, or fail to credit each one with a sense of self-respect and a

conscience like our own. Think of the sacrifices
that they had made beyond measure in a cause which
they believed to be just, and remember that now at
last, notwithstanding all, they were face to face
with defeat, which meant that social, domestic, and
economic conditions were bound to be disrupted
into utmost chaos. Think it all over, broad-minded
reader, as you evoke the scene.

And so, then, nephew Fitzhugh, and you, Gordon, and Longstreet, hero old and tried, what next?
Shall the Army of Northern Virginia, after all its
confident assertion and reassertion of ultimate victory, lay down its arms, and the South acknowledge
that it has been utterly defeated? For with this
army's surrender the Confederacy plunges into an
abyss beyond reach of recovery.

And with that dire result a fact, what political
steps will necessarily follow? Are we and the leaders civil to be disfranchised till death overtakes us?
And are the sins of the fathers to be visited upon their
children?

And how about the states? Are they to be held
as conquered provinces and never allowed to take
their places again, clothed in their native sovereignty, in a Union which they had helped to form?
And how about the future of the slaves themselves?
What is to be their status? Are they to be granted
and we denied the right of suffrage?

Again, whatsoever the terms which Grant may

make, how far will they bind his government? Has it not notified him peremptorily, "You are not to decide, discuss, or confer upon, any political question "? Our arms laid down, let the implacable radicals cry for vengeance: what will the government do then? Will it yield to them and invoke the penalties of treason? — Treason! You are a dread old word, whether heard under the oaks of England or under the oaks of Virginia; and when has there ever been a rebellion in England that the land did not groan under the shadow of gibbets? Had not these men, brought up on the *Spectator* and lovers of Shakespeare, more than once read Prince John of Lancaster's cruel speech to the rebellious Scroop, Archbishop of York? —

Moreover, what is to be the character of the ceremony of surrender? — Is it unfair to assume that Longstreet and Gordon had read Livy? Fitz Lee at least had had to study Blair's *Rhetoric* in his course at West Point, while his uncle Robert E. was superintendent, and surely was familiar with the story of the legions' anguish at the prospect of having to pass under the yoke after the Caudine Forks. — And was their beloved commander Robert E. Lee on Traveller to head the Army of Northern Virginia in a like march of humiliation before the Army of the Potomac? These were questions stalking round that fire like grim spectres, and calling on the members of that last council for an answer. Do not be deceived. This is not fancy; they were there in sternly eager reality. Gordon himself says that " if all that was said and *felt* at that meeting could be given, it would make a volume of measureless pathos."

But let us come to the main issue. There was one chance left. It was possible, if cavalry alone disputed the way, for them to break through and continue their onward march either to the Roanoke or to the works and supplies at Lynchburg. And, if that were impossible, then, with the fragments which might elude capture, keep up a desultory guerrilla warfare till the government should grow weary and grant a peace of considerate terms. It is needless to speak of how Longstreet's, Gordon's and Fitz Lee's pride, and self-respect, and the wounds they bore, — for each of them had been carried bleeding from the field, — clamored in favor of this course, or that the council decided that the attempt of clearing the road should be tried, and if it failed, then Lee was to see Grant and accept terms.

Fitz Lee claimed, in justification of withdrawing his cavalry after the flag of truce was raised, that it was fully understood at the council that he should do so in case of their failure to break through Sheridan. But let this be as it may, his men scattered to their homes and he in a few days came in and gave himself up, convinced that, with his chief gone, all was over.

There is every reason to believe that Lee was glad when Longstreet, Gordon and his nephew Fitz decided as they did; and I am glad, too: for the sake of enduring peace, I am glad that the Army of Northern Virginia took war's last hazard, notwithstanding that scores of noble-spirited youths on both sides lost their lives. For when Victory finally illumined the torn banners of the Union, nowhere within the range of endeavor's vision was there a single lost opportunity to save the Confederacy; all had been done by the Army of Northern Virginia that fortitude and courage could call upon it to do.

To carry out the decision they had reached, Gordon and Fitz Lee, accompanied by four or five batteries, were to move at one o'clock, get into position by daylight, and then attack Sheridan. Longstreet was to follow after them with his heroic corps, and in case they were successful, take a stand at the Court-House, and hold Humphreys back till the trains were out of the way, Mahone meanwhile guarding their left.

Then the three corps commanders left to rejoin their shattered, sleeping forces. Gordon, while thinking intently and rapidly over the coming enterprise as he rode away, suddenly bethought him, " Where, after throwing off Sheridan, shall I halt and camp for the night? "

It was an important question, and he sent one

of his staff back to Lee to have him settle the matter.

"Yes," said Lee, after hearing the serious aide, "tell General Gordon that I should be glad for him to halt just beyond the Tennessee line," — which was only about two hundred miles off to the west, amid the Alleghany Mountains!

Lee, as the world knows, was not inclined to be facetious, but this reply under all the circumstances bubbles with such spontaneous humor that I am sure that it will bring him closer to my readers.

Thirty guns from Carter's, Poague's, Johnson's and Stark's battalions of artillery were ordered to support Gordon, and at a very early hour they, with the infantry and cavalry, took up the march. Fitz Lee's cavalry having bivouacked east of New Hope Church, had to pass through Longstreet's tired, sleeping veterans, whose waning camp-fires were faintly twinkling by the roadside, — for in those dark, still hours the fairy spinner, Mist, was weaving her veil deeply over the face of the fields and woods. Lee's staff, and a part of Gordon's and Longstreet's, lay down on the ground near the roadside, after the conference, with saddles for pillows, their horses picketed to the trees and gnawing every little while at the bark for want of better provender.

Lee rose at three o'clock and rode forward through the rear of Fitz Lee's and Gordon's troops to a commanding point overlooking the misty valley below. There he reined up and waited, as they filed down the road past him; and the time must have seemed long till dawn. But at last it came, and with its approach, the pale fog, as if it had heard a mysterious signal, began to lift slowly, and the surrounding region became visible.

Meanwhile Grimes of Gordon's corps, a square-faced, resolute man with eyes wide apart and penciled brows, to whom Bushrod Johnson's divisions had been assigned, had crossed the river, and passing through the village, had formed athwart the Lynchburg road.   James A. Walker's division also of Gordon's corps, drew up in the fog-gray darkness on Grimes's left, and Evans, with his Georgia, Louisiana, and Virginia brigades, under whose command was all that survived of the old Stonewall brigade, on Walker's left.

Grimes put Bushrod Johnson on his right, Cox's brigade of North Carolinians holding the extreme flank. The batteries assigned to accompany Gordon took their places; cannoneers mounted, ready to follow Grimes. The cavalry formed on the infantry's right, first W. H. F. Lee's division, then Rosser, and then the young, gallant Munford, all under the command of stocky, blue-eyed, full-rusty-bearded, jolly Fitz Lee, — but he was not in a joking mood that morning. A little before daylight Gordon accompanied by Fitz Lee, came to where Grimes stood, and began in his presence to talk

about what should be done. Grimes says Gordon
was of the opinion that the troops before them were
cavalry, and that Fitz Lee should begin the attack;
Fitz Lee thought they were infantry, and that
Gordon should attack. They discussed the matter
so long that Grimes got impatient and blurted out
that it was somebody's business to attack at once,
and that he was sure he could drive our forces
from the Bent Creek road, which it had been
decided the Confederate trains were to take.

It may help to vivify the landscape if we stand
where Gordon and Grimes stood and look at it
through their eyes. They were within one hundred yards of the McLean house, on the edge of the
village and facing south. Before them, spread out
like a tilted fan, old fields, veiled with mist and
creased with gentle folds, rose toward the south,
crowned at last with dark circling woods. About
midway of the incline, the Bent Creek road strikes
off westward from the Lynchburg, but after a while
rambles back into it again beyond Appomattox
Station. It will be remembered that the First
Maine's videttes, carbine in hand, were posted along
it, and that their division, Crook's, was up in the
woods a half mile or more to the rear, dismounted,
their horses browsing, and some of the men behind
a line of temporary defenses of rails, brush, and
pieces of old logs, whose centre was on the Lynchburg road; and that while Gordon and Grimes

were having their interview, Mackenzie's small division was moving under orders from Sheridan to take position on Crook's left.

" Well! " replied Gordon, to Grimes's soldierly, blunt remark, " drive them off! "

" I cannot do it with my division alone," observed Grimes.

" You can take the other two divisions! " responded Gordon.

Grimes then rode to Walker on his left and asked him to go with him while he pointed out Crook's position and explained his plan of attack.

Meanwhile Gordon and Fitz Lee settled on the following plan: the cavalry should bear to its right, then circle to the left till it got well on Crook's left and rear, and as soon as they were ready, Grimes was to advance, and they together make an attack on Crook and clear the road. But the cavalry's movements were sluggish, and it was not till my classmate " 'Jim " Lord, by order of Colonel Smith of the First Maine, let drive a few rounds from his battery, pushed well up on the encircling ridge, down in among the swarm of cavalry, infantry, and wagons dim in the enshrouding fog, that any advance was made. Thereupon Grimes started a light force up the pike and drove the videttes from the Bent Creek road back on the main line.

The road clear, the right of Fitz Lee's command, Rosser and Munford, took it, moving briskly, and

Grimes with lines extended waited for them to get to Crook's left. Meanwhile, the sun rose, as did the fog, and the dewy tree-tops on the timbered hills, which zigzag round the head of the Appomattox, began to loom free against the fresh sky of that Palm Sunday morning, a sky that soon, north and south, would hear the bells of many a steeple ringing.

XII

But before Fitz Lee strikes — it should not be forgotten that at that very time Mackenzie was moving toward Crook's left — let us turn to Ord's troops, who had bivouacked at midnight within four or five miles of Appomattox Station. They were called from their slumbers at three A. M., and although weary and foot-sore, and without breakfasting, — "but a few had had anything to eat since noon of the previous day," say the *War Records*, — fell in without murmuring, and resumed the march. Foster's division of Gibbon's corps was in the lead; behind him Turner's, of the same corps, the Twenty-fourth, and then Griffin, with the Fifth corps.

About the time Gordon was replying to Grimes, Foster had reached the vicinity of Sheridan's headquarters, the little frame house just south of the Station, and halted for breakfast. Their fires were barely started when Ord rode up, dismounted, and, after a short consultation with Sheridan, started Foster on at full speed and then rode back to hurry on the rest of the infantry, for word had just come in that the enemy were moving.

Rienzi was stamping in front of the door; Sheridan mounted him, and dashed for the front. Having gained a point where he could get a good view of Gordon's infantry, he halted. They were now advancing firmly with colors, and there were so many standards crimsoning each body of troops, — to their glory the Confederate color-bearers stood by Lee to the last, — that they looked like marching gardens blooming with cockscomb, red roses, and poppies. One glance told Sheridan that Crook and Mackenzie could not possibly hold their ground, and he sent word to them to fall back slowly. He also sent orders to Custer and Devin, who, after their severe trials of the night before, had retired for a little rest near his headquarters, to come on the field at once.

Meanwhile, the Confederate batteries which, under Alexander, had jarred earth and sky at Gettysburg just before Pickett's charge, had opened and were thundering well. And as I loitered last October on the spot where they stood that Sunday morning in 1865, the spirits of Confederate cannoneers approached me, asking, " Can you tell us where we can find our old commanders, Pelham, Alexander, Dearing, ' Joe ' Blount, Brown, and Carter? " Yes, if you will follow a road upward, upward past moons and stars, the road that the sound of the church-bells took that Palm Sunday morning, it will lead you at last to where you will find them all, in the land o' the leal.

The sound of the firing reached Ord's column, stepping briskly, and with cheers they broke into double-quick. Pennington of Custer's division, who had not found rest until after midnight, was fast asleep on a quilt of pine-needles in a grove traversed by the sunken road on which the men were marching. Their eagle-like scream awakened him, and as far as he could see, the road was packed with men, their faces grimly ablaze, colors flying, and over them, like a wavering shield of steel, were their muskets at right-shoulder-shift, as they trotted forward to the sound of the now booming guns; for Gordon's and Fitz Lee's veterans were answering the last call of the Confederacy with their old-time spirit.

Fitz Lee, having gained his position, assailed Mackenzie violently, and swept his small brigade out of the way before he could establish due connection with Crook — reader, for the sake of a boy's love for another, let me say that Ronald S. Mackenzie (we always called him Mack) graduated at the head of my class, and that a braver, less self-conscious or truer-hearted boy never lived, and that many and many a happy hour I passed with him and our fellow classmates as we sat and smoked and talked, — oh, so young and care-free! — before call to quarters at West Point. Poor Mack! His mind became clouded, but death released him at last, and I know he rests in peace, for Honor and Valor saw to it that his pillow was soft. I shall never forget his riding up to Meade's headquarters in the Mine Run campaign, the red blood dripping from his horse's shoulder. The bullet that made the wound was fired at Mackenzie while making a reconnaissance of the enemy's line.

Well, at about Mackenzie's critical moment, Grimes, supported by four or five batteries under Colonel Thomas H. Carter, struck Crook in front, and, although his dismounted men held on stubbornly, they were forced to give way finally, and mighty fast, too, at that, for W. H. F. Lee was charging squarely against their left flank and rear. Back through old fields and heavy copses of young pine and shaggy jack-oaks, Crook and Mackenzie were driven, their led horses and batteries retreating in great confusion, leaving a gun, and perhaps two of them — for the number is in doubt — in the enemy's hands, captured by Beal's and Roberts's brigades of W. H. F. Lee's division. Meanwhile Devin, who was on the Le Grand road commanding Sheridan's first division, seeing the trouble Crook and Mackenzie were in and Gordon's infantry moving up the Lynchburg road in two lines of battle, formed his men to attack Gordon's advancing left opening on it a rapid and effective fire with his artillery. Crook and Mackenzie out of their way, Grimes wheeled his first line of battle to the left and brushed Devin back to Plain Run and the Le Grand road.

The Lynchburg road was clear, and the tattered forces that had cleared it burst into cheers.

But their victorious shouts had hardly broken before on through the mob of Crook's fleeing cavalry came Foster's division of Gibbon's corps, and, with the greatest promptness, and without regard to its own flanks, his leading brigade, Osborn's, — Thirty-ninth Illinois, Sixty-second and Sixty-ninth Ohio, — sought and rushed at the flanking cavalry. To Osborn's right and left the other brigades of Foster's division, Dandy's and Fairchild's as well as Turner's division, and the brigades of colored troops, hurried, and forthwith all fought their way to the open, where rested the right of the main body of the Confederate infantry. Several batteries now, at point-blank, fired shell and canister into Gibbon's men, and held them for a while, but were quickly driven from their position with the loss of several guns, captured by the Eighth Maine, Fairchild's brigade, and 199th Pennsylvania, of Osborn's brigade, Foster's division.

Meanwhile, the Fifth corps, Chamberlain's brigade in front, on reaching the Station had been deflected to the right, and soon Pearson's brigade, second in line of the front division, was ordered to line up alongside of Ord's right. Obliquely to the northwest into double-quick they broke, and orders from General Joseph J. Bartlett came sharp and fast: "One Hundred and Fifty-fifth Pennsylvania, for-

ward as skirmishers!" "On centre!" "Take
intervals!" and away they go to the front, the cavalry parting and falling back through them. When
deployed, their right was near the Trent house.
Chamberlain continued the march rapidly up the
Le Grand road, heavy guns answering each other
fiercely, their lordly roar mingling with the spiteful
crack of carbines and muskets, which every little
while were drowned in the crash of a volley. One
of Sheridan's staff dashed at full speed up to the
gallant Chamberlain, exclaiming, "General Sheridan wishes you to break off from the column and
come to his support. The rebel infantry is pressing
him hard. Our men are falling back; don't wait
for orders through the regular channels, but act
on this at once."

At a run they followed the staff officer to where
Sheridan sat on fiery Rienzi, partially enveloped in
the smoke of the batteries, man and horse living
embodiments of tumultuous energy.

I do not know just where Sheridan stood that
morning, but for a clearer understanding let us paint
the view that was swept by his ardent dark eye.

There is a little brook a couple of miles long, called
Plain Run, which has its source in woods not far
from Appomattox Station, and, after creeping out
into the sunshine, flows northeastwardly in a shallow
valley to the Appomattox. Along the western rim
of the brook's cradle is the Lynchburg road. On

the eastward rim, which is somewhat higher, is a country road that starts at the station, and after traversing three or four large plantations, the Inge, Sears's, and Le Grand's, enters the Walker's Church road within less than a mile of the Court-House; thence the two glide on together down to Plain Run, which at this point is only a few hundred yards from the faint-beating heart of the old hamlet. Thus the shallow valley is bounded by these roads. On its gently-sloping sides are fields that last October were covered with dun broom-grass, some dotted with low, green-tufted pines, and some tented with rows of corn in the shock. By the Trent house and then the Sears, the run wanders at the foot of these fields, and a lowing cow on its banks in the still hours of the night can be heard from road to road.

When I visited the field I went to the Sears house and from thence to the run itself, a few hundred yards away, for I wanted to see it at about the point where Chamberlain crossed it. I found it stealing through willows and alders, and under half-grown trees interlaced with wild grape-vines. The water, like that of Shiloah, was flowing softly, softly, from one shadowed pool to another. A little alarmed bird was chirping nervously in the alders, a yellow butterfly wavered by me to join a colony, sitting close together with upright, bladed wings, gilding a spot on a black, damp bar, — all of them resting as though in the dream of a distant summer day, —

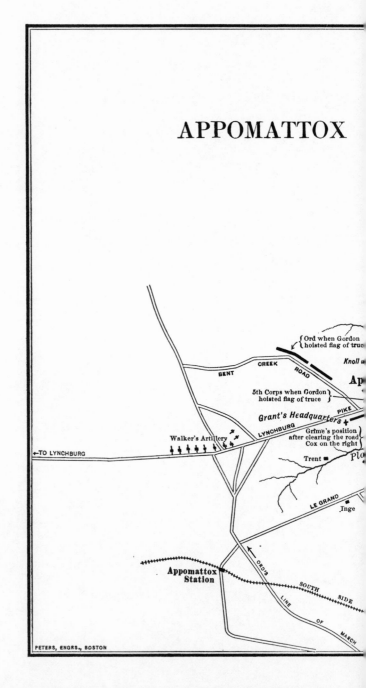

APPOMATTOX

Ord when Gordon
hoisted flag of truce

Knoll w

Ap

CREEK
BENT ROAD

5th Corps when Gordon
hoisted flag of truce

Grant's Headquarters PIKE

LYNCHBURG

Grime's position
after clearing the road
Cox on the right

Walker's Artillery

←TO LYNCHBURG

Trent ■ Pl

LE GRAND
Inge

ORD'S

Appomattox
Station

SOUTH SIDE

LINE

OF

MARCH

PETERS, ENGRS., BOSTON

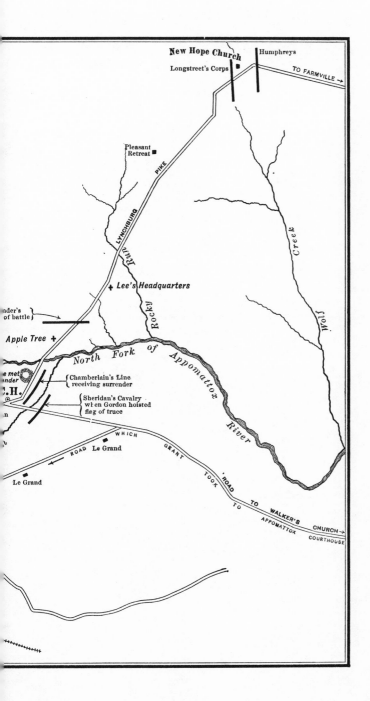

New Hope Church

Humphreys

Longstreet's Corps

TO FARMVILLE →

Pleasant
Retreat

LYNCHBURG

PIKE

Creek

Lee's Headquarters

Rocky

Run

Wolf

nder's
of battle

Apple Tree +

North Fork of Appomattox

e met
nder
C.H.

Chamberlain's Line
receiving surrender

River

Sheridan's Cavalry
when Gordon hoisted
flag of truce

WHICH

ROAD Le Grand

GRANT

Le Grand

TOOK

TO

'ROAD

TO WALKER'S

APPOMATTOX

CHURCH →

COURTHOUSE

and from the direction of the Court-House came faintly the intermittent jangle of a cow-bell.

I went back, up to the Le Grand road, and there lay the scene swept by Sheridan's blazing eye. And what did *he* see? His cavalry falling back down the sloping fields from the Lynchburg road, and on their crest Gordon's men cheering, shrouded in the smoke of battle, with scores and scores of crimson banners flying. Oh, stormy sea of four long years! Your last triumphant wave is breaking; but not, not forever, like a shadow, are you gone, for there is a beach in men's hearts which God in his wisdom hath made to respond to echoes of wars like this, and that creative, musical beach is emotion.

War's tumult is loud, volleys are crashing, hills and woods are throwing back madly each sullen cannon's roar, men are falling mangled and bleeding; the ultimate crisis of the war is at hand. Ord's left is drawing near the Bent Creek road. Gibbon, Turner, Ayres and Bartlett are all surging through the timber toward the cheering Confederates.

But hark! Abruptly that cheering stops; stops as abruptly as though a deadly pang had struck each breast, or a sheeted ghost had risen before them. Whence and from whom has come the pang or what has evoked the forbidding spectre to change the mood of those cheering veterans? Lo! a mighty host with colors, fields of stars and bands of white and crimson, is pouring from the green leafy depths of the woods, and in full view across the valley the old Fifth corps has risen up out of the earth, as it were, and in two lines of battle is swinging down past the Sears house with flags rippling gaily; flags that waved so opportunely on Round Top that second day at Gettysburg; and the cheering stops.

Sheridan's bugles are calling triumphantly shrill; the scattered cavalry respond to their notes and gather in high spirits promptly to their standards; and Custer, at the head of the clanking column, gallops up the Le Grand road, drawing sabres for a charge toward the Court-House itself. Sheridan, as he leaves Chamberlain to join them, grits out, "Now smash 'em, I tell you; smash 'em!" and gives the bit to the champing, restless, head-tossing Rienzi.

As Chamberlain crosses the little run, all the troops on his left press forward, and the whole Confederate line, now full of despair and heartache, begins to fall back. But as they retire, Cox gives to his North Carolina brigade the command, "Right about face!" Behind them their young, stately commander stands, his body bearing the scars of eleven wounds. As one they whirl. Firmly rings his voice again: "Ready! Aim! Fire!" and from levelled guns pours the last volley that will be fired by the Army of Northern Virginia. Manly was he in the morning of life; manly is he in its evening;

and his heart still youthful notwithstanding its weight of seventy-odd years. Here is my hand, gallant Cox, and may your last days be cloudless and sweet!

And reader, while the smoke of his brigade is billowing up, let me tell you a monument marks the spot where that last volley was fired; and, if ever you visit the field, — and I hope it will be in October, — do go to that stone: the tall, slender, gray-bodied, twilight-holding young pines that have grown up thickly in front of it, and the purple asters blooming round it, if you lend your ear, will welcome you to its proud record.

In vain is Cox's volley, for invisible hands are loosening the curtains that in a few minutes more will fall on the drama, ending the long, fierce struggle. Yes; let the last volley roar on past Gordon. He will wonder whether it was fired by friend or foe; but whichsoever, it matters not: his hope has flickered and gone out, for he sees Ord beginning to form up in the fields along the Bent Creek road; Gibbon's, and Griffin's corps, veiled by musketry and artillery smoke, coming out from the timber; Custer on the point of charging down into the village, threatening to cut off all communication between the wings of the Confederate forces. The sight was appalling, and Custer's threatening charge called for immediate action. Gordon sent a brigade of engineer troops, under that mild and well-bred gentleman, Colonel

Talcott, to stay him, and ordered Grimes and the cavalry to fall back to the village.

Fast now they recoil, leaving many a brave comrade behind them. They pass, on their way, the spot where a gun (or guns) was captured; and there lies Wilson, the color-bearer of the Fourteenth Virginia cavalry, mortally wounded, his beautiful bay mare standing beside him. He has just bade his friend Moffett good-bye, murmuring, " Moffett, it is hard to die just as the war is over! " And so it was, dying color-bearer; and when I stood where you fell, Wilson, my heart beat tenderly for you. Autumn flowers were blooming there, and a mist, like that of the morning when you made your last charge, was drenching the field, and here and there it had gathered like tears at the tips of the bending grass.

The galloping column of cavalry, with golden-locked Custer at its head, has almost reached the Walker's Church road; drawn sabres are glinting; guidons are fluttering; foam is spotting the breasts of the horses who spring to the bugle-notes ready for the charge.

A Confederate battery gallops up to the edge of the village, unlimbers its right section in front of the rear door of the Peet house and opens at Custer and Chamberlain's right, firing shell and shrapnel as fast as the cannoneers can load the guns. Longstreet, watching Gordon's attack from the other side of the river, and seeing that it is failing, tells

Alexander, who is at his side, to form a line quickly as a rallying-point for the retreating forces. Alexander plants battery after battery, and Wilcox and the fragments of Hill's old corps and of Pickett's and Kershaw's divisions form in line. Heth takes his place on the left; and Heth, by the way, was a young, spare-faced, blue-eyed, and very lovable West Point man. His portrait now adorns the walls of the Westmoreland Club in Richmond.

The historian of McGowan's South Carolina brigade says of the formation of this last line of battle which the Army of Northern Virginia ever made: " The nature of the campaign of the past week was easily read in the countenances and gait of the troops. Their faces were haggard, their step slow and unsteady. Bare skeletons of the old organizations remained, and those tottered along at wide intervals."

A command about two hundred strong moved up in the rear of McGowan's brigade, and at once lay down; thereupon some one asked, " Whose regiment is that? " A soldier in the prone line replied with a grim smile, " Kershaw's division." Only two hundred and fifty left of the heroic division that turned the tide in the Wilderness, and whose volleys I can hear as I write these lines!

Meanwhile, Ord's troops and the Fifth corps, led on by Griffin, are quickening their steps at every moment. Now they are all out in the open across the Lynchburg road, coming like a mighty wave ready to break at any moment upon the disorganized, retreating Confederates. Alas, the garden of poppies, red roses, and cockscombs that marched up so gaily is broken into patches and drifts back fast on the out-going tide of defeat.

It is now about nine o'clock, and many a village and country church-bell is ringing for morning service, their tones dying away over blooming orchards and over fields where lambs are frisking; but where no smoke of battle rises, and no poor boys are breathing their last, their young blood staining the lea as at Appomattox.

XIII

GORDON has been through four or five dreadful hours, and they must have been trying hours to Lee also, who, when we left him, was waiting for dawn to come, and for Gordon to attack.

On account of the mist it is doubtful if Lee, from his position beyond the river, could see Grimes as he mounted the fields to the Bent Creek road and thence on to the timber. Yet he could hear the guns and the uppermost question must have been: Has Grant been able to out-march me, and will Gordon encounter infantry? Yes, General Lee, Grant had out-marched you, and I think the world will hold that he out-generaled you, too, in this last campaign. Minutes, quarters of an hour, went by; the firing seemed to hang at one spot, and every one who has been at an army headquarters during an engagement knows that when that is the case the advance is, momentarily at least, checked. Lee could stand the anxiety no longer, and sent the accomplished Venable, of his staff, to Gordon to ask him if he thought he could cut his way through. Gordon replied emphatically, " Tell

General Lee that my command has been fought to a frazzle, and I fear I can do nothing unless I am heavily supported by Longstreet's corps!"

Venable galloped back with the discouraging response, and says that Lee exclaimed, "There is nothing left me but to go and see General Grant, and I had rather die a thousand deaths."

Rather die a thousand deaths! Rather die a thousand deaths! Here we have about the first and only recorded spontaneous, right-out-of-the-heart, furnace-glowing utterance from that remarkably self-poised man; and, if true, it is a mighty interesting revelation. For what was there in the occasion so painful as to wring this burst of feeling from his habitually deliberate lips? It could not have been surprise. Had not these very circumstances, for the last year, cast their shadows before? In fact had he not within less than twenty-four hours told his old friend of West Point days, Pendleton, that from the beginning he had doubted the ultimate success of the South if the Confederacy were not recognized by the powerful of the foreign governments? Again, when at midnight that same old West Point friend got back from his somewhat troublesome experience with Custer's cavalry, and seeing Lee in full uniform remarked upon his spick and span appearance, had Lee not answered, that he might have to meet Grant before the day closed? Spick and span! Nelson on the day of Trafalgar

put on all the medals, orders, and rich decorations
he had won, and Cæsar, as he felt the stabs of
Brutus and Cassius, arranged his toga that he
might fall gracefully. It does not seem, then, that
the pain he felt could have come from the suddenness
of surprise. It must have had some other source.

Rather die a thousand deaths than to go and see
Grant! What keenly sensitive point in this truly
great nature had been pierced? Was a natural
pride rebellious and mad that, after all those brilliant battles, — Gaines's Mill, Manassas, Antietam,
Chancellorsville, the Wilderness, Spottsylvania, and
Cold Harbor, — he should have to go and ask on
what terms that valiant army might lay down its
arms, as the armies of Buckner and Pemberton
before him had done? Or, if the exclamation sprang
from a dread of humiliation, had he a right to
harbor such a thought? Had not Grant said to him
in the note received the evening before: " Peace
being my great desire, there is but one condition
I would insist upon, namely, that the men and
officers surrendered shall be disqualified from taking
up arms against the Government of the United
States until properly exchanged " ? Was there
anything in those terms to justify a fear of humiliation in their execution?

In view of the fact that his going would bring
peace to the land, whence came the keen pang?
Had not he himself said in his reply to Grant's note,

quoted above, that, "The restoration of peace should be the sole object of all "? Why should he prefer a thousand deaths, then, rather than go to see the man at the head of an army which, through its multitude of men, had overcome the Army of Northern Virginia, when that visit would bring peace, peace, "the sole object of all "? Venable was an honorable man; but, in the light of the fact that it was an hour when greatness called for greatness, I wonder and wonder if Lee ever made just that remark. If he did, it only tells me this, — that beneath all glamour and earthly glory lies the common clay of our natures.

Well, he at once sent for Longstreet, whose forces during the night had moved up till the trains at New Hope Church impeded their further progress, and who were then throwing up a line of intrench-ments, breast-high, with an abatis in front across the road, the left of the works resting on the head-waters of Devil's Creek, flowing north into the James, the right on those of Wolf Creek which soon finds its way through dense, wild-turkey-haunted woods to the Appomattox.

Longstreet rode forward. In his memoirs he says that Lee " was dressed in a suit of new uniform, sword and sash, a handsomely embroidered belt, boots, and a pair of gold spurs; " but adds that " the handsome apparel and brave bearing failed to conceal his profound depression." Lee, after

gracefully saluting Longstreet, — this old hero still
had his right arm in a sling from the almost fatal
wound he received in the Wilderness, — told him
that Gordon's men had met with a formidable force
through which he could not break, and sought his
views as to what should be done. Longstreet,
with his usual inflexible resolution, asked if the
bloody sacrifice of his army could in any way help
the cause in other quarters. Lee said he thought
not. " Then," replied Longstreet, " your situation
speaks for itself."

They were standing near an almost burned-out
fire. Lee called Mahone, who was near by. The
brave little blue-eyed man came forward, and Lee
put the same question to him; but, before answering,
Mahone kicked some of the embers together, and
then affirmed Longstreet's judgment.

Lee in his note of the night before had appointed
ten A. M. as the time when he would like to meet
Grant on the road beyond New Hope Church, and
while waiting for the hour to come, and no doubt
longing every minute for an answer from Grant, he
had a talk with Alexander.

Lee, from the roadside, as Alexander was riding by,
called to him, and when Alexander joined him, Lee,
after peeling off the bark, took a seat on a felled oak.
He then produced a field-map and said, " Well, we
have come to the Junction, and they seem to be
here ahead of us. What have we got to do to-day? "

A long and interesting interview followed, that can be found in Alexander's most admirable military memoirs, which, like those of Stiles and Sorrel, breathe sincerity.

Alexander was glad of the chance to talk with Lee, for, ever since the afternoon before, when Pendleton told him, as they rode side by side, of his going to Lee with the self-appointed council's suggestion, he had been mulling over the matter, and had thought out a plan of his own to save Lee and them all from the ignominy of surrender. I know just how he felt, for he was a man of fine grain, and I shall never forget its manifestation during an interview I had with him in Richmond at the time of the undraping of Jefferson Davis's monument. We were at the Jefferson Hotel, and that stately and capacious hostelry was thronged with ex-Confederates, all proudly dressed in their gray, and cheering to the echo every time the orchestra struck up one of their favorite Southern airs.

At Alexander's suggestion we had withdrawn to an alcove under the stairway; and while we were talking over West Point days he told me of a row he had had there with a classmate just before graduation, a row so bitter that neither spoke to the other on parting from the Academy. Now it so happened that this classmate was the senior aide to the chief of artillery of the Army of the Potomac, to whom, at Appomattox, the Confederate batteries under Alexander had to be turned over. On first going to headquarters officially in regard to details the day after Lee met Grant, Alexander said that he had made it a point not to notice his classmate, whose face wore a look of friendly greeting. The next day he had to go there again, and his classmate, standing at his tent-door, beckoned to him. Alexander, after a struggle with his West Point hate, turned his steps toward him, wondering what he wanted. To his surprise, his old-time enemy drew a large roll of bills from his pocket, stripped off a goodly number, and held them out, saying, " Aleck, you are welcome to this; I have more than I want, and you may need it."

" Do you know, Morris," said Alexander, his soft voice trembling with emotion, " I declined the money, although I had hardly a cent in the world, I felt so badly and ugly over surrendering; but I see now that I did myself and him a great wrong."

He paused. I glanced at his face, and his eyes were swimming. My only excuse for allowing this episode to delay the narrative is that the reader may get some idea of the man who was talking with Lee, and what surrender meant to him and the Southern army.

Well, Alexander developed his plans warmly to Lee, finally urging with the desperation of youth, that the men should take to the woods, understanding that they were to rally on Johnston or report armed to the governors of their respective states. Lee listened quietly, and then replied to this obviously impracticable scheme that he had not over fifteen thousand muskets, and that even if all should report for duty their numbers would be too small to accomplish anything, and it would end in nothing but a destructive, malignant, guerrilla warfare. He then added, " General, you and I as Christian men have no right to consider only how this would affect us; we must consider its effect on the country as a whole; if I took your advice we would bring on a state of affairs it would take the country years to recover from. . . . I am going to meet Grant at ten A. M. and surrender the army on the condition of not fighting again until exchanged, and take the consequences of my act."

Now we have the Lee of Venable and Alexander, but it is only fair to the former to complete his account of what was said after Lee's exclamation about dying a thousand deaths. " Convulsed with passionate grief," goes on Venable, " many were the wild words which we spoke, as we stood round him. Said one, ' Oh, general, what will history say of the surrender of the army in the field? '

" He replied, ' Yes, I know they will say hard things of us.' (No, no, General Lee, you were mistaken: no one ever has said or will say hard things of you or your gallant army for surrendering

in the field.) ' They will not understand how we
were overwhelmed with numbers.' (Yes, the world
thoroughly understands that we had five men to
your one.) ' But that is not the question, colonel
[Venable was a colonel], the question is: Is it right
to surrender the army? If it is right, then I will
take all the responsibility.' "

In these portraitures by Venable and Alexander,
what living examples we have of how enthusiasm
and love build up and festoon this world's heroes.
But I find no fault. Climb on, blooming glory,
round the pure-minded and dignified Lee! climb
on, and ever climb on, around the modest, peace-
bringing, and magnanimous Grant.

Lee finally mounted Traveller and, without
notifying either Longstreet or Gordon, set off to
meet Grant. His course was toward the rear, that
is, along the road toward New Hope Church. He
soon met a battalion of artillery withdrawing from
its bivouac by the side of Rocky Run, and one of
its officers says that it was about nine o'clock,
and that Traveller was finely groomed, his bridle
and bit polished until they shone like silver. Lee
was accompanied by a courier and Colonels Marshall and Taylor of his staff.

Up the leaning ridge that faces the midday sun
and pours its summer showers and melting snow
down into the little murmuring run, went Lee.
Captain Outlaw and the officers of the Eleventh

North Carolina saw him, and from his unusual
dress concluded that he was on his way to surrender,
and that in that case the hour had come to carry
out their resolution of two nights before, namely,
to commit their colors to the flames; and soon, up
among the fresh green leaves of spring went the
smoke of their destruction, but not quite all, for
Captain Outlaw tore off a little piece for a memento
that now, from time to time, in his ripe old age, he
holds in his hand and looks at with warm eyes and
welling heart. On went Lee and soon came to
Longstreet's line of intrenchments; and as he passed
through them that intrepid corps gave him cheer
upon cheer. Go ask the field of Manassas, Gettysburg, far-away Chickamauga, and the Wilderness,
and they will tell you with pride where every one
of its colors flew.

After clearing the rear-guard, the orderly bearing
the flag of truce was put in front and Lee proceeded
slowly on his distressful journey; and I can imagine
Traveller, with ears alert, looking down the red
streak of road bordered on both sides by still woods.
Great was the hour, and great was the man he bore,
but who knows what was passing through his
rider's mind? Never had Traveller carried him on a
mission like this. For the comfort of Lee I wish
that, as he rode, the reality of the present had by
some magic come and enveloped him, and then,
instead of Sheridan's and Gordon's angry guns, he

would have heard from Southland and Northland the mighty song of the triumphs of Peace.

Before long a staff officer from the front overtook them. Lee, after hearing what he had to say, asked him to go back and notify Longstreet and Gordon that he was on his way to see Grant, and rode on.

Meanwhile, Gordon had made repeated applications to Longstreet to come to his aid, which Longstreet could not do; but, as soon as Lee's message was received, Longstreet sent it to Gordon by Captain Sims, who had been serving on his staff since the untimely death of his own commander, A. P. Hill, telling Sims to say to Gordon that, in view of his inability to come to his aid, he might, if he thought proper, ask Sheridan to suspend hostilities till they could hear the result of the conference between Lee and Grant.

Sims set out for Gordon, whose forces by this time were threatened with immediate rout, for, save Munford's and Rosser's brigades of Fitz Lee's cavalry, who, on the repulse of the main attack, with Fitz Lee himself at the head, had fled up the pike toward Lynchburg, all the infantry and remaining cavalry had fallen back till their skirmish line lay within three hundred yards of the Court-House, and Ord, the Fifth corps and Sheridan were on the point of completing their destruction.

And now, while Sims is hastening to Gordon, let

me say that a stone marks the spot where this last
skirmish line lay, and that, when last October, in a
fog heavy and cold I stood beside it, the chilled
crickets beneath the sere matted grass at the foot of
the stone were responding feebly to the silence of the
fields, and in a small pasture, near a couple of old,
unpruned apple trees not far from where Gordon
stood, a perfectly white cow, and beside her a red
one with a white scarf adown her shoulder, were
grazing peacefully. The haggard apple trees, the for-
lorn, red-chimneyed houses behind them — there
are less than a dozen in the historic old village and
in the yard of one of them, near the McLean house
ruins, I saw a lean, aged, black and tan hound outstretched fast asleep — well, houses and hills and
the woods beyond the river, all loomed mysteriously
in that cold mist. But, while standing there gazing
around, a puff of wind came by and the mist began to
steal away, and I thought I was fortunate in seeing
the field of Appomattox clothed as Gordon saw it
that other morning so long ago.

When Sims galloped up to Gordon — the battery
at the Peet house was firing rapidly — and by
word of mouth shouted Longstreet's message, Gordon was, as we already know, in a most trying
position, for he expected disaster to break upon
him at any minute. His discomfited, down-hearted
men were drifting by him in shoals, he could
see our infantry ready like shrieking hawks to

swoop down upon him, batteries going into position on every knoll, the cannoneers running to their posts alongside their frowning guns, and the flash of Sheridan's sabres as they were drawn preparatory for a charge.

What a contrast with that morning at the breaking out of the war when he marched through Atlanta at the head of a company of Georgia mountaineers wearing coonskin caps and some one from the admiring mob lining the side-walk asked him, " What company is that, sir? " and, on Gordon answering proudly, " This is the Mountain Rifles," one of his men, a tall Georgia cracker, exclaimed, " Mountain hell! We ain't no Mountain Rifles, we're the Raccoon Roughs."

Yes, it was a contrast; gone was his smile at the answer; gone were the hopes of the crowd that had cheered him at the head of the Mountain Rifles; Atlanta a pitiable ruin; and now he was about to close the eyes of the dying Confederacy.

On receiving Longstreet's message, all of his aides being away on duty, Gordon begged Sims to go at once to Sheridan and ask him to suspend hostilities. Off dashed Captain Sims, and as soon as he had passed Gary's small Confederate brigade, for want of a flag of truce, or even a handkerchief to display, he tied a new white crash towel to the tip of his sword and proceeded on his way. A piece of that towel, and of the drawer of the table on which Lee signed the terms of surrender, Mrs. Custer has kindly given me, and they, with a piece of the flowing red flannel necktie which her husband wore that morning, hang framed on my wall.

It took only a few strides of Sims' horse, after having passed through Gary's line, to bring his rider to a group of the Seventh Michigan cavalry, Devin's division, near whom, dismounted, stood Colonel Whitaker, Custer's chief of staff. " Where is your commanding officer, General Sheridan? " asked Sims, " I have a message for him." " He is not here," replied Whitaker, " but Custer is, and you had better see him."

" Can you take me to him? " inquired Sims. " Yes," answered Whitaker, mounting his horse. They soon struck Custer's division pressing at full gallop up the Le Grand road toward Gordon's left, and hurried to the head of the column. As they rode up to Custer, he turned on Sims and asked, " Who are you and what do you wish? " Sims replied, " I am of General Longstreet's staff, but am the bearer of a message from General Gordon to General Sheridan asking for a suspension of hostilities until General Lee can be heard from, who has gone down the road to meet General Grant to have a conference." Custer exclaimed, " We will listen to no terms but that of unconditional surrender. We are behind your army now and it is at our mercy." Sims asked, " You will allow me to

carry this message back?" "Yes," responded
Custer. "Do you wish to send an officer?" inquired Sims. Custer, after a little hesitation,
directed Col. E. W. Whitaker, his chief of staff, and
Major George G. Briggs, 7th Michigan cavalry,
to go with Sims. Whitaker, in a letter to me, says
that Custer gave him the following message. "Take
that truce and go with the officer to General Lee,
and say to him that he (Custer) could not stop the
charge unless an unconditional surrender is made,
as he (Custer) is not in command on this field."
At the same time Custer sent another aide to Sheridan with the news, and Sheridan says the aide-de-
camp, hat in hand, dashed up to him exclaiming,
"Lee has surrendered; don't charge; the white
flag is up."

Whitaker having reached Gordon, Gordon asked
him to go with two of his aides, Jones of Alabama
and Brown of Georgia, and stop our infantry still
on the move. Fast they galloped, Brown displaying Sims' towel, and as they passed Wells'
brigade of cavalry in line of battle, Whitaker cried
out, "Lower your carbines, men, lower your carbines; you will never have to raise them again in
this war."

Striking Chamberlain's line, Whitaker cried out,
"This is unconditional surrender; this is the
end!" And then on.

One of his Confederate companions reined up,

and drawing near Chamberlain, said, "I am just from Gordon and Longstreet, and Gordon says for God's sake stop that infantry or hell will be to pay."

Chamberlain had to tell him that he had no authority to stop the movement, that Sheridan was in command. "Then I'll go to him," said the officer; and off he went, and the humane Chamberlain ceased pushing his division.

Gordon, on Sims' return, sent orders by Major Parker of Huger's battalion to Lieutenant Wright of Clutter's battery at the Peet house to cease firing.

Let us pause a moment. The last shot has been fired; the gun is still smoking, and its fated projectile goes muttering over Whitaker and the bearers of the flag of truce, on toward our lines, where with bated breath and in joy of heavenly expectancy our own men are awaiting the oncoming flags. Blind to everything but its deadly purpose, on past the heralds of peace, rushes that dooming projectile, on and plunges through the breast of Lieutenant Clark of the One Hundred and Eighty-fifth New York. Inscrutable Fate, as the blood spurted from that youthful heart, I hope you were satisfied.

At about that very same moment, too, when not another life need have been sacrificed, a musket-ball sped from the Confederate lines, and mortally wounded William Montgomery of the One Hundred and Fifty-fifth Pennsylvania. Fate's victim in this case was less than sixteen years old, and out of his photograph, now before me, gazes a boy with a pure, sweet, hauntingly earnest face.

Soon all firing ceased; but the ranks did not stop till they had gained a position from which they could overlook the Court-House and the remnants of Gordon's troops falling back in utter and hopeless confusion beyond the river. With this scene before them, they halted, guns were brought to an order, colors were planted, and all stood looking, wrapped in flooding joy. It meant the end of the war, and a gray-haired officer exclaimed, " Glory to God! " and Chamberlain replied, " Yes, and on earth peace and good-will toward men."

Sims had barely reached Gordon on his return from our lines before Custer appeared and, with his usual assurance, demanded in the name of General Sheridan the unconditional surrender of all Gordon's troops. To this abrupt demand Gordon replied with boldly defiant resolution that he would not pledge himself to any such terms, and that if Sheridan in the face of the flag of truce insisted on fighting, the responsibility for bloodshed would be on Sheridan and not on Gordon. Custer then asked to see Longstreet, and Major Hunter, a fine type of the Virginia gentleman, a member of Gordon's staff, escorted him to the old hero.

On Longstreet Custer made the same peremptory demand for unconditional surrender. Longstreet told him that he was not in command of the Army of Northern Virginia and, annoyed by Custer's brusque manner, — the old fellow naturally was in no humor that morning to stand impertinence, and especially that of a brassy, yellow-haired boy, — gave him to understand that he was entirely out of his place, and finally let fly some English that was quite vigorous. Custer was acute enough to see that his boyish game of bluff would not work, and I can fancy his laughing, contagious smile as he parted with the indignant old general, who assigned Major Wade Hampton Gibbs, one of Custer's West Point friends, to show him out of his lines.

Meanwhile Sheridan, who was about three quarters of a mile from the Court-House, noticing a large group of officers about it, and supposing that Custer was among them, started to join them. He had his headquarters flag behind him, and as soon as he drew near Gordon's lines, was fired on. Sheridan halted, and taking off his hat, called to them that they were violating the flag of truce; but the firing did not stop, and boiling mad, he took refuge in a ravine. Later he sent the sergeant back with his flag and an aide to Gordon's group, demanding what their conduct meant.

Gordon rode forward to meet him, and says that Sheridan was mounted on a very handsome horse — yes, we know about Rienzi. The interview was not very pleasant, for Sheridan did not have a gracious manner. But after explaining the situation and reaching a mutual understanding, they dismounted and sat together on the ground. The silence that had begun to reign was broken suddenly by a roll of musketry. Sheridan jumped to his feet, glaring fiercely at Gordon, and asked, " What does that mean, sir? " " It's my fault," replied Gordon. " I have forgotten to notify that command."

As none of his staff were available, Vanderbilt Allen, of Sheridan's staff, and one of my fellow West Point cadets, was sent to Gary's lines directing him to cease firing. And do you know that Gary insisted on " Van's " surrender, and when he learned that the army was about to lay down its arms, took off his sword and slipped away, away from his colors and comrades, and from sharing the greatest event in the history of the Army of Northern Virginia, for it was its transfiguration.

Well, I will not cumber the narrative with all that happened in the next hour and a half at the Court-House; let it suffice that Longstreet, Wilcox, Heth and other West Pointers from the South, joined Ord, Sheridan, Griffin, Custer and Pennington from the North, in the friendliest spirit, and agreed to wait till Grant and Lee had met. But Longstreet could not rest easy till word of the situation was sent to Humphreys, who, he feared, would attack his lines at New Hope Church; and Sheridan sent his chief of staff, " Tony " Forsythe, escorted

by Colonel Fairfax of Longstreet's staff, back through
the Confederate lines with a message to Meade of
the agreement they had reached.

"Tony," for so everybody called him, was a tall,
statuesque West Point man of light complexion,
very companionable, dignified, but with an under-
current of natural gaiety. I wish now that I had
asked him all about this ride when, with boon companions, I sat till late hours in the City Club of
Columbus, Ohio, with Governor Powell, John Taylor,
Galloway, and Dennison, and heard him talk of
Arizona jack-rabbits, as we sipped some fragrant
old Scotch.

Meanwhile the troops were resting on their arms;
those of the Army of the Potomac, to their manhood
and honor, showing no wild or barbaric elation, and
the privates of Lee's Army, heavy at heart, speculating wistfully on what was to be their fate. One
of their number has written that there was an in-
describable sadness over them all, but that they,
feeling their common misfortune, were very gentle
in their words to each other, sharing liberally the
little food that remained.

XIV

AND now let us return to Lee.

Having gained a mile or so beyond Longstreet's lines, he halted and dismounted, and sent Colonel Taylor, preceded by the courier, forward. The courier soon met my friend, Colonel Whittier of Humphreys' staff, bearing a flag of truce. Whittier was an uncommonly fine-looking and prepossessing young fellow, with charming manners; and somewhere on the campaign from the Wilderness to Petersburg he shared my tent one night, and by its lone candle we talked long, and when he rode away in the morning he carried my heart with him.

The courier asked him if he had a letter for General Lee, and if so, offered to deliver it; but Whittier told him he must deliver it in person. They soon came up with Taylor, who led the way to Lee, standing a little off, beside the road. The letter read as follows: —

"April 9, 1865.

"GENERAL: Your note of yesterday is received. I have no authority to treat on the subject of peace.

The meeting proposed for ten A. M. to-day could lead to no good. I will state, however, that I am equally desirous for peace with yourself, and the whole North entertains the same feeling. The terms upon which peace can be had are well understood. By the South laying down their arms, they would hasten that most desirable event, save thousands of human lives, and hundreds of millions of property not yet destroyed. Seriously hoping that all our difficulties may be settled without the loss of another life, I subscribe myself, etc.,

"U. S. GRANT, Lieutenant-General.
"General R. E. LEE."

This communication must have brought great disappointment to Lee, for I am sure he had been confident, if Grant would only meet him, of securing terms for a general peace that would save him and the army from the pain of surrender, and the South from a dismal remembrance of unqualified defeat. But this straightforward, kindly note completely dashed any such hopes; the surrender of the Army of Northern Virginia was inevitable; and to give the hard stony fact emphasis, Whittier says that, while Lee was reading the letter, Sheridan's angry guns from the direction of the Court-House could be distinctly heard.

Lee, without reading Grant's letter a second time, began to dictate to Marshall the following reply:

"GENERAL: I received your note of this morning on the picket-line, whither I had come to meet you and ascertain what terms were embraced in your proposal of yesterday with reference to the surrender of this army. I now ask an interview, in accordance with the offer contained in your letter of yesterday, for that purpose.

"R. E. LEE, General.

"Lieutenant-General U. S. GRANT.

"April 9, 1865."

While the above was being written, an aide from Longstreet, Colonel Haskell, with a message to Lee, swept by like the wind, not discovering Lee till he had passed him; and, having but one arm, the colonel was unable to check his horse at once. But as soon as he got control he reversed her course and, on nearing Lee, threw himself to the ground. The mare's large pink nostrils were flaring wide, and she was panting fast as, with lowered head, she walked by his side.

Lee hastened toward him exclaiming, "What is it? What is it? Oh, why did you do it? You have ruined your beautiful mare!"

The history of that mad ride is as follows:

After Lee had left Longstreet, Fitz Lee sent in word that he had found a gap for the escape of the army, and Longstreet felt that that news was so important that he told Haskell to overtake Lee and bring him back before he saw Grant, if he had to kill his mare. This favorite blooded animal, so Longstreet tells us, had been led all the way from Petersburg and, for the first time, had been saddled that very morning, Haskell intending to call on her to fly with him, if necessary, from the impending surrender.

I am truly glad to tell you, reader, that the beautiful, high-bred, and high-spirited creature soon recovered. What! Break down under a single heat carrying a message on a field like that, and perhaps the blood of Sir Henry in her veins! And had he not worn the colors of the South against American Eclipse? No, no! She was sold the following day to one of our officers for a good round sum in gold, but I suspect that visions of Traveller and the fields of Virginia passed before her as in her Northern stall she dreamed of that heat.

Lee did not credit Fitz Lee's report, and his judgment was soon confirmed by the arrival of another aide from Longstreet, saying that it was a mistake. He finished his letter and Marshall handed it to Whittier, with the request from the general that he would ask Humphreys not to push his lines. Humphreys forwarded the letter to Meade, and Meade, thinking time and some good might result from so doing, opened it, and then sent it on to Grant, suggesting that it might be well for him to see Lee, and that he had granted a short truce.

Meanwhile, Humphreys, not hearing from Meade, moved on, sending Whittier ahead to notify Marshall that he had had no orders to suspend hostilities. Marshall again pleaded that Humphreys should not persevere, for it meant a useless sacrifice of life, but Humphreys, with his line of battle deployed, would not listen to any delay and actually was sending word to Lee, who was in plain sight, to get out of the way, when fortunately Forsythe appeared, directly from Sheridan. Lee sent Taylor with Forsythe to Meade, who, having heard his story, agreed to an armistice until Lee could go and see Grant. It was this detached duty that accounts for Taylor's not being with Lee at the McLean house, for I have no doubt that he would have asked this deeply attached and seasoned aide to go with him.

Lee thereupon rode back to within about three quarters of a mile of the Court-House, where he dismounted, and sat down at the foot of an apple tree by the roadside. Alexander, who was near by, with thoughtfulness for Lee's comfort, had some fence-rails laid or piled under the tree, and covered them with red artillery blankets for him to rest upon.

Meade selected for the bearer of Lee's letter to Grant, Lieutenant Pease, an aide to Seth Williams, and many were the happy days I passed with him and others at Meade's headquarters. He was above middle height and firmly built, had dark-brown, earnest eyes and reddish hair.

When Pease overtook Grant, his party were breathing their horses near an open field, and he and Rawlins were sitting on a log. Pease gave him Lee's letter. Grant tore off the end of the envelope and drew forth the note. After reading it, without a change of expression, he passed it to the pale and worn Rawlins at his side, one of the best friends that any man like Grant ever had in the world, saying, "Here, General Rawlins."

When Rawlins had read it, Grant asked, "Well, how do you think that will do?"

Rawlins replied emphatically, "I think *that* will do."

Grant at once wrote to Lee as follows:

"April 9, 1865.

"General R. E. Lee,
        "Commanding C. S. Army:

    "Your note of this date is but this moment (11:50 A. M.) received, in consequence of my having passed from the Richmond and Lynchburg Road to the Farmville and Lynchburg Road. I am at this writing about four miles west of Walker's Church, and will push forward to the front for the purpose of meeting you. Notice sent to me on this road where you wish the interview to take place will meet me.

        "U. S. Grant, Lieutenant-General."

Grant gave this dispatch to Babcock, directing him to take the shortest road he could find to reach Lee.

That was a famous duty Grant put on his young and loyal aide, and there was something mysteriously fitting in the choice. For a youth with a gentler face or with more of the natural bloom of charity and good-will in it, or with less reprehensive blue eyes, could not have been found in the army. Grant at once set off for the Court-House.

Meanwhile, Lee, joined by Longstreet, had expressed to the latter his anxiety lest Grant, on account of his first proposition not having been accepted, might now insist on harsher terms. Longstreet tried to reassure him that he knew Grant well enough to say his terms would not be harsher than Lee might demand under like circumstances. But Lee's concern as to how Grant would deal with him, for some reason, was not laid. Whence came his distrust of Grant? Was it because camp gossip of old associates had drifted to Lee, in substance not unlike that which I heard myself from old army officers at Fort Monroe, after Donelson and Shiloh, that Grant was a rather common and inoffensive fellow? And I wonder, too, if the fact that Grant had piled up his dead, and apparently without mercy, before the works of Spottsylvania and Cold Harbor, had tended to confirm in Lee's mind the gossip as to his character? Might not the heart of that " common "

fellow be vindictive as well as cold? Oh, the refined
and hidden qualities in the clay of those called
common! and the scornful indifference that has
been shown them! In the most sublime of the
Psalms, the nineteenth, we read, " Keep back thy
servant from presumptuous sins; let them not
have dominion over me."

Or was Lee's concern as to the terms because he
had caught the eye of that member of the inner
court which sits in judgment, day and night, on
the deeds of men — the judge who had argued
silently, with benevolence yet with warmth, on
the Farmville hills, that, defeat being inevitable,
he ought to accept his fate without the loss of
another life, — a responsibility which Grant had
raised in his first note and repeated in his last?

Lee's heart was tender, and, on more than one
occasion in his loneliness (for no head of any army
ever led a more isolated life), we know it had bled se-
cretly over the sorrowful state of his men and of the
Southern people; yet it was not of the kind to tor-
ment itself over exquisite condemnatory abstractions.
No, as he sat there on the bank by the roadside
waiting to hear where he should meet Grant and
lay down his arms, *that* was not the source of his
mind's worry. The trail to it will be struck, as I
believe, in less subtle fields of quest. Why, after
the fall of Petersburg, Richmond, and the overwhelming disaster at Sailor's Creek, should his

hope of ultimate success have lived or even flickered
for a moment, and why did not that epitome of
the manliness of his day yield at Farmville? What
carried him on from there against the pitchy darkness and steep desperation of the situation, on,
resolutely, after the heads of divisions and corps
had virtually told him that, in their opinions, the
end had come? And above all, when he knew that
his army had wasted away to a mere shadow and the
few who remained were worn out with hunger and
fatigue? What qualities in his being were at the
helm, blind to facts and deaf to reason?

Although I fully realize that as a soldier he was
bound to effect a junction with Johnston if possible,
yet to me, as he appears leading on that fragment
of the old Army of Northern Virginia, from whose
heart hope had fled, leading it on in the face of that
utterly dismal and starless situation, there is something so fraught with doom in his conduct that a
shadow of brooding awe falls over this page, and
lo! I see Æschylus, soldier of Marathon and Salamis,
taking his place in the silent, hollow-eyed, famished
column; and, as on through the darkness following
Lee, I see him, hear him murmuring the preludes
of his immortal tragedies; and over Lee hover the
spirits of Agamemnon, Orestes, Prometheus, and
the pursuing, unappeasable Erinnyes.

And now let us draw near to Lee and give him a
steady, kindly, searching look, unmindful of the

showering stars of yellow, red, and green that are falling about him from, so to speak, exploding bombs of eulogy. Nor as to an idol or a marvel let us draw near, but as to a fellow mortal, genuinely true to the real in every, and the best, sense of the word; one who, though famous, was not honeycombed with ambition or tainted with cunning or cant; and though a soldier and wearing a soldier's laurels, yet never craved or sought honors except as they bloomed on deeds done for the glory of his lawfully constituted and acknowledged civil authority; in short, a soldier to whom the sense of duty was a gospel, and a man of the world whose only rule of life was, that life should be upright and stainless. I cannot but think that Providence meant, through him, to prolong the ideal of the gentleman in this world.

And now to those high moral standards, warmest family affections, imperial qualities, — Lee had a bearing that would have made him at home among princes, — add wealth, station, an imposing stature, a noble countenance, and abilities of the first order, and, as the background of those preëminent attributes, a glowing series of rare victories in the cause of the Confederacy with its appealingly tragic life and death, and it is easy to see why, through the natural impulses of our nature, Lee has become the embodiment of one of the world's ideals, that of the soldier, the Christian, and the gentleman. And

from the bottom of my heart I thank Heaven, since
the commercial spirit of our time has grown into a
sordid, money-gorged, godless, snoring monster, for
the comfort of having a character like Lee's to look
at, standing in burnished glory above the smoke of
Mammon's altars.

But we are not seeking the sublimation of his
mortalness; rather we would see the ingrained
qualities of his nature which carried this modern
Prometheus, those last two days of the Confederacy,
on to the storm-battered crags of Scythia.

In manner and mood becoming his native gentleness of character and unsullied life, and above all,
the tender associations of the morning (it was Palm
Sunday and the church-bells of the land were calling
from steeple to steeple), let us look at him as a
fellow mortal, look at him and find, if we can, the
reason why, as he sits there by that Virginia roadside amid the wreck of the Army of Northern
Virginia, nothing Longstreet does or may say as to
Grant's magnanimity of character assuages his
troubled mind. With this end in view then, and in
order that our survey may be direct, true and substantial, let us detach him from his surroundings,
penetrate the glamour and deal with his personality,
that marvellous compound the secrets of whose
making are in the breast of Nature herself, and
which she in her wisdom turns over from the cradle
into the unfeeling hands of Destiny to direct to its end.

So, note, if you will, the stately angle at which he holds his head, and the peremptory silencing gaze of those potent eyes, studded with the light of conscious personal worth and a distinguished ancestry; eyes which, as those of all men of like parts, aloofness and dignity, are ever quietly on their guard. And do not fail to note, also, how quickly his winning openness of address shelves into an unfathomable ocean of reserve; the open gate, the blooming meadow, figuratively, closing, like a floe in a polar sea. This cold simile is not overdrawn: he greeted his fellow men with charming, dignified kindliness, but that was the end of it, and there is no one among the living or dead, outside of his own family, who has ever claimed to have been on close confidential relations with him.

Under the habitually unruffled composure of that ocean of reserve, and dominated, as I believe, by two master spirits, stands the authentic Lee. And who were those master spirits, which, blind to facts and deaf to reason, drove him on from Farmville? Were they creations of his own? No, not at all. Nature herself had planted them. And what were they? One, an all-pervading unconscious pride, a pride not sordid or arrogant, but lofty. The other, sovereignly cogent and diffused through his whole being and pulsing in every vein, namely, a burning, even fierce enthusiasm. These, in my judgment, were the ingrained, controlling temperamental qualities in Robert E. Lee. The former could not stand the hoar frost of defeat in a cause he believed right; the latter converted him at danger's first challenge, as was again and again displayed in the field, into a prompt and inveterate fighter. As for instance, at Antietam, although he had met and stood off McClellan, yet with such carnage that it was in effect a defeat, still for a day after the battle he held his ground among his dead, silently, yet resolutely, proclaiming to his adversary to come on if he dared. So, too, he stood for a day at Gettysburg, after his frightful repulses, inviting Meade to attack; and when with his bleeding army he reached the flooded Potomac after Gettysburg to find every bridge swept away, undismayed he turned his back on the raging stream and, planting his colors, defiantly bade the Army of the Potomac to strike. Who can forget, either, how quickly he accepted Hooker's gage of battle in the Wilderness, and how a year later (the violets were just in bloom again for the first time in the blood-stained woods) he plunged at Grant. No, no eagle that ever flew, no tiger that ever sprang, had more natural courage; and I will guarantee that every field he was on, if you ask them about him, will speak of the unquailing battle-spirit of his mien. Be not deceived: Lee, notwithstanding his poise, was naturally the most belligerent bull-dog man at the head of any army in the war.

XV

AND now, as there by the roadside he sits, his nature distempered by the balk of its two masterful, earthy, incarnated spirits, we discover the reason why nothing Longstreet can say assuages his troubled mind; and why the idea of surrender is so galling.

Not then, and peradventure never, did it dawn on Lee that it was not Grant primarily, but a country with a destiny against which he had drawn his sword, that had cast him down. And mistake not, by the significance of this fact Lee mounts the dire, footworn steps of Tragedy, one of the worthiest characters that ever passed through its dread portal.

Fate! you never drew a harder lot than that you drew for Robert E. Lee. For he did not believe in Slavery at all; in fact, to him it was repulsive, and an institution antagonistic to the South's ultimate political weal; yet you put him at its head in its last struggle with Freedom in this world! From this point of view, and detached from all sentiment, Lee stands out to me like a vast fire-swept temple, desolation staring out of its charred, flame-shattered windows.

The speculation as to the temperamental and in-grained qualities of Lee may be wide of the mark; but I think not; for, as certainly as we live, when lofty pride and burning enthusiasm in human nature are struck, they, like sterling, will ring true. This, at least, we are sure of, that the one thing he dreaded, and was ready to lay down his life rather than sub-mit to, was a studied humiliation; and let us be thankful that a place has been provided in human breasts for that kind of pride, a pride which not only rebels at abasement but at what is almost as intolerable, patronizing, sniffing condescension, come from whomsoever, or how, it may. And while you and I, reader, may not even dream of putting ourselves in the company of the great, yet, in so far as we have that kind of pride and show it when we should, we claim, with uncovered heads in their presence, a common brotherhood.

And now, before the narrative journeys on, one final word as to Lee. Had the war ended favorably for the South, he would inevitably have been called upon and forced to head its government, which, in the very nature of things, could not have enjoyed peace. For so long as slavery existed, it would have had implacable enemies, many within, millions without, and sooner or later, torn by internal dis-sensions, the Border States would, one after another, on account of commercial advantages, have deserted the Confederacy; and Lee's fame would probably have gone down in the general wreck.

But, be this as it may, the failure of the Confederacy to establish its independence broke the heartstrings of thousands of high-minded Southerners, and, for reasons already hinted at, I believe that its failure broke Lee's very heart itself, and the wonder is that death did not come sooner to him.

Well, conversation between Longstreet and Lee as to Grant's prospective terms continued in broken sentences till Babcock was seen approaching, and then, as Lee still seemed apprehensive of humiliating demands, Longstreet suggested to him that, in such an event, he should break off the interview and tell Grant to do his worst. "The thought of another round" says Longstreet, "seemed to brace him, and he rode with Colonel Marshall to meet the Union commander." So closes Longstreet's account of that unfolding incident.

Lee directed Marshall to ride ahead and find a suitable house for the conference; he chose McLean's, the best in the town, a brick, with locusts and elms about it, and rose bushes blooming on the lawn. The old mansion, with a cool, inviting veranda, stood facing west, and was the first to the right on going into the village from the south.

Marshall, having made his choice, sent his orderly

back to notify Lee, and soon Lee, Marshall and Babcock were seated in the parlor, the left-hand room as you enter the hall. Meanwhile Traveller's humane groom removed the bridle-bit and the famous war horse began to nip the fresh springing grass in the dooryard, while Babcock's orderly sat mounted out in the road, to notify Grant on his arrival. Ord, Sheridan, Custer, Griffin, Merritt, and their staffs, and among them my friends Woodhull and Winne, were up the road only a few hundred yards away, and in full view.

Grant, after dispatching Babcock with his note to Lee, mounted at once and followed the Walker's Church till he came to the Le Grand road. This he took to the left, and then struck down across Plain Run to the Lynchburg road. As he passed the left of the First New York Dragoons, some one shouted, " There comes General Grant." He rode directly to Sheridan's group, saying as he reined up, " How are you, Sheridan? "

" First-rate, thank you; how are you? " replied Sheridan, with an expressive smile, and then told Grant what had happened, and that he believed it was all a ruse on the part of the Confederates to get away.

But Grant answered that he had no doubt of the good faith of Lee, and asked where he was.

" In that brick house," responded Sheridan, pointing to McLean's.

" Well, then, we'll go over," said Grant, and asked them all to go along with him.

Cincinnati, with his delicate ears, high and thorough-bred port, — he was sired by Lexington, King of the Turf, — led the way, and at his side was Rienzi, carrying Sheridan. For some reason or other, perhaps because as a boy I played with the colts on the old home farm, those horses, from the day I saw Grant on Cincinnati, and Sheridan on Rienzi in the Wilderness, have seemed like acquaintances to me; and now it pleases my fancy to put them with Traveller in a pasture, far, far beyond the reach of thundering guns or lamenting bugles sounding taps — a pasture that remains eternally green.

As Grant mounted the steps and entered the hall, Babcock, who, through the window, had seen his approach, opened the door. Sheridan, Ord, and the other officers remained outside and took seats upon two benches, one on either side of the door and upon the steps of the veranda.

Grant, about five feet eight inches tall, his square shoulders inclined to stoop, was without a sword, wore a soldier's dark-blue, unbuttoned, flannel blouse, displaying a waistcoat of like material, and ordinary top-boots with trousers inside. Boots and clothing were spattered with mud, and, in his memoirs, with his usual unstudied frankness, he says, " In my rough travelling suit, the uniform of

a private, with the straps of a lieutenant-general
[bullion-bordered rectangles, supporting on their
ground of black velvet, one large and two smaller
stars], I must have contrasted strangely with a man
so handsomely dressed, six feet high, and of fault-
less form. But this was not a matter that I thought
of until afterwards."

Never, let me say again, was a great man less
self-conscious than Grant, yet, as I have observed
elsewhere, he maintained his dignity day in and day
out at the head of the Army of the Potomac, without charging the air of his headquarters with the
usual pompous military fuss. This I know from
experience, and although I was a mere boy, had he
shown any affectations I believe I should have noticed
them.

The kind and cut of his beard, deep-brown in
shade, the way his hair lay, and the outline of his
face, are familiar; but his eyes, so charitably direct,
his voice, so softly vibrant, veracious and sweet,
must have been seen and heard to be duly appreciated. But under the depths of his quiet and artless reserve, lay a persistent and intense doggedness
of purpose, as prompt and unconquerable as Lee's
pride and burning enthusiasm. And thus strangely
balanced, stood Grant and Lee, types and creations
of American society of their generation, facing each
other.

" Grant greeted Lee very civilly," says Marshall;

and I have no doubt that he and his sublimely austere chief at once felt the charm of that gentle, autumnal composure which every crowned head of the world, who afterward met him, felt and remarked upon.

Lee said to Grant, with his customary urbanity, that he remembered him well in the old army; to which Grant, with his usual modesty, replied that he remembered *him* perfectly, but thought it unlikely that he had attracted Lee's attention sufficiently to be remembered after such a long interval.

Lee soon found himself in a stream of pleasant reminiscence with Grant about the Mexican War; and it could not have been otherwise; for there was something so quietly companionable in Grant's manner that every one whom he met informally and socially always joined him in his unpremeditated talk.

I think I can see Lee's brown, vigilant eyes, filled with the same marvelling, inquisitive wonder, that had filled Meade's and every officer's eyes, save Sherman's, who had known Grant in the old army and the reason why he had left it, on meeting him after he had won the laurels of Fort Donelson, Vicksburg and Chattanooga. And now he was undergoing the same searching scrutiny from Lee that he had had to undergo from others, but he stood before him, as he had stood before all, mild, unselfconscious and unpretentious; and yet, about to receive from him the surrender of the Army of Northern Virginia! Thank God, Obscurity cannot claim an unbroken realm!

It was Lee who finally had to remind Grant of the object of their meeting and suggest that he put his terms in writing, — another proof of Grant's inherent delicacy, which made him reluctant to broach a painful subject.

Grant asked for his manifold order-book and, on receiving it, took a seat at the little centre-table and rapidly, with only a single momentary pause, wrote his terms. He says that when he put his pen to its task, he did not know the first word he should make use of in writing the terms. They were as follows:

"APPOMATTOX CT. H., VA., April 9, 1865.
"GENERAL R. E. LEE,
    "Commanding C. S. A.
"GENERAL: In accordance with the substance of my letter to you of the 8th inst., I propose to receive the surrender of the Army of Northern Virginia on the following terms, to wit: Rolls of all the officers and men to be made in duplicate, one copy to be given to an officer to be designated by me, the other to be retained by such officer or officers as you may designate. The officers to give their individual paroles not to take up arms against the Government of the United States until properly

[exchanged], and each company or regimental commander to sign a like parole for the men of their commands. The arms, artillery, and public property to be parked and stacked, and turned over to the officers appointed by me to receive them. This will not embrace the side-arms of the officers nor their private horses or baggage. This done, each officer and man will be allowed to return to his home, not to be disturbed by the United States authorities so long as they observe their paroles, and the laws in force where they may reside.

"Very respectfully,
"U. S. GRANT, Lieutenant-General."

When he came to the end of the sentence closing with " appointed by me to receive them," he raised his eyes from the page; they fell on Lee's lion-headed, stately sword, and then he continued, " This will not embrace the side-arms of the officers nor their private horses." (Grant probably thought of Traveller, and the pang it would give him, Grant, to part with Cincinnati were he in Lee's place.)

Grant's pen goes on to the end of the most pre-potent task it ever was put to; he rises, goes to Lee and hands him the open order-book. Remaining seated, Lee lays it on the table beside him and with deliberation takes his spectacles out of their case and adjusts them. Slowly and carefully he begins to read line after line. All eyes are on Lee.

It is a brooding hour, a hush quiet as death pre-
vails and Lo! a storm-beaten figure is at the door,
haggard and in ravaged garments. It is easy to
read in her face that it was once the playground of
passion; it is easy to see the ashes of burned-out
hopes in those blood-shot but once soaring eyes;
and it is easy to see, too, where care and disappointment have ploughed deeply her once rose-blooming
cheeks. With lean hand and long, trembling finger,
her eyes flashing the urgency of immediate com-
pliance, she beckons imperatively across the room
to Destiny. With his still and inevitably onward
step he makes his way toward her. Clutching him
close, she whispers in quick, feverish breath, " What
paper is that he is reading? "

" Who are you? " Destiny asks, fixing his cold-
gray eyes on her.

Half-way resentfully and half-way proudly, she
straightens up and exclaims, " I am the Southern
Spirit that launched the Confederacy. It was I
who made their capitals ring as state after state
left the Union, who, four years ago almost to this
very day, fired the first shot at Sumter, and it was
I who beat the Long Roll at every cross-road and
before every door of the Southland! Awake, awake!
come back, come back, oh, drum-throbbing days! "
But suddenly turning her eyes to Lee, and changing
the tones of her voice, she asks, " What paper is
that he is reading? I am persuaded there must be

something dire in it, for I hear the bell in my breast, here, sounding a knell."

" Those are Grant's terms for the surrender of the Army of Northern Virginia," coldly answers Destiny.

"Stop him! stop him!" implores the spirit wildly.

Destiny shakes his head; she staggers backward, death rattling in her throat. But as she is about to fall, Charity puts her kindly arms around her and, then, stroking her pale, tired brow, leads her away. (Oh, what a life is ours!)

Barely have they cleared the door when another figure appears, gaunt, reeking of the lair, and in-veterate malice flaming in his hard, stony face. He needs no Plutonic herald to proclaim him Re-venge. But note that darkening frown on the noble countenance of broad-shouldered Magnanimity as he approaches the newcomer and asks in subdued tones, loaded with reproach, " What are *you* doing here? "

With a look of scornful hatred, " What does Grant mean," growls the figure, " by giving such terms to these damned rebels! "

"Rebels, damned rebels! " exclaims Magna-nimity; " why, they are kith and kin! sons of Washington, Jefferson, Marshall, Madison, and Pinckney! Oh, you malignant, unforgiving crea-ture! "

He seizes Revenge and flings him far; and great

Nature approvingly allows his crunching bones to break her silence as he falls on the jagged cliffs of Hate. Courage and Manliness greet their brother proudly as he reënters the door, and Mercy, "the sweetest virtue ever ascribed to God or man," walks up to him and, lifting her smiling face, puts her hand in his.

Lee kept on reading slowly and carefully, and when he came to the end he raised his eyes from the book, looked at Grant, and remarked, "This will have a very happy effect upon my army."

Grant then said he would have the terms copied in ink, unless he had some suggestions to make. Lee replied, one only, — that the cavalry and artillery-men owned their own horses, and he would like to understand whether or not they would be allowed to retain them. Grant told him the terms as written would not allow this, but, as he thought this was about the last of the war, he would instruct the officers in carrying them out to allow every one claiming to own a horse or a mule to take the animal to his home, so that they could put in a crop to tide them through the next winter, which he feared might be one of want and suffering, owing to the wide devastation.

Lee is reported to have then said, "This will have the best possible effect upon the men. It will be very gratifying, and will do much toward conciliating our people."

When on my visit to Appomattox last autumn, I had proof of Lee's prophecy from the lips of one of Virginia's well-bred matrons, the wife of Colonel Abbitt, who commanded a regiment in Wise's brigade. During a call of respect to her and her mild-faced, battle-tried husband (we were on the porch; before us a long-stemmed red dahlia was in bloom, the shadows of venerable oaks mottled the sward, and the old plantation lay dreaming), she said, with gentle voice, " I never like to hear our people speak unkindly of Grant, for the armies had stripped us of everything we had in the way of food, and I think the supplies we got from the officers he left saved us from almost starving. No, I never like to hear any one abuse Grant."

It is needless for me to point out the political significance of the last sentence, binding as it did the passions, and pledging the honor, of his country. In short, it meant that there should be no judicial bloodshed, no gibbets, and no mourning exiles. These terms, in the light of all that might have happened after the assassination of Mr. Lincoln, which took place within five days of the surrender, lent elevation, repose, and dignity to humanity, and, I have no doubt, the eyes of the Country's guardian angel welled over them with tears of joy.

The terms were put in writing by Colonel Parker of Grant's staff, a full-blooded Indian, a chief of the historic Six Nations, whose empire England, in the

early days, had recognized. Parker's stature was
imposing — he was as tall as Lee, and heavier;
his eyes were coal-black, and his face had the broad
commanding features of his race. He carried the
table which Grant had used to the opposite corner
of the room, and Colonel Marshall, a gentleman
through and through, let him have his small box-
wood inkstand and pen.

While Parker was copying the terms, Ord, Sheridan, Rawlins, and others, were presented to Lee, but
the only one whom he greeted with any cordiality was
Seth Williams; to the others he bowed formally.
When Williams, with his usual spontaneous spirit
of comradeship, referred to something amusing
that had happened during their service together at
West Point, one as adjutant, the other as superintendent, Lee's only response was a slight inclination
of the head.

A paraphrase of what Grant says in his memoirs
of Lee and his manner at this interview, may be
pertinent: namely, that Lee was a man of much
dignity, and with a face so impassive that Grant
did not know the character of his feelings, and that,
whatsoever they may have been, they were entirely
concealed from observation. He goes on to say:
" My own feelings, which had been quite jubilant on
the receipt of his letter, were sad and depressed. I
felt like anything rather than rejoicing at the downfall of a foe who had fought so long and valiantly

and had suffered so much for a cause, though that cause was, I believe, one of the worst, for which there was the least excuse. I do not question, however, the sincerity of those who were opposed to us."

The cause which Grant had in mind was obviously slavery, and Grant was right, but while slavery was the primal cause of the war, yet the people of the South did not lay down their lives in defense of the right to buy and sell human beings; and to charge them now with that offense, is to my mind doing them a wrong. No; Slavery, as property, or as a lawfully acknowledged institution, went up with the smoke of the first house that was burned, and the animating principle then, and to the end, was the defense of home and the rights of the States to govern themselves.

While the terms were being copied, Lee told Grant that he had a number of prisoners whom he should be glad to release, as he had no provisions for them or his own men, who had been living for the last few days on parched corn and what they could gather along the route. Grant asked him to send the prisoners within his lines, and said that he would take steps at once to have Lee's army supplied, but was sorry to say that he was entirely without forage for the animals. On inquiring as to the number to be fed, Lee was unable to answer, and then Grant asked, " Suppose I send over twenty-five thousand rations, will that be enough? "

" More than enough," replied Lee.

Grant directed Morgan, his chief commissary, to see that Lee's army was fed.

By this time the terms were copied, and, when they were signed, it was about half-past two or three o'clock. Lee shook hands with Grant, bowed to the other officers, and left the room. Colonel Paine of Ord's staff says: " As Lee came out of the room, and stopped for a moment in the doorway, those of us on the porch arose and complimented him with the usual salute to a superior officer. He seemed pleased at this mark of respect and, looking to the right and the left, raised his hat in recognition of the attention. As he drew on a pair of apparently new gloves, he stood so close to me that his initials, worked in white silk upon the guard of the gauntlet, were plainly observed."

Having signalled for his horse, Lee stood on the lowest step of the veranda while the groom was rebridling Traveller, and from time to time, Lee's eyes swept the leaning fields blooming with the Stars and Stripes, colors he had helped to place triumphantly on the walls of Chapultepec, and he smote his gauntleted hands together unconsciously. When Traveller was led up, he mounted him at once. Grant just then stepped down from the veranda and, as he passed Lee, touched his hat. Lee returned the salute and rode away. Marshall says that, if General Grant and the officers who were present at the McLean house had studied how not to offend, they could not have borne themselves with more good breeding.

On Lee's departure, General Grant mounted Cincinnati, and, having ridden some distance, on being reminded that he had not notified the War Department, dismounted, called for pencil and paper, and briefly telegraphed Stanton, Secretary of War, that the Army of Northern Virginia had surrendered to him on terms proposed by himself. He then remounted and went to his headquarters, which meanwhile had been pitched on a knoll to the left of the road, toward Appomattox Station, a mile or so from the Court-House.

When I visited the spot, on that misty morning already referred to, the ground about was covered almost knee-high with a stubble of tall, intermatted, coarse grass and weeds, chiefly asters with stunted white blossoms. Crawling here and there up to the mist-drenched tops of the weeds and grass were vines like morning-glories, with now and then on their wavering stems a single bell-shaped, pink flower. The field, a pretty large one, which has an oak wood across the road to the west, declines to the east, and in the rising field beyond, a pasture dotted with trees and colonies of young sassafras and persimmon, stood an old deserted tobacco-house veiled in the mist. Cattle, twenty or more, with bells of different tones, were grazing toward the south.

XVI

ALMOST as soon as Grant reached his headquarters,
the trains carrying rations started on their humane
mission, and with them went a hamper from Custer
to his classmate " Gimlet " Lea, colonel of a North
Carolina regiment, and its historian says that Lea
invited some of his officers to join him at luncheon.
By the time the order announcing the surrender
was promulgated, the rations were being issued. It
was then nearly four o'clock, and the official an-
nouncement of the surrender was made.

Joy overflowed every heart of the Army of the
Potomac. Men threw their hats in the air and
cheered themselves hoarse, bands played, and officers,
young and old, embraced each other, not in exulta-
tion over their foe, but because, at last, after four
long years in defense of their country, the end had
come — victory with healing on its wings.

The official news reached Meade on Humphreys'
front at five o'clock. Major Pease was the bearer
of the happy tidings. Webb, Meade's chief of staff,
at once led three cheers with swinging hat, and then
three more for Meade, who of all men should have
been present at the McLean house. He had been

unwell and, for a good share of the day, had lounged in an ambulance; but on receipt of the joyful news he mounted his horse and, preceded by a bugler sounding rejoicingly to clear the way, rode down through his men, whom he had led so long and so well; and Lyman, who was riding at his side, records that the color-bearers brought up their flags and waved them, and that the patient, silent old Army of the Potomac burst into a frenzy of excitement, rushing to the sides of the road and shouting till his very ears rang with the cheering.

Pretty soon Wright, commanding the Sixth corps, which it will be remembered was with Humphreys beyond New Hope Church, ordered the heroic, brown-eyed Cowan, a man of noticeable presence and stature, whose ancestors brought him a child from the land of Wallace and Bruce, to fire a national salute. The guns began to roar, and Bernard of Petersburg, author of an interesting book entitled *War Talks of Confederate Veterans*, and who was on furlough, says that as he and his party, on their return, jogged along near Amherst Court-House, the sound of distant artillery from the direction of Appomattox Court-House reached their ears, " But there was an ominous regularity in the firing of the guns." The guns were Cowan's, and Grant, as soon as he heard them, sent orders forbidding salutes. Nature has her mysteries, and she has carefully hidden her final purposes from the ken of men, but in one respect she has been benignantly open and wise, — she has left the traits of the gentleman unmistakable to us all.

Lee, on riding back from the McLean house, established his headquarters for the afternoon by the roadside in the orchard, under one of whose trees he sat in the forenoon so troubled over the terms Grant would give him. Now there is only a tree or two left in the southeasterly sloping field.

W. W. Blackford, in the appendix to Volume II of *Memoirs of the War*, a rare and valuable book, says that his command, the Engineer Brigade, under the refined and scholarly Tallcott, was resting near by in the orchard. Blackford records:

" There were many details about the surrender demanding attention, one of which was securing rations for the army from General Grant's supplies, and officers were going and coming all day. General Lee's staff were bivouacked in the shade of an apple tree near the road, and there Colonel Taylor or Colonel Venable received all visitors. General Lee was under the shade of a tree a little farther back, where he paced backward and forward all day long, looking like a caged lion. General Lee usually wore a plain undress uniform and no arms, except holster-pistols; on this occasion, however, he had put on his full-dress uniform and sword and sash, and looked the embodiment of all that was grand and noble in man. We, the field officers of the First,

occupied a tree near General Lee's staff. Colonel
Tallcott had been a member of General Lee's staff
up to the time he took command of our regiment,
and consequently there was a good deal of social
intercourse between regimental and army headquarters, and during this day we were all much together, so we were kept posted pretty fully about all
that was going on.

" General Lee seemed to be in one of his savage
moods, and when these moods were on him it was
safer to keep out of his way; so his staff kept to
their tree, except when it was necessary to intro-
duce the visitors. Quite a number came; they were
mostly in groups of four or five, and some of high
rank. It was evident that some came from curiosity
or, as friends in the old army, to see General Lee.
But the General shook hands with none of them.
It was rather amusing to see the extreme deference
shown him by them. When he would see Colonel
Taylor coming with a party toward his tree, he
would halt in his pacing and stand at ' attention '
and glare at them with a look which few men but he
could assume. They would remove their hats entirely and stand bareheaded during the interview,
while General Lee sometimes gave a scant touch
to his hat in return and sometimes did not even do
that."

At first sight, there is something a bit discordant
in this account with the popular conception of Lee;

but to me it only makes the man more real and adds to my admiration for him. Does not out of the same mellow and blessed summer sky come the growling thunder and the speeding lightning? And what are we, if not human? Where is there any one, with a drop of red blood in his veins, who, with a cause so dear, and after leading an army like that of Northern Virginia so long, — we know how bravely, — could, in the face of what Lee had just gone through with, wear the look of a saint and curtain his natural feelings with a lace-work of hypocritical smiles, — and Cowan's guns booming! — and above all, in the presence of the curious, who, next to the supercilious rich, are the most obnoxious of beings. No, unless a man be a cool, smooth, tricky sham he cannot suppress his feelings under an awful trial like that. And on the contrary, and in justification, God has set times for us all when anger's fires shall kindle quickly and blaze in every feature. I am surprised that any of General Lee's old friends should, at that hour, have sought to renew acquaintance; they should have known better.

Late in the afternoon, when Gordon saw Lee mount Traveller to go back to his permanent head-quarters up on the timbered ridge at the foot of the majestic oak, he sent word for his men to give their loved commander a cheer as he passed, for he told them that Lee was feeling badly. Longstreet says:

"From force of habit a burst of salutations greeted him, but quieted as suddenly as they rose. The road was packed by troops as he approached, the men with hats off, heads and hearts bowed down. As he passed they raised their heads and looked upon him with swimming eyes. Those who could find voice said: ' Good-bye; ' those who could not speak, and were near, passed their hands gently over the sides of Traveller. He rode, with his hat off, and had sufficient control to fix his eyes on a line between the ears of Traveller and look neither to right nor left until he reached a lone, white oak tree, where he dismounted to make his headquarters and finally talked a little."

Alexander says: " He [Lee] told the men that in making the surrender, he had made the best terms possible for them, and advised all to go to their homes, plant crops, repair the ravages of the war, and show themselves as good citizens as they had been good soldiers." And all who were present say that tears were in Lee's eyes. He then appointed Longstreet, Gordon, and Pendleton as commissioners to meet Gibbon, Griffin, and Merritt, of our army, to formulate details for carrying out the terms of capitulation.

Meanwhile Grant, according to Porter's most realistic account of what took place at the McLean house, seated himself in front of his tent, on reaching camp. No cheers greeted him as he rode thither

(had it been McClellan the army would have gone
wild and their voices would have shaken the skies
over him). Well, Grant seated himself in front of
his tent, and what do you suppose he talked about?
The surrender, of course. No, he turned to Ingalls
and inquired, —

"Ingalls, do you remember that old white mule
So-and-so used to ride when we were in the City
of Mexico?"

"Why, perfectly!" exclaimed the diplomatic Ingalls, one of the best poker players of the old army,
who, having to draw suddenly on his wits (it is
barely possible that he had never even heard of
the old mule before), filled his hand as usual.

Ingalls was clever. I used to look at him with a
boy's keen interest. A man of the world, true as
steel to his friends, and a most efficient officer.

Grant, until supper was ready, went on recalling
the antics of the long-eared, nimble-footed patient
beast of those far-back times; times and mule
doubtless evoked by his interview with Lee. His
unstudied naturalness and summer calm in this
hour of victory, I could not believe possible, had
I not seen him day after day on the field.

After supper, to the surprise and disappointment
of his staff, who were looking forward to witnessing
the ceremonial of surrender, Grant announced that,
on the following afternoon, he should start for
Washington. He also expressed, with customary

informality, his conviction that all the other Confederate armies would now lay down their arms and that peace would soon prevail. And thus, without vainglory, before his camp-fire on that knoll, where now the asters and the bind-weed bloom, Grant ended the great day when the sun of the Confederacy set, one among the greatest days, I think, in the annals of our country.

Meanwhile, night had fallen, and the camp-fires had been lit, but no moon or stars looked down softly on the field of the last act of the tragedy. For nature, as if in sympathy with the moods of the broken-hearted, had let fall a dark, responsive curtain, and the expanded heavens were black, draped as with a pall.

And now, as the bivouacs of the armies come into view, they are, as you see in every field, on every slope and by every brook, their gleaming fires surrounded by figures of men, some upright, some prone, and many sitting with clasped knees; those in blue looking into the fires with home-going dreamy joy, those in gray with sad and moistened eye, and, as all this breaks on my vision, a sense of loneliness comes over me. I know that I ought to feel glad, glad that the North conquered, that democracy had won her triumph, and that peace had come; but for some reason or other, as the field of Appomattox lies before me with its two old armies, the pitchy darkness fretted with their lonely camp-fires, my

heart beats low. Back come again those war days
when, as a boy, I followed the flag; back come the
nights of Chancellorsville, the Wilderness, Spottsylvania, and Cold Harbor; and the slender chords that
nature has strung across the abysses of my weak
heart are vibrating sadly.

And listen! The bands are playing " Home,
Sweet Home."

Come, dear reader, let us withdraw, — the feeling is too tender; let us go beyond the reach of
those pathetic notes, up to that oak-timbered ridge
which rises steeply west of the Court-House, and
there sit down till the bugles sound " taps."

How the dry leaves scuffle under our feet as we
disturb them in their quiet beds! But here we are;
let us sit down on this fallen stub, once in the van-
guard of the venerable trees, to greet the morning
sun. No wind is astir; dogwood, oak, beech, ma-
ple and gum about us, are holding their blooming spring-time festival; for it is April. Deep is
the silence of their infinite joy, and deep is the quiet
of the night about us. The Appomattox, which
rises at our feet, is murmuring the news it will tell
to the sea, and a little frog, free from man's troubles,
pipes child-like in the sedges.

We can see nearly all of the camp-fires of the
Army of the Potomac. There is Grant's; but we
cannot see Lee's, for it is up in the woods at the
foot of that large white oak. But we can see those

of his men who are bivouacking in the gullied fields pitching gently down to the river. And how all of the fires glow through the darkness like lonely topazes! The sight of them, with all they mean to those about them, will outlast many a memory; for each one of our intellectual faculties has its own special treasure room, and, thank God, when the winds of fortune blow too chill, the humblest farmer's boy can withdraw in his old age to the picture galleries of his youth!

Night with her noiseless step has moved on. The fires are burning low, and only here and there can we see a man with clasped knees still looking into the failing blaze. Hark! the first bugle is sounding "taps," and let me tell you, reader, that if you have never heard it blown on the field, you will not realize the depth of its moving tones; that call, to be at its best, must be heard on the edge of a battle-field and in the presence of an enemy. Then the night-enveloped neighboring fields and woods, and the vaulted skies seem to lend each note some of their own subdued, sweetly-lamenting loneliness. One by one, camp after camp, battery after battery, is sounding the call, and now the last one — oh, trumpeter, you nor any other will ever blow its like again — is dying away, dying over the field of Appomattox — its last note lingers as if reluctant to go, it is fading, it is gone.

But before we leave this spot, let us not forget

that it is a Sunday night, and that in many a country home, North and South, the little sleepy ones are assembled for evening prayer, and fathers, — or too often it is a pale, widowed mother, — on bended knees, with palm to palm, are thanking God for mercies, asking Him to watch over them during the night, imploring Him earnestly to bring peace once more to the land, and adding with low, trembling voice, a prayer that " He will protect and guard the absent soldier-boy."

To-morrow they will hear that the war is over. Speed, speed on, glad tidings, to every door in the land! Unworthy as we are, let us kneel and join in a silent prayer of thankfulness that the end of the strife has come and that no more homes, North or South, will hear the blighting news of a son who has died in a hospital or been killed in battle; but ere we rise, let us thank Him that the North had the courage to fight for their country, and ask Him to send His comforter to our enemies, the broken-hearted Confederates of the Army of Northern Virginia; and, I think, I can hear from mountain ranges and wave-breaking beaches a respondent, " Amen, and Amen."

A peevish voice hails, — it sounds to me like that of a carping professor of literature: — " I thought we were to have an account of a famous military campaign and he has led us to a prayer-meeting! He does not seem to have the first idea of true narrative continuity!" Well, perhaps not; but continuity or no continuity, which would you rather follow, a canal, or some insignificant rivulet wandering from field to field, which, although without depth, yet for a moment now and then, besides its little actual world reflects cloud and star, and once in a while breaks into a low little gurgle of its own?

The narrative might linger in the shadow of the four years of war that had been waged so bitterly by the two sleeping armies, sponsors now for all their absent, valiant dead, dwelling on what Appomattox meant in the way of progressive national life. But what the contest meant between North and South historically and politically, that I shall leave to other pens, with this single suggestion only, that it is not in our country's stupendous growth and world-recognized power that the war finds its true measure. It has other terms than those of commerce and wealth. In short, it supplies to our countrymen what Grote says the Iliad did to the Greeks, " a grand and inexhaustible object of common sympathy, common faith, and common admiration."

Sleep on, then, Army of the Potomac, and Army of Northern Virginia, and sleep well; your countrymen's " common sympathy, common faith, and common admiration," will, through the powers of mind and heart, camp you together on a field higher than this.

XVII

THE following morning, Monday, a rain began
which lasted off and on for several days. Grant,
with his staff, peace-loving Ord and Gibbon, set
out, preceded by a white flag and bugler, to call on
Lee. But on reaching the Confederate sentinels
at the river, they halted him, having orders to
allow no one to pass, and requested that he wait
there till his presence could be made known to Lee.
Grant and his party then turned in to the little
knoll at the left of the road: a tablet marks the
spot. As soon as Lee heard that Grant had been
stopped on his way to pay him his respects, he
mounted and came down from his camp at a gallop,
and, as he rode up, lifted his hat. Grant lifted his
and stepped Cincinnati forward; Lee wheeled Traveller to Grant's left, and the staff fell back into a
semi-circle, out of hearing.

There they talked for well-nigh an hour, and
Grant says in his memoirs, that " Lee referred to
the extent of the Southern country and that the
armies of the North might have to march over it
several times before the war entirely ended, but
he hoped earnestly that that would not be necessary,

involving, as it would, further destruction of property and useless sacrifice of life." Grant, in view of this truth, suggested to him that if he, Lee, would say the word, so great was his influence, every Confederate army would lay down its arms, and the suspended political life would soon resume its peaceful sway. To this Lee replied, with his usual reverence for authority, that he could not usurp executive functions without consulting Mr. Davis.

Marshall says that Lee observed to Grant, in the course of his interview, that if he, Grant, had met Lee at Petersburg, or at any time later, they would have ended the war then and there. Marshall does not give Grant's reply, but it was doubtless that he had orders from the War Department not to assume to make terms of peace, which Lee as a soldier would have recognized as a complete answer.

At the end of the interview, Lee requested that such explicit instructions be given to the commissioners as to paroles and the carrying out of the details of the terms that there might be no misunderstandings. He then lifted his hat and said good-bye.

He and Grant parted, and they never met again, but for a moment when Lee, with some friends, called to pay his formal respects to Grant as President.

The question as to who was the greater, Lee or

Grant, is no longer an open one: the aristocracy of England and a great number of our own people have apparently decided irrevocably in favor of Lee. But, nevertheless, I cast my vote unhesitatingly for Grant, and on the substantial ground that he was intuitively great; and I can think of no foundation for greatness so unchallengable and so elemental as intuition.

Grant after his interview with Lee rode back to the McLean house, and there met Longstreet, Wilcox (who had been his groomsman), Heth, Gordon, Pickett, and others, all of whom, except Gordon, were fellow West Point men. Longstreet says that, as he "was passing through the room, General Grant looked up, recognized me, rose, and with old-time cheerful greeting, gave me his hand, and after passing a few remarks offered a cigar, which was gratefully received."

At noon Grant shook hands with all of the Confederates, saying good-bye, and then started for Washington, bivouacking that night at Prospect Station.

Meanwhile Meade, with his son George, Webb, and Colonel Theodore Lyman, had set out to see Grant, intending to pay his respects to his old friend Lee on the way. As Field, a large and handsome man, whose hair was very black and worn long, was in command where they entered the Confederate lines at New Hope Church, Meade went to

his headquarters first. And here is what Lyman
says in his diary:

" He [Field] guided us to Lee's headquarters, in a
small wood, and consisting only of a flag with a
camp-fire before it. His baggage had perhaps been
burnt the night before, along with much more; we
saw many burnt wagons here and there. The rebel
infantry was camped or rather bivouacked along
the road, with their muskets stacked and the regimental colors planted. They appeared to have
very little to eat and very few shelter tents. The
number of men actually equipped seemed small,
the bivouacs did not appear larger than those of a
weak corps. Lee was away, but as we rode along
we met him returning. He looked in a brown
study, and gazed vacantly when Meade saluted
him. But he recovered himself and said, —

" ' What are you doing with all that gray in your
beard? '

" ' As to that, you have a great deal to do with
it! ' said our general promptly.

" Lee is a tall, strongly-made man, with a florid,
but not fat, face. His thick hair and beard, now
nearly white, are somewhat closely trimmed. His
head is large and high, the eye dark, clear, and unusually deep. His expression is not that of genius
or dash, but of wisdom, coolness, and great deter-
mination. His manners are courtly and reserved,
now unusually so, of course. Though proud and

manly to the last, he seemed deeply dejected. Meade talked with him some time."

Meade then went on to the McLean house, hoping to find Grant, but he had left. While there, and Lyman was talking to Gibbon, a voice behind him said:

" How are you, Ted? "

It was " Roonie " Lee, the General's second son, W. H. F., who had been a college mate of Lyman at Harvard. I never saw this son of General Lee, but often heard his old army friends speak of him with warm affection.

That night Lee sat before his camp-fire with Marshall, and told him to prepare a farewell order to the troops, which on the following day was read and was in these terms:

" HEADQUARTERS,
" ARMY OF NORTHERN VIRGINIA,
" April 10, 1865.

" After four years of arduous service, marked by unsurpassed courage and fortitude, the Army of Northern Virginia has been compelled to yield to overwhelming numbers and resources. I need not tell the survivors of so many hard-fought battles, who have remained steadfast to the last, that I have consented to this result from no distrust of them, but, feeling that valor and devotion could accomplish nothing that could compensate for the loss that would have attended the continuation of the contest, I have determined to avoid the useless sacrifice of those whose past services have endeared them to their countrymen.

"By the terms of the agreement, officers and men can return to their homes, and remain there until exchanged. You will take with you the satisfaction that proceeds from the consciousness of duty faithfully performed; and I earnestly pray that a merciful God will extend to you his blessing and protection.

"With an increasing admiration of your constancy and devotion to your country, and a grateful remembrance of your kind and generous consideration of myself, I bid you an affectionate farewell.

"R. E. LEE, General."

A few hours before Lee left, on the following morning, Captain Colston, who has been mentioned before, went to see him to say good-bye, and asked him as a favor to write his name on the fly-leaf of a New Testament which he had carried through the war. Lee willingly complied, and the Testament, and the almost sacred autograph, are still in Colston's possession in Baltimore, and when death comes to the gallant captain, may all the sweet promises of the book be realized.

Lee, about ten o'clock, accompanied by Marshall, Taylor, and Venable, rode off the field of Appomattox, off into the radiant field of glory; and I think the towering white oak followed him and his staff with tender interest till they disappeared behind the timbered ridges of wildness and beauty in Buckingham. And who knows that on many and many a night, as the stars shone down, and all the younger generations of oaks, pine, and gum were asleep, the venerable, majestic tree did not commune with itself, wondering how it was going with Lee?

XVIII

AT an early hour on the following day, the 12th,
General Chamberlain, of Maine, to whom the honor
had been given of receiving the surrender of the
arms and colors of Lee's forces, formed his line
along the road from the Court-House to the river.
I believe the selection of Chamberlain to rep-
resent the Army of the Potomac was providential,
in this, that he, in the way he discharged his duty,
represented the spiritually-real of this world. And
by this I mean the lofty conceptions of what in
human conduct is manly and merciful, showing in
daily life consideration for others, and on the battle-
field, linking courage with magnanimity and sharing
an honorable enemy's woes.

The division he commanded was the first of the
old Fifth corps, — Warren's: the unfortunate Warren, to whom, however, with Chamberlain, has
fallen the honor of saving Little Round Top and
Gettysburg. And yet, mournful as the grave that
Warren fills, yet to clouds, wandering winds, and
the glimmering silence of the marching stars, that
little wooded hill at Gettysburg repeats with exul-
tation the story of its broken-hearted hero.

Well, Chamberlain led his division to its post
along the road to within a stone's throw of the
Appomattox. On the right of his line stood the
Thirty-second Massachusetts, sponsor for Lexington and Bunker Hill, for Adams, Hancock, Franklin,
and the old, unconquerable Puritan spirit. Puritan
Spirit! Deep, deep is the blending in our country's
life of the hopes and aspirations that have stirred
the heart in all ages. Read the annals of New England, read the annals of Virginia, and it will be
made known to you how the Spirit of Liberty
made her home here with the Puritans, there with
the Cavaliers, who fled from Old England for practically the same reasons that drove the Puritans
to New England and the Catholics to Maryland.
Yes, there at those hospitable hearths she sat
where slaves were treated almost as members of
the same family, tears falling down black cheeks
as well as white, when death struck either master
or slave; there she sat, stirrer of big hearts, kindling Virginia's torch to light the way to the Declaration.

Chamberlain's troops, facing west, and in single-
rank formation, having gained their position, were
brought to an " order arms." The Confederates, in
plain view, then began to strike their few weather-
worn scattered tents, seize their muskets, and for
the last time fall into line. Pretty soon, along Chamberlain's ranks, the word passed: " Here they come! "

And as, in my mind's eye, I see them heading down that road, their colors dotting the gray column like tiger-lilies, my heart beats tenderly. I know how the color-bearers feel at the thought that they are to lay down their banners and part with them forever, banners which I saw so often floating defiantly.

On they come, and Gordon is riding at the head of the column. On he leads the men who had stood with him and whose voices had more than once screamed like the voices of swooping eagles as victory showed her smile; but now he and all are dumb. They are gaining the right of Chamberlain's line; now Gordon is abreast of it, his eyes are down and he is drinking the very lees, for he thinks that all those men in blue, standing within a few feet of him at " order arms," are gloating over the spectacle. Heavy lies his grief as on before the line he rides, and now he is almost opposite Chamberlain, who sits there mounted, the Maltese cross, the badge of the Fifth corps, and the Stars and Stripes displayed behind him; lo! a bugle peals and instantly the whole Federal line from right to left comes to a " carry," the marching salute.

Chamberlain has said: " Gordon catches the sound of shifting arms, looks up and, taking the meaning, wheels superbly, making with himself and his horse one uplifted figure, with profound salutation as he drops the point of his sword to the boot-toe; then, facing to his own command, gives word for his successive brigades to pass us with the same position of the manual, — honor answering honor. On our part not a sound of trumpet more, nor roll of drum; not a cheer, nor word nor whisper of vainglorying, nor motion of man standing again at the order; but an awed stillness rather, and breath-holding, as if it were the passing of the dead!"

Great, in the broad and high sense, was the cause battled for, and spontaneous and knightly was this act of Chamberlain's, lending a permanent glow to the close of the war like that of banded evening clouds at the end of an all-day beating rain. It came from the heart, and it went to the heart; and when "taps" shall sound for Chamberlain, I wish that I could be in hearing, hear Maine's granite coast with its green islands and moonlight-reflecting coves taking them up in succession from Portland to Eastport, and as the ocean's voice dies away, hear her vast wildernesses of hemlock, spruce, and pine repeating them with majestic pride for her beloved son.

After passing, the Confederate brigades, one after another, came into line, dressed carefully to the right, and then the last command was given — "Stack arms." The guns were planted, the bayonets writhing in each other's grasp; equipments were taken off, and then the colors were laid lovingly on the stacks. The color-bearers cried as they turned away from them; and my eyes swim, too.

Longstreet's men, the men of Chickamauga and Gettysburg, came last; and bringing up the rear was Pickett with the remnant of his division; and the banners which, I suspect, valor has planted on the peaks of History from Thermopylæ down, waved as the old fellows marched by with their torn standards. God's blessings on every one who wore the blue and the gray that day; in peace, sweet peace, I *know*, rest the dead.

It was not mere chance that Chamberlain was selected, and that he called on the famous corps to salute their old intrepid enemy at this last solemn ceremonial. Chance, mere chance! No, for God, whenever men plough the fields of great deeds in this world, sows seed broadcast for the food of the creative powers of the mind. What glorified tenderness that courtly act has added to the scene! How it, and the courage of both armies, Lee's character and tragic lot, Grant's magnanimity and Chamberlain's chivalry, have lifted the historic event up to a lofty, hallowed summit for all people. I firmly believe that Heaven ordained that the end of that epoch-making struggle should not be characterized by the sapless, dreary commonplace; for with pity, through four long years, she had looked down on those high-minded, battling armies, and out of love for them both, saw to it that deeds of enduring color should flush the end.

The ceremony of laying down arms took up the whole day, and all that night men in relays were printing the paroles for the Confederates on a shambling little field-press. On the following morning, as fast as the paroles were distributed, the men set off for home. And with each departing step a deeper stillness comes over the field, and in corresponding mood the current of this narrative slows down; for, a few more lines, and its course is run.

Major William A. Owen, adjutant of the Washington Artillery of New Orleans, in his diary thus describes the scene. After receiving the paroles, he assembled his battalion and read Lee's farewell order to them.

" The men listened with marked attention and with moistened eyes as the grand farewell from their old chief was read; and then, receiving their paroles, they every one shook my hand and bade me goodbye, and breaking up into parties of three or four, turned their faces homeward, some to Richmond, some to Lynchburg, and some to far-off, ruined Louisiana.

" I watched them until the last man disappeared with a wave of his hand around a curve in the road, then mounted and rode away from Appomattox."

With this last scene of the great tragedy — that Confederate cannoneer outlined against a golden evening sky, and waving a long farewell — to soft and low falls the beat of my heart. Gone are the Armies of the Potomac and Northern Virginia, the long white trains and the rumbling wheels, the dreaming colors and the thundering guns, gone to a field which the mind of man by the wings of imagination alone can reach.

THE END.